To Maria, Geoffrey and Nikos

SOCIAL HISTORY

Also by Miles Fairburn

The Ideal Society and Its Enemies: The Foundations of Modern New Zealand Society, 1850 1900

Nearly Out of Heart and Hope: The Puzzle of a Colonial Labourer's Diary

Social History

Problems, Strategies and Methods

Miles Fairburn

Professor of History
Canterbury University
New Zealand

First published 1999 by
MACMILLAN PRESS LTD
Houndmills, Basingstoke, Hampshire RG21 6XS
and London
Companies and representatives throughout the world

ISBN 0–333–61586–7 hardcover
ISBN 0–333–61587–5 paperback

A catalogue record for this book is available from the British Library.

This book is printed on paper suitable for recycling and made from fully managed and sustained forest sources.

10   9   8   7   6   5   4   3   2   1
08 07 06 05 04 03 02 01 00 99

Printed in Hong Kong

 Published in the United States of America 1999 by
ST. MARTIN'S PRESS, INC.,
Scholarly and Reference Division,
175 Fifth Avenue, New York, N.Y. 10010

ISBN 0–312–22123–1 clothbound
ISBN 0–312–22124–X paperback

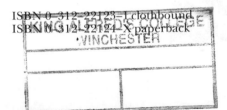

Contents

Acknowledgements

This book arose out of a fourth-year History Honours course I taught at Victoria University in 1994 and 1995. I am most grateful for the assistance and encouragement I received in teaching it from good friends and colleagues in other Departments. They included John Pratt (Criminology), David Pearson, Kevin White and Bob Tristram (Sociology), and Ed Mares and Kim Sterelny (Philosophy). I also owe a great deal to the students who took the course and stimulated my thinking on various issues. My debt to John Morrow (Politics Department) and Bob Tristram is particularly heavy: they not only persuaded me to take on the book but went to the trouble to read and criticise closely an earlier draft. The contribution of Dr Trevor Burnard (one of my new colleagues at Canterbury) must also be acknowledged since he provided invaluable information and advice on several points. Lastly, I must thank Pauline Wedlake for her secretarial assistance.

MILES FAIRBURN

Introduction

During the last two or three decades, social history has become the fastest growing and the most fashionable area of professional historical writing, research, and teaching in the English-speaking world. The growing popularity of the subject has brought in its train a large and expanding body of discussion about what social historians have done, what they are doing, and about what they can, might and should do. Although the subject-matter of all this discussion about the discipline is quite diverse, the bulk of it focuses on a more restricted range of concerns.

The first concern is with straightforward historiography. This discussion is of a basically descriptive kind. It variously covers the origin, rise, present condition and prospects of the discipline as a whole, or of one of the many sub-disciplines or 'schools' within the discipline. Typically, such discussion details the aims, approaches, backgrounds and major works of the leading practitioners, the influences upon the practitioners, the defining characteristics of particular sub-disciplines or of branches within a sub-discipline, and how social history is different from what has been called the 'old' history (political, administrative, diplomatic, constitutional and biographical history, generally presented in a narrative fashion).

Falling into a second category is the discussion that has dwelt on the relationship of the discipline to the social sciences. Some of this discussion has set out simply to introduce historians to the different concepts and theories of the social sciences (notably sociology and anthropology) and to show how particular studies by practising social historians have employed these concepts and theories to advantage. A large portion of the discussion, however, has become a debate about the whole identity of social history in relation to the 'old' history and to the social sciences. On one side of the debate have been those who have claimed that history and sociology (or anthropology) have a natural affinity; and those who have dismissed the 'old' history as impressionistic and have urged that social history should model itself upon one or a combination of the disciplines of sociology, anthropology and geography. On

1

the other side of the debate, have been the followers of the 'old' history who have argued that history and the social sciences are incompatible; and some social historians who have criticised the influence of the social sciences on their discipline, saying (for instance) that the social sciences have no capacity to explain what is central to the past, change over time, or that social science theories are too deterministic, and so forth.

Critical discussion of the discipline forms a third category. Some of the criticism has been directed towards the more popular of the sub-disciplines (notably the history of *mentalités*). Other criticism has been directed at the whole discipline, saying (amongst other things) that practitioners too often study trivial topics and neglect politics and elite ideas which exercised (it is asserted) a far greater impact on ordinary people.

A further category of discussion is made up of 'bedrock' arguments by social historians about what society is, how it can be known (if at all) and the language that should be adopted to talk about it. The arguments, that is to say, have been over the nature of people as social beings, and about what 'schools' of social history, approaches and varieties of theory provide the best ways of examining and talking about people as social beings. Frequently such arguments have arisen during the course of debates over particular interpretations of the past. Very often the arguments have spilt over from anthropology, sociology, speculative philosophy and, increasingly of late, literary theory. There have been arguments, for example, about whether **quantification** and **models** are appropriate devices for representing collective human activity; whether the social past should be written in narrative form (**event-oriented history**) or in analytical form (**structure-oriented history**); whether social historians should study large-scale structures or minute localised settings; whether culture/ideology is more fundamental to a society than its material forces or its social arrangements or its power structure; whether the job of social historians should be to explain the causes of peoples' outward behaviour or to understand peoples' intentions and social meanings; whether the concepts which are used to analyse a society should be drawn from within it or from outside it; whether gender has primacy over class as a social category; whether language ('discourse') makes (or 'constitutes') the social world.

There also exists discussion of an advisory nature, on the mechanics and techniques of collecting and processing information. Most of this discussion provides instruction to readers on how, for example, to do oral history, to apply a range of statistical techniques to numerical data, to compile computerised data-bases of different kinds tailored for specific purposes, to handle certain sources of raw data such as census manuscripts and parish records, etc.

Then there is the last category of discussion on the discipline: that dealing with its methodology. And this brings me to the subject of this book.

The book's discussion of methodological problems is based on a particular concept of methodology.[1] Some practitioners and students associate 'methodology' with a particular research field or a specialised sub-discipline or genre. Hence, when they ask 'What is your methodology?' they mean something like: 'Do you work in women's history?', or 'Are you doing research in economic history?', or 'Are you bringing to the history of nineteenth-century Britain a focus based on social history?', or 'As you are a social historian, are you working within the genre of the history of *mentalités*?' But my definition excludes notions of fields, genres and sub-disciplines. They are far too broad.

Another notion often associated with methodology is the way we gather information and process it. Hence, oral history is sometimes called a methodology, as is the employment of mass quantification techniques.[2] But while this notion is closer to my definition, it is far too narrow.

The definitions that I will use in the book are variants of each other. One is *the relationship between the aims of an enquiry and its data, concepts and forms of reasoning, and their justification*; the other *the system of data, concepts and forms of reasoning which are used to solve a problem, and their justification*.

Discussion of the methodology of social history in the senses in which I use the term has hardly been extensive. Christopher Lloyd has produced a magisterial survey of the different 'schools' of the philosophy of knowledge and their broad relationship to the explanatory mechanisms adopted by certain groups of social historians. Theda Skocpol and her co-workers have theorised about the applications of the **comparative method** to social history. The historiography on a particular sub-discipline or 'school' of social history will often contain information on the aims which those working in it have collectively set themselves, and on the means by which they seek to achieve these aims by drawing on certain sorts of sources of data, techniques, concepts, and theories. But no comprehensive text on the methodological principles of social history has as yet been published, at least not in the Anglophone world. Several journals cater for specialist interests in the techniques of data collection and processing, but there are none that deal with the broader methodological problems faced by social historians.

Moreover, it is rare for a work by a practitioner to begin with an introduction that systematically states and justifies the aims of the enquiry in relation to its sources of data, its concepts, its methods of reasoning. There are exceptions of course. Among the most notable were the works by various cliometricians in the 1970s on patterns of collective protest and social mobility. Perhaps the most striking exception is G.E.M. de Sainte Croix's monumental work, *The Class Struggle in the Ancient Greek World* (London, 1981), which begins with a long and brilliant reflection on methodological issues, including theories of class, and justifies the applicability to that era of a Marxist class analysis based on the concept of exploitation.

Most book-length works have an introductory section on 'method', but it usually runs to no more than three or four pages, and is restricted to a discussion of sources, with perhaps a passing comment on theory and the salient literature in the field – the concepts, the methods of reasoning, and their justification, are left to speak for themselves in the main body of the text. In addition, as the work proceeds we rarely find the author identifying *major* problems in the concepts, theory, evidence and analytical framework as they arise (which they inevitably do), then outlining the options for solving each problem *and defending* the preferred problem-solution. This is not to say that social historians generally turn a blind eye to the problems in the concepts, theory, evidence and analytical framework as they arise in the text and never advance problem-solutions; the contrary is the case. What I am saying is that the way they write about these matters is far more likely to be implicit and *ad hoc* than explicit and systematic. Interestingly enough, the growth of interest in what is called 'theory' has not made much difference to practice: theory, to most social historians, is a system of generalisations or a set of propositions about the world. The term theory is rarely employed to describe abstract discussion of the methodological problems we encounter when formulating, demonstrating and testing the propositions and the generalisations.

But would a more reflective approach to social historical methodology of social history be feasible, fruitful or necessary? As some practitioners might say 'no', I will now try to anticipate their arguments.

One such argument is that a more reflective approach is unfeasible. Social history as a discipline has no unity, indeed it does not really exist, since it is composed of an extraordinarily large number of different sub-disciplines and 'schools'. These include the history of crime, *mentalités*, the family, demography, sex, popular culture, women, gender, children, popular protest, poverty, peasants, sensibility, health and medicine, diet and consumption, work, towns, social organisation, sport and recreation, the *Annales* 'school', **microhistory**, to name but a few. But I do not think this is a convincing argument. Each of the social sciences has also splintered into a myriad sub-discplines; and none, with the partial exception of economics, is a 'paradigmatic' discipline (based on a consensus about the validity of its core theories, how the social world works, what the entities in the social world are, how it should be studied, and the problems that need to be investigated), let alone a standardised vocabulary of technical terms. Yet this has not prevented the establishment of journals, of textbooks and university courses on the philosophy of the social sciences with a strong methodological bent.

Another possible argument is that a more considered approach to methodology is pointless. We have no independent access to the past as the past, everything we say about it is completely subjective, that all our accounts of the past are fictions, and we are fooling ourselves if we think that a more reflective approach to methodology would make any difference. This line of argument has become very fashionable. It is one that has been pressed by post-modernist theorists, and not a few practitioners have gone along or flirted with it. At the core of the argument is a relativist notion that objectivity is impossible, that our observations of the past (or of anything for that matter) are 'discourse-dependent', predetermined by the ideas in our minds which are fixed by the connotations of the language used by the society or sub-group of which we are members. The same relativist notion is often expressed in other ways. It is often encountered in the **hermeneutic circle** theory of interpretation, that what people see and how they interpret what they see is determined ('prefigured') by what they already know and by their existing interpretations. It is also manifested in the view that 'observation is theory-laden', that we select and organise evidence according to our prior beliefs, theories and ideological commitments. But irrespective of how it is expressed, the basic relativist notion is the same: that we cannot observe the world as it is (whether it be the world of nature or the social world of the present) or the world as it was (the social world of the past) since our observations are biased by our preconceptions.

The exact nature of the claims being made by relativists is frequently unclear. There is a radical difference between saying that our observations of the past are *shaped* or influenced by preconceptions and saying that our observations are *determined* by them. I entirely agree that the ways we see the past are shaped by preconceptions and that as a result total objectivity is impossible to achieve. But that does not mean that we should not strive to be objective, nor that everything is entirely a matter of opinion. As will be shown later in the book, although it is impossible to know the 'truth' about the social past in any absolute sense, we can nonetheless under certain conditions make propositions about it which are reliable to varying degrees.

The more extreme claim, that our observations are determined by preconception, is quite untenable. For one thing, it is self-refuting – incoherent. As the statement 'all observation is determined by preconceptions' is itself an observation, it too must be determined by preconceptions. An analogy would be the statement 'There are no words'; or the notorious book, *Against Method* (London, 1975), written by the relativist philosopher of science, Paul Feyerabend, which employed the standard methods of inductive and deductive reasoning to argue against any kind of method to make claims about knowledge. Of course, the hardline post-modernists who claim that it is impossible to be objective might also imply that they are exempt from the implications of their own claim. But if they imply that, they have to explain why they have this privileged status, or concede that other people are exempt as well. For another thing, the more extreme claim is confounded by our own research experience. If expectations determined observation, we would never see anomalies (data that are inconsistent with our preconceptions), we would never change our minds when we encountered the primary sources, and we would never be surprised by what we saw in them. Patently, however, we often see anomalies, change our minds as a consequence, and make surprising discoveries, despite our preconceptions.

Another possible argument is that social history does not require a self-conscious methodology since it has inherited from the 'old' history a well-established and effective set of conventions about how the past should be studied, conventions which where necessary have been suitably adapted to fit the particular needs of social historians. Some of these conventions consist of basic scholarly rules – such as 'getting the facts straight', consulting all the relevant source materials, providing adequate references, giving reliable summaries of factual minutiae, quoting accurately, and ensuring that quotations are not wrenched out of context. Other conventions relate to the techniques of verifying the authenticity of texts and the accuracy of their observations through 'external and internal source criticism'. There are also conventions about what social historians study (usually large collectivities of people and their constituent social categories, consisting of the subordinate elements); the need to give proper representation to the people 'lost from history' (women and ethnic minorities, for example); the need to avoid anachronism; the main grounds on which social historical explanations should be evaluated; and the obligations to document major contentions with empirical evidence, to distinguish matters of opinion from matters of fact, and to argue coherently.

How well does this argument hold up? There is no doubt that some of the conventions are well defined, well established and indispensable – notably, those relating to the basic rules of historical scholarship. Moreover, although the standard techniques of internal and external source criticism are not as widely applied by social historians as they might be, they are nonetheless most useful – and some practitioners have modified them in quite ingenious ways to solve evidential problems specific to social history. However, many of the other conventions have not been so useful. Some are too loose and thus not at all clear. Others have logical implications which make them difficult if not impossible to follow.

Moreover, several that work well in the context of the 'old' history, have been applied without modification to social history, where they do not. To illustrate the last point, let me put it in a broader context. Social history, according to one of the conventions, is generally (but by no means always) concerned with the behaviour, actions, customs, desires and values of large aggregates of subordinate people. Almost invariably, however, these people are inherently difficult for the social historian to understand since their cultures are so different from the one to which the social historian belongs. Also, the amount of reliable information that the social historian can discover about them is inherently minute since they usually generated few surviving records about themselves. Lastly, making plausible generalisations about them is inherently difficult since the social historian usually wants to generalise about the whole collectivity and not about a few of its individual members. But the subject-matter of traditional biographical, political, intellectual and diplomatic history, is quite different. The result is that the methods which the practitioners of the 'old' history have developed to solve the problems associated with their subject-matter, are not equipped to solve the problems associated with the subject-matter of social historians. To understand the mind-set of the elites they study, traditionalists follow the practice of 'immersing themselves in the documents' produced by the elites; but how can social historians follow this practice when the bulk of the available source material about the mind-set(s) of the people they want to understand was not generated by these people themselves but by the dominant elements and their institutions? Moreover, the confirmatory method favoured by traditionalists to support their claims, is to cite a few relevant examples; but the same method proves nothing when applied by social historians since their claims usually refer to large collectivities of people, not to a single individual, a handful of key personalities, a single institution or a small number of institutions. Yet as this book will show, social historians have tended to apply both these conventions to their subject-matter without adequate modification. They have mistakenly assumed that as the conventions worked well for the 'old' history, they must be appropriate for social history.

The intention of this book is not to criticise the conventions nor the practitioners who use them unreflectively. Instead it has other, more positive, aims. One is to suggest ways in which many of the conventions can be tightened, clarified, improved and enriched. Another aim, which is linked to the first, is to discuss seven standard methodological problems that occur in social historical enquiry and to outline a range of options for addressing each one. I will also attempt to demonstrate why some strategies and procedures for dealing with these problems are better than others. My overall objective, however, is to persuade readers that methodological inventiveness and skill are often as important to the growth of knowledge as the ability to formulate original hypotheses and the discovery of new and rich sources of raw data; and that we can construct better arguments in support of our claims, design our research more purposefully, ask sharper questions, deepen our understanding of what is going on inside the texts produced by others, and to make our own works more interesting, by being much more conscious of methodological principles.

Before outlining the seven standard problems several points need to be made clear. In the first place, the book is not about *research* methods – the techniques for collecting, compiling and processing data. In the second place, the book is aimed at advanced students, especially those engaged in thesis work, and all practitioners who take a problem-centred approach to social history. Moreover, the book will be of little interest to hardline post-modernists since I, unlike them, start from the premise that there is a world independent of our ideas and language and that we can know it, though often not without difficulty. Also, much of the discussion has been influenced by the philosophy of science and the social sciences; but where I have felt the need to refer to larger philosophical matters, I have tried to keep the discussion simple, brief, and free from jargon since this is not a book about the philosophy of knowledge and it is not aimed at philosophers but working social historians. However, I have used many technical terms and concepts, and as readers may not be familiar with many of them, I have highlighted the more abstruse when they first appear and defined them in a glossary of terms at the back of the book. In addition, the end of each chapter provides an annotated and highly selective list of works for further reading.

To make the discussion of each problem area as plain as possible, the points in nearly every chapter will be illustrated with an analysis of a small number of works by practitioners. In some instances I will refer to the complete work, in others to a section of it. Frequently, I will show how each exemplifies the problem and either fails to deal with it effectively, goes a long way in solving it, or solves it satisfactorily. This, I hope, will also provide students with a critical purchase on a range of important works of which they may not have heard, or which they have read but not studied in depth. Although it is beyond my scope (and expertise) to talk at length about the primary sources relevant to each work, this certainly is not intended to imply that methodological problems have nothing to do with the handling of primary sources – on the contrary. Very often a scrutiny of the primary sources which the author has used or an investigation of new sources will throw up additional methodological questions.

Readers might well have doubts about what I have suggested so far. Do they not have enough to do without worrying about methodological 'niceties'? How can these possibly be as important as doing good research and getting the facts straight? Would not greater attention to the problems of methodological strategy and procedure take the subtlety out of writing about the past and make it harder for practitioners to express themselves in stylish prose? Does it not give insufficient scope for the formulation of new and interesting ideas about the past? Would it not also make history tedious and less accessible to the non-specialist reader? Do my suggestions mean practitioners have to give up narrative history and replace it with analysis? Is it not the case anyway that the facts speak for themselves and do not need such heavy-handed methodological treatment?

Now I have to agree with the implication of the first question – striving to be rigorous does make the job of the social historian more demanding. At the same time, however, I think that attention to the problems can facilitate the job by making it more directed and focused. Doing good research and getting the facts straight are important but surely these things are not ends in themselves: if they were, history would be no different from antiquarianism. The best way to harness facts is to yoke them to the demonstration or testing of interesting ideas. I cannot agree with the assumption behind the claim that there is something unsubtle and unstylish about expressly addressing methodological problems. There is surely a virtue in writing lucid and explicit prose:

such qualities are much to be preferred to subtlety and stylishness if these mask and excuse obscurity of meaning and defective thinking. Nor do I think it right to assume that addressing methodological problems is a mechanical task that reduces the scope for creating new and interesting ideas about the past: attending to these problems can require a great deal of ingenuity, is often essential if the ideas promise to transform a domain, and may (as we shall see) stimulate new ideas rather than discourage their formulation. Some non-specialists could find that tackling methodological problems makes history less accessible and interesting; but this all depends on how the practitioner approaches the problems (the more interesting problems, for example, can be presented in the text, the least interesting left to an appendix). I have to admit that greater attention to the problems would demand more analytical writing; but I do not think that this entails the end of narrative history: depending on the subject-matter, there are a multitude of ways a good writer can combine analysis with narrative. Then there is the old cliché that tackling the problems is quite unnecessary since the facts speak for themselves. Social facts are seldom unproblematic and I doubt whether they do speak for themselves: the historian has generally selected them according to some notion or other which should be brought out into the open and defended.

The last issue that needs to be clarified is perhaps the most obvious: how do I know that there are seven standard methodological problems faced by social historians? I have to confess that I doubt whether there are only seven such problems; I am sure there are others; and none of the seven could be as famous as the 23 unsolved mathematical problems that were listed in a famous international conference of mathematicians in 1900! Moreover, my claim that they are the standard problems is not based on any kind of scientific sampling. Nonetheless, I have reasonable cause to say that they are the standard ones since I see them crop up continually in the criticisms which practitioners make of one another's works in reviews for learned journals, in debates on controversial works, and in exchanges at conferences. They also happen to be the sorts of things that I first look for when I read other people's works, that I have become increasingly aware of in my own publications and research, that I am now most interested in teaching, and that I think all students taking advanced courses in social history should know something about.

So the seven standard methodological problems we will be discussing, are these:

1. The problem of absent social categories. Should we always attempt to include in our accounts of the past every category of person that lived there? Are there justifiable grounds for excluding some and giving prominence to others?
2. The problem of generalising from fragmentary evidence. How can reliable claims be made about the general case in past time when the evidence we have for the general case usually consists of particular instances and when the typicality of these instances is usually unknown?
3. The problem of establishing causal importance. How can we know what factors had the greatest influence on an event, a state of affairs or a trend when a myriad different factors were usually involved?
4. The problem of establishing differences and similarities. Given that few social phenomena are exactly the same, how do we know when they should be put in the same class and when in different classes?
5. The problem of socially constructed data. Most data on subordinate and deviant groups in past time were generated by the dominant groups and their agents. Can these data tell us anything about the actual values, actions and beliefs of subordinate/deviant groups, or do the data only tell us something about the perceptions and responses of the dominant groups?
6. The problem of appropriate concepts. Should the concepts used for analysing a past society come from that society or can they be exterior to it or even come from the present?
7. The problem of testing competing explanatory accounts about the same phenomena. What criteria should we use for determining which account is the best?

■ *Chapter 1* ■

The Problem of Absent Social Categories

As I indicated in the Introduction, the subject-matter of social history usually consists of large aggregates of people (or collectivities) and of the social categories that make up these collectivities. The term collectivity may refer to a whole society, a cluster of societies, an empire, a civilization, a large segment of people within a society, a local community, an institution and so on. The term social category refers to a subset of a collectivity. Thus the peasants in a society could be taken as a social category, as could its urban population, its men over sixty, tribes-people living by lakes, children with red hair, the top quintile of income-earners, home-owners, the people born in a certain series of years (a 'cohort'), women who have given birth to two children and so forth and so on. I will distinguish a social category from a social group by stipulating that a category consists of people who do not necessarily know each other, interact, engage in reciprocity, have the same beliefs and values or have a common identity, whereas the people belonging to a group necessarily possess these attributes. Thus while many social categories may also have the attributes of social groups, by no means all will; a great many will be purely abstract entities, having no group life at all. Social historians do not always study large collectivities and social categories; they also study individuals as well as families and other very small groups. But when they do their purpose is generally to contribute to our knowledge of a collectivity.

Apart from taking large collectivities as their subject-matter, another convention followed by social historians is what I shall call the inclusionist convention – the notion that our accounts of collectivities should include, or at least strive to include, all categories of people belonging to the collectivity. The notion is usually most visible in critical discussion of books under review, of historiography, and of the state of the discipline. For example, in a discussion of gender, Leonore Davidoff, a well-known British practitioner, wrote that consciousness of how the past contributed to the present, 'must include everyone's past, humble as well as mighty, colonized as well as colonizer, children as well as adults, women as well as men.'[1] In an overview of the state of play in the discipline in *Reviews in American History* in 1996, one practitioner proclaimed,

> Social historians should study everybody. They should resist any temptation to replace a history that celebrates selected elites with one that celebrates selected groups. The social history of America in the twentieth century...involves all of the ways that ordinary people have responded to and shaped changing ideas about, race, gender, family, community, sexuality, ethnic, regional, and national identity, religion, work, and more.[2]

A standard practice in critical book reviews is to draw our attention to the failure by the works under discussion to mention this or that sub-section of the population. Sometimes reasons are given for these opinions: the critic might demonstrate, for example, that the absent sub-section did not fit the overall picture painted by the work. Sometimes, however, the critics fail to say why an absence is bad: they take it for granted that readers will know why it is bad since the convention is integral to the discipline. Certain stylised expressions have evolved to describe accounts with conspicuous absences. The labels include 'not full', 'gives inadequate attention to variations', 'neglects differences', 'overgeneralised', 'prone to overgeneralisation', 'lacking in nuance', 'overlooks the range of social experience', 'coarse-grained', 'sociological', 'not a complete history'. Some kinds of absences, however, attract more critical comment than others, and many are seldom mentioned if ever. The most frequently criticised are those related to the concepts of rural/urban, class, ethnicity, regionality, and gender.

To be sure, the convention is not universally held; different practitioners have quite different grounds for adhering to it; and the value attributed to it varies substantially. Moreover, most practitioners recognise that where the primary sources are particularly patchy, the convention cannot be followed to the letter. Further, they would not expect an account to categorise people in ways that were manifestly inappropriate – such as categorising a social stratum made up of illiterates according to the books they had read, or categorising the members of a male workhouse by gender, or categorising the English middle classes in the late nineteenth century according to the size of their slave workforces, and so forth. Thus, the convention is not a rigid convention, but a loose one, subject to diverse interpretations. Even so, if pressed, most practitioners would say, I think, that a bad social historical account is one that, either through faulty research and/or acts of conscious suppression, has absences.

In this chapter I want to argue that the convention needs modification, that it is inappropriate to apply it in a blanket manner, and that the demands for its blanket application stem from a mistaken view about the aims of social historical enquiry. I will begin the discussion by suggesting how the inclusionist convention might have arisen. I will then demonstrate that the convention has certain logical implications which makes it impossible to follow, and that our accounts of social life are necessarily selective in their coverage of categories. Following this, I will look at the problems involved in selecting categories, and indicate how a certain strategy will allow us to make justifiable category selections. Lastly, I will illustrate the points with two case studies.

The origin of the convention can be attributed to many factors. One is the long-held and widespread view – a view which prevails in the humanities and the social sciences – that history and, by extension, social history, is an **idiographic** not a **nomothetic** discipline. The term idiographic refers to the concern with particularities – particular individuals, particular events, particular places. The term nomothetic refers to the concern with generalities – with general classes of things. Thus history is viewed as an idiographic discipline in the sense that its subject-matter consists of specific entities – specific events and specific historical actors – and not of generalities. The reverse, however, is claimed of the social sciences: these are nomothetic disciplines in that they do not deal with specific entities but with general classes of things and with determining the regularities, the laws, governing the relationships between these general classes of entities. J.H. Hexter has devised a more homely way of describing these differences: historians, he says, are 'splitters', they split the social world up into tiny pieces, whereas social scientists are 'lumpers', they lump the pieces of the social world together. (This is discussed further in Chapter 5.) Irrespective of the rights and wrongs of this view, the point is that it has encouraged social historians to believe that it is not appropriate for them to study each collectivity as a single unit; that way of doing things is the approach of the social scientists; instead they should break each collectivity into all its constituent social categories and study them all. In short, one factor that has led social historians to follow the inclusionist convention is the influence of a traditional view inside the academy about the division of labour between the disciplines. It is not the business of history to generalise but to deal with specific entities. Historians do not study large aggregates; social scientitist do. Social scientists treat large aggregates as undifferentiated masses; historians disaggregate them. By extension, therefore, social historians in their accounts of the social past must endeavour to include every category of person who lived there.

Another influence upon the inclusionist convention came from the mother discipline itself – the 'old' history. Social history partly arose in reaction against what was perceived as the narrowness of the 'old' history – especially its preoccupation with events, politics, and elites ('kings, battles and treaties'). But the reaction did not by any means lead to the overthrow of everything associated with the 'old' history. A key goal of the 'old' history was to 'recover things as they actually were' in the past; in the famous phrase of von Ranke, the object of historical scholarship was 'wie est eigentlicht gewesen'. Now what this goal entailed was the idea that every historical work should be appraised by seeing how far its narrative structure corresponded to the actual events recorded in the archival documents. According to this standard, narrative structures that did not *correspond* to the actual events contained in the documents were wrong and therefore bad; while works that did correspond were true and therefore good. When social history emerged in France in the late 1920s and in the Anglophone world three or so decades later, it took over the correspondence principle. However, since it rejected the narration of political events and replaced it with the study of social collectivities, it had to apply the principle in a different way. Accordingly, its method for appraising studies of collectivities, was to see how far they corresponded to the actual composition of collectivities as revealed by the source materials. Since collectivities are composed of social categories, the test of a good account therefore was its capacity to represent every category of person belonging to the collectivity.

Perhaps, however, what did most to establish the convention in the Anglophone world were two radical movements within the profession. The first arose in the late 1940s. Consisting of the members of the Communist Party Historians' Group in Britain, its most notable figures were E.P. Thompson and Christopher Hill. Rejecting the 'elitism' of the 'old' history, its goals were to bridge the gulf between popular and academic history, and to show working-class people of the present how their forebears had resisted exploitation in the past. To these ends, their works attempted to recover in detail the experiences and 'everyday life' of the common people who had made their own history. The second movement was a composite one which arose from about the 1970s. It consisted of feminist historians in Britain, and feminist and black historians in the United States. Reacting against the 'old' history's fixation with the 'white male elite', and inspired by the political mobilisation of women and of blacks at that time, the goal of the second movement was to write compensatory history, revealing the gendered and racial dimensions of oppression in the past. As a result of the influence of both waves, it became virtually compulsory for studies of collectivities to cover the categories of the subordinate classes, women, and (in the United States) blacks. For example, in a special supplement to the *Journal of Social History* in 1995 dealing with the attack on the discipline by the American right wing, one contributor insisted that social history is a 'inclusive history': it 'dwells upon diversity, struggle, and the arbitrary exercise of power', it is 'the history of women, of African Americans, of working class America'. Another contributor observed: 'Social History in the United States originated in, and still devotes most of its attention to, the study of disenfranchised groups: workers, slaves, women, immigrants, racial and ethnic minorities.' Peter Stearns, the editor of the *Journal*, and a prominent practitioner, wrote: 'of course, social historians do see large groups of people, including lower-class and racial minority groups, as significant subjects of historical study and as significant actors in the past. ... Regardless of our special topics, which do not always focus on the masses, this inclusiveness forms a card-carrying test of social history.' And speaking from a 'central European viewpoint', J. Kocka said, 'Social historians are trained and

inclined to take a close look at the concrete patterns of social inequality, at the conditions under which large groups of people
live, at the hopes and fears of ordinary men and women of different class positions and different ethnic affiliations.'[3]

A variety of trends have reinforced the convention. They
include the disillusionment with quantitative social history in the
1970s which had attempted to study collectivities as undifferentiated mass aggregates; its supersession by cultural history which
has specialised in retrieving the separate identities of tiny groups
and communities; the belated discovery by Anglophone historians of the highly prestigious French *Annales* school of historians,
with its holistic approach to history, embracing all levels of human
experience; and the diversification of social history into a myriad
sub-disciplines, many of which are committed to the investigation
of highly specific social categories – children, the aged, rural women, prisoners, lunatics, paupers, prostitutes, transients, lesbians,
homosexuals, to name but a few.

It is not hard to understand the appeal of the inclusionist convention. For one thing, it seems democratic and sensitive to the
voices of the oppressed. For another, the convention appeals to
our humanistic convictions. By striving to be inclusive, we acknowledge cultural diversity and the richness of human experience. In
addition, the convention seems to make good sense. It appears to
be in tune with the historical realities of the pre-modern world.
Unlike the modern world where social life everywhere is subjected to strong external influences, in the pre-modern world
international institutions and the forces of economic and political integration were much weaker, allowing a host of peripheral
societies to develop distinctive cultures.

But as well-meaning and reasonable as the convention might
seem, it nonetheless has certain inherent problems which prevent
even its most ardent followers from observing it properly. At the
root of these problems is the nature of social categories. The convention presupposes that the types of social categories which can
be used to classify past people are relatively few in number and
immutable. The presupposition, however, is wrong: the types of
social categories are huge in number and highly unstable. How
then can we properly observe the convention? No matter how
hard we try, our accounts of the social past are doomed to exclude
many categories of person who lived there. Despite our best

efforts to be inclusive, the very nature of social categories guarantees that our accounts will contain multitudes of absences.

To elaborate and demonstrate the point that category types are innumerable and highly unstable, let me start by listing just the most basic types of categories. Now, the list will, of course, contain regionality, ethnicity, class, and gender. But why should the list stop there? People can also be classified according to many other basic types. They can be categorised by place of birth, age, marital status, religion, amount of schooling, level of marketable skills, consumption habits, dietary patterns, sexual preferences and behaviour, physical and mental health, medical history, their physical characteristics (weight, height and so on), personality structures, cognitive structures, pastimes, military service and record, the size of settlements they live in, the length of time they have dwelt there, the structures of the households they live in, the range and kinds of informal networks they belong to, the ways in which they have been brought up, their methods of child raising, their institutional affiliations, their relations to authority, the distance they travel to work, their working hours, the physical characteristics of the dwelling they live in, their vocabulary range, speech patterns, their manners, their genealogies, and so on.

But these are only the most basic types of categories we could divide people into. Each of these basic types can be fragmented into a long series of more specific types. Take the example of the 'consumption habits' basic type. Let us say that we define this in terms of total consumer expenditure and divide people belonging to this basic type into five percentiles of spenders, making five categories of people in all. Let us say, too, that in addition to dividing them into these five basic categories, we take the people in *every* category, and split them again into four grades of spenders according to how much money each person spent on four different groups of consumer items (food, rent, entertainment, and clothing). Let us now determine the total number of possible categories of people we have created, by multiplying the five basic categories by the four sub-categories of spenders by the four groups of consumer items. The sum total is 80 separate possible categories of people! But this is only the beginning of how we could proliferate categories from just the one basic type.

Remember that we started with five basic categories of spenders; had we devised six basic categories of people and divided them into the four percentiles covering the four groups of consumer items, we would have ended with the sum total of 96 separate categories of people. There would have been an even larger number had we taken five groups of consumer items, each with five percentiles of spenders.

More than that, we could continue to disaggregate the 80 categories by dividing the people belonging to each, into types made up of sub-sets of each of the four consumer items. Take the food item. This could be split into different five types of food – fish, meat, fresh fruit and vegetables, and bread. Under the fish item, we could divide all the fish eaters into those that ate haddock, those that ate herring, those that ate whiting, and those that ate every other sort of fish. In turn, the people belonging to the haddock-eating category, could be divided according to how they cooked the fish. Thus, we could have fryers of haddock, boilers of haddock, those who made haddock stew, and those who made the haddock into soup. Does the this reach the limits of the disaggregation process? No, it does not. The people, say, in the haddock-frying category could be divided according to the weight of the haddock they fried for each meal: one division consisting of those who fried less than half a pound and another division consisting of those who fried half a pound or more. But why stop there? The people who fried less than half a pound of haddock, could be split up into any number of other types of subsets – by the amount of time it took them to fry the haddock, by the amount of salt and vinegar they poured on the haddock, whether they fried the haddock in fat or oil, whether they ate the haddock with knife and fork or with their fingers, the size of the plate they ate from, whether they cooked the raw haddock in batter or rolled it in flour, whether they ate the haddock with the family, how many times a week they had a fry-up of haddock, whether they fried the haddock in a frying pan or a chip basket, how they disposed of the remains of the haddock, the degree of freshness of the haddock, the places where the haddock-fryers lived, the gender of the haddock-fryers, their ethnic origins, their class origins, whether their fathers ate fried haddock – need I gone on?

The point I am driving at is that, with sufficient ingenuity, we can take any one of the basic types and, by subjecting its constituent categories to a process of disaggregation, end up with a collectivity consisting of a vast number of different categories of people.

The reason we can do this is that social types and social categories are convenient abstractions. Unlike, therefore, a biological species, social categories are inherently plastic – highly unstable. If we want to disaggregate them until we reach their irreducible elements, we have to divide them a large number of times. In most instances, the process of division, if taken far enough, will not lead us to an irreducible category, but to the individuals who comprise the whole collectivity. The divisibility of social categories, in other words, allows their number to be multiplied in an exponential fashion, like a pyramid scheme.

The inherent plasticity of social categories, in consequence, makes the inclusionist convention unworkable in its present form. For one thing, given that their inherent instability entails their proliferation, how can we be expected to think of all their possible number when we describe them in our accounts of past social life? Irrespective of how much we try to be inclusive, we are bound to overlook some of them and thus violate the inclusionist convention.

For another thing, supposing we endeavoured to think of every conceivable category of person and we largely succeeded, how could our accounts possibly discuss all these myriads of categories in an intelligible fashion? The convention forbids generalising about the collectivity as a whole, from talking about averages and treating people as undifferentiated mass aggregates – real social life is not like that, we are told. This being the case, then every time we wanted to make a point about the collectivity, all those categories we had been able to think of would have to be mentioned, swamping discussion of the point in a morass of data. Not only, however, would each point be lost in the detail, but the whole account would become shapeless and inordinately lengthy – hardly a good way of pleasing the examiners of our theses, the editors of the journals to which we submit our articles, or the publishers which we hope will publish our manuscripts. In short, the inclusionist convention, if carried to its logical extension, prevents good – clear and concise – communication. An account that endeavours to include everything, can be read by no-one. An account that faithfully followed the inclusionist convention would be as unintelligible as a novel involving fifty characters that told the reader how every single episode in the plot affected each of the fifty characters.

To be sure, most practitioners who believe in the convention might respond to the argument so far by saying that, of course, no-one should follow the convention to the absolute letter – a total adherence to the convention was never a part of the convention. What the convention means, they might go on to say, is that our accounts of the social past should judiciously select its categories of people, but taking care to include, or giving prominence to, the most important categories. Moreover, they could conclude, the convention indicates what the important category types might be, namely, class, regionality/locality, ethnicity, and gender.

There are several rejoinders to this. The first rejoinder is the most obvious: is it a fact that the inclusionist convention means all these things? I suspect it does, but I cannot be sure. The second rejoinder is to suggest, in regard to the concluding point, that the list of important category types is too narrow. It is far from obvious that these are more central to past social life than many of the other basic types I mentioned earlier. Take religion: was that not central to social life before the modern era? What about military service and record: was this not crucial to the organisation of warrior societies? Then there is age: in most societies, is there not a strong relationship between age and the distribution of resources and rewards? And could we not go on through the other basic types and think of societies where one or more of these other basic types was important to it in some sense or other?

The third rejoinder is to point out, again in relation to the concluding point, that the convention may (presuming it does take ethnicity, class, gender and regionality/locality as the most important basic types) lead us in some situations to overgeneralise! They are, after all, very sweeping types, and the categories of people under each type are quite capable of being highly diverse. It would, for example, be highly misleading to claim in a gender-based account of a society that that there were marked disparities in average incomes between the genders, when the disparities within each gender may have been as great or greater.

The last rejoinder is to suggest that the whole idea of splitting people up into *the* important types of categories puts the cart before the horse. It tells us what the important categories must be for any given collection of people in the past irrespective of whether or not we know anything about them and irrespective of the objectives of our investigations.

So far we have seen that the inclusionist convention gives rise to a threefold problem for our accounts: one is the problem of conceiving of all the possible categories of people that *should be included*; the second is the problem of writing coherently about all the myriads of categories of people that we know *could be included*; and the third is the problem of knowing what the most important categories are so that they, at least, *will be included*.

What I now want to do, is to suggest a strategy for dealing with the problems – one that does not involve the abandonment of the convention, but its reorientation. Methodology, it will be remembered, is the specification of the aims, reasoning and evidence needed to solve a problem and the justification of the methodology. The strategy focuses on the aims part of the specification. *It presupposes, in essence, that the mode of enquiry governs category selection, and that the problems associated with the inclusionist convention solve themselves when a much more reflective approach is taken to setting aims.* The strategy, in other words, claims that taking a highly focused approach to the study of social life automatically filters out the extraneous categories and catches all the necessary ones, which should usually be limited and manageable in number.

But how do we go about following a highly focused approach? An apt analogy here could be drawn with the practices of the exponents of the 'old' history. Although they often say that historical narratives must correspond with 'what things were actually like', they nonetheless select their material according to the purpose which is expected of the form of history they are writing. The political biographer, for example, only includes material germane to the subject's role in a series of political events. The biographer is not expected to count the number of hairs on the subject's ears, or dwell on the subject's manner of walking, or spend pages describing the subject's eating habits, unless it so happens that these matters influence the political decisions made by the subject or the attitudes and actions of other actors towards the subject.

What we need, then, is something equivalent to these 'forms' and practices of 'old' history. If we had them, then we would know what the ground rules were for making acceptable breaches of the inclusionist convention. The difficulty, however, is that we have not evolved clearly defined conventions about what our modes of enquiry are, so that we can engage in a highly focused approach to social life that permits us to make acceptable choices of social categories according to the expected purposes of each mode. However, these modes are latent in a good deal of the work by social historians, and in a few instances they have been the object of considerable theoretical discussion and have given rise to programmes of research. Hence, one of the functions of the strategy is to clarify and make explicit these various modes, to codify them in a sense. To do so, I have drawn heavily on the ideas of particular disciplines – notably, the philosophy of history, the philosophy of the social sciences, and certain of the social sciences – since they have reflected more on these modes and are more conscious of methodological principles than are social historians.

In a moment I will describe these modes, their corresponding objectives, and how each mode solves the problems of category selection; but before doing so, several things need to be clarified. By modes of enquiry, I do not mean the genre (sub-discipline) or specialist area we happen to work in: the history of towns, demographic history, the history of crime, the history of leisure, the history of *mentalités*, cultural history and so on. My notion of a mode of enquiry instead can be thought of as a way of studying things that is appropriate for a certain field of problems. A mode of enquiry, thus, is bounded by certain rules or guidelines.

It also needs to be made clear that engagement in any one of these modes of enquiry critically depends on the availability of suitable source material; a clear understanding of the mode's rules or guidelines; and a belief in the value of question-driven and problem-centred investigation. By definition, the strategy is irrelevant to accounts that are wholly or strongly antiquarian in character. These include social historical writing in the 'slice of life' or descriptive realism vein, the dominant objective of which seems to be to document as faithfully as possible, like a display of museum photographs, the specifities of the past existence of ordinary people, letting the facts speak for themselves, with a minimum of analysis and argument. 'Slice of life' accounts are a common and quite legitimate way of doing social history but by their very nature generate all the troubles associated with the inclusiveness convention.

Another prefatory point that needs to made is that there are many different ways of operating in some of these modes and that therefore their 'rules' are not unitary nor clear-cut. In addition, although operating in these modes allows us to solve the problems of category selection, it does not solve other kinds of methodological problems. Indeed, many of these modes have been the centre of debate and have been strongly criticised, sometimes rightly, sometimes not. In subsequent chapters I will discuss these modes in much greater detail, drawing attention to the standard criticisms that have been advanced against them and indicating how they might be handled.

There are five modes of enquiry. I have treated them as 'ideal types' in the sense that my descriptions, for the sake of clarity, have accented their main features and ignore their complexities. Moreover, although the modes could be used in varying combinations in an account, I have discussed them separately.

■ Modes of enquiry

□ *1. The* hermeneutic *mode*

The overarching objective of this is to understand the alien ways in which people belonging to a past culture understood themselves and understood the world. Essentially, then, hermeneuticians endeavour to see a past society from the 'native's' point of view. To fulfill this objective, they characteristically examine in minute detail the actions and the concepts behind the actions of one person or of a tiny group of people. Hermeneutic social enquiry has been most developed by anthropologists, and has strongly influenced a specialised genre of social history called 'microhistory', the subject of a later chapter.

By its very nature, microhistory seldom has a problem with category selection. The reason for this is simple and it stems from the hermeneutic objective of attempting to see things only from the perspective of a tiny group of actors. When seeking to understand the actors' idea of themselves and of the world, the microhistorian does not impose exterior concepts or theories on the actors. Instead the historian works within their system of concepts, including their ways of categorising people, and uses these categories in the same way the actors do, attempting to make sense of them by seeing how the categories made sense to the actors themselves. Of course, when subsequently writing about the actors, the historian will have to translate their language of concepts so that the reader finds them intelligible, but the translations have to be as close to their original meanings as possible. The hermeneutic mode of enquiry makes category selection easy since it stipulates that the only appropriate way of selecting categories is within the framework of concepts of the people being studied. The hermeneutic rule of category selection, as with everything else, is thus very clear: when in Rome, do as the Romans do.

☐ 2. *The* intentional explanation *mode*

The objective of intentional explanation is to account for a specific action by recovering the *conscious* reasons of a specific historical actor, assuming the reasons were well-founded. To recover these conscious reasons, the investigator looks closely at the conscious desires, values, aims, purposes of the actor and relates these to the actor's conscious beliefs about how the desired ends could be brought about. Intentional explanations generally, though not always, entail hermeneutic enquiry since recovering the reasons requires an understanding of the culture that shaped the aims and beliefs of the actor. As the actor's situation is only seen from the actor's point of view, an historical account of the action selects social categories according to the actors' own perceptions of who those social categories were in that particular situation. As in the case of hermeneutic enquiry, thus, the rules of category selection under intentional explanation are very simple: again, the principle is, when in Rome do as the Romans do. The basic model of intentional explanation and its rules were formulated by a philosopher, W.H. Dray, specifically for historians, and by another philosopher, Karl Popper, for the social sciences and history. (For a discussion of Dray and Popper, see Chapter 8.)

☐ 3. *The* causal explanation *mode*

The standard objective of this mode is to explain social behaviour as driven by forces which people are usually unconscious of and over which they have no control. The mode assumes that the preconditions of the behaviour occur in many other cases, and where they do the same behaviour will always result. A very close relation to causal explanation is **probablistic explanation;**

this accepts that there will be exceptions to the explanation. Another close relation, **statistical explanation**, employs quantitative data to measure the strength of the association between preconditions and expected behaviour across a large number of comparable cases. The comparable cases which investigators in these modes analyse usually consist of social categories or collectivities belonging to the same class. Hence, broadly speaking, the objective of investigators is to establish that in all or most comparable cases (categories or collectivities belonging to the same class), the same attributes or circumstances comprising the preconditions of a given behaviour will be found in conjunction with that behaviour. In contrast to the hermeneutic and intentional explanation modes of enquiry, it is the investigator, not the people being investigated, who decides what categories or collectivities will be chosen for the investigation. The rules of causal explanation and statistical explanation are complex and were developed from about the mid-nineteenth century onwards by a series of theorists belonging to a tradition in the social sciences called the naturalistic or positivistic. A sub-discipline within social history called 'historical sociology' represents the tradition.

Category selection under these modes can be far more problematic than under the hermeneutic and the intentional explanatory. As I will discuss the reasons for this in more detail in later chapters, I briefly mention the most obvious. One problem is presented by the internal diversity of cases. If one of the cases contains a great diversity of people, its apparent conformity to the general model could be quite misleading since most of its overall expected behaviour may have come from extreme manifestations of the behaviour by an exceptionally small sub-section of people affected by extreme preconditions. Another problem is finding comparable cases that are truly comparable. Causal analysis relies on finding the same patterns in cases belonging to the same class. But it is seldom easy demonstrating that they do so, especially if they are composed of large aggregations of people.

☐ *4. The* 'how-possibly' *explanation mode*

The objective of accounts in this mode is to establish that things which appear to be impossible or strange are not once we look at them in their proper context. 'How-possibly' explanations are not concerned to show *why* things happened. Rather their objective is either to dispel our preconception that something could not have existed, or to remove our belief that some event or state of affairs was 'odd', 'incredible', 'puzzling', 'bizarre' and so on. 'How-possibly' problems arise when we say 'I cannot believe that so and so happened' or we ask 'How on earth could this have occurred?' The writer may try to dispel the preconceptions and remove the belief by showing where our preconceptions and beliefs are wrong. Alternatively the writer can overcome our incredulity by providing us with additional information about the phenomena in question, demonstrating perhaps that the entity or state of affairs is possible or normal when we consider the logic of the situation. By their very nature, 'how-possibly' explanations do not present problems of category selection where the puzzle affects an event or an attribute associated with a category of people. As the problem is specific to those people, we do not have to select categories. 'How-possibly' modes of enquiry are well recognised in the philosophy of science.[4]

□ *5. The* focused information-gathering *mode*

The objective of this mode is obvious enough. It is not to explain or to analyse but to find and compile the maximum amount of reliable information on a precisely defined and pre-designated subject. The mode is, of course, very common. We engage in it every time we go into primary sources knowing exactly what kind of information we want. We engage in it, for example, when we want to know whether a contemporary rumour about the occurrence of a particular event had any foundation, what the size of the casual labour force was in particular area, what books a certain collection of people had read, how many people were unemployed in a certain year in a given place, what the average age of life expectancy was in a certain time and place, when certain institutions in a place were founded, what festivals a particular local community had over the year, and so on and so forth. To be sure, such enquiries often involve asking questions about the social composition of a collectivity ('what categories of people did so and so'). But we can lessen the problems associated with category selection by showing that differences within each category were not greater than those between them.

To illustrate the points that have been made, we will now examine two very famous texts, E.P. Thompson's *The Making of the English Working Class* and Fernand Braudel's *The Mediterranean and the Mediterranean World in the Age of Philip II*. In the case of Thompson's work, however, we will illustrate our points less by examining his text than by scrutinising the criticism that it fails to consider that the experiences of women were different from those of men.

history from Below [handwritten annotation]

The case of E.P. Thompson's *The Making of the English Working Class*[5]

E.P. Thompson was labour history's most influential figure and his *The Making of the Working Class* (first published in 1963) is one of the most cited books in the humanities and the social sciences. The central objective of *The Making* is to tell the story of how 'In the years between 1780 and 1832 most English working people came to feel an identity of interests as between themselves, and as against their rulers and their employers.'[6] The huge reputation of this giant text (it runs to over 800 pages) stems partly from the extraordinary range of the subjects it covers, partly from its self-conscious attempt to tell the story from the viewpoint of the actors, partly from the passion with which it is written, but mainly from its bold reinterpretation of orthodox Marxist accounts of how class consciousness arises.

According to orthodox Marxist history, the material base in any given society (its economic forces and productive relations) *determines* the superstructure (everything else in society including the formation of social classes and their sense of identity – or 'consciousness'). Although a committed Marxist, Thompson criticises the determinism in the orthodox account and the primacy it attributed to economic factors. In *The Making* he gives far more weight to two other factors. Firstly, he plays up the ability of working people to make their own history, that is, to reflect upon and take action against their economic exploitation and their political oppression (this ability is otherwise broadly known as **agency**). Secondly, he claims that the 'culture' of working people played a crucial part in motivating and enabling them to engage in these struggles.

The whole implication of *The Making* is that culture is the source of agency and that culture is very loosely tied to the economic base and can arise independently of it.[7] Thompson, however, does not repudiate the role played by economic factors in class formation. As he sees it, economic and cultural factors play equally important but different roles. In his famous formulation, productive relations, the pattern of exploitation, gives rise to the 'class experience' of working people (by class experience he means their physical and emotional condition). But the manner in which they *understand and respond* to their exploitation is moulded and governed by their cultural experiences (which he defines very broadly as 'traditions, value-systems, ideas, and institutional forms').[8]

The Making is divided into three parts. In the first, he details the stock of ideas that English working people possessed by the late eighteenth century and that subsequently helped to shape the growth of their class consciousness. These ideas included the traditions of dissenting religion, the unwritten codes of popular justice, the notions of the 'Englishman's birthright' (liberty from arbitrary government), the myth of the Norman Yoke, and most important of all, the democratic ideas of a contemporary radical, Thomas Paine (*The Rights of Man,* 1791). Stimulated by the French Revolution, skilled workers (artisans) throughout England embraced Paine's ideas and established the first working-class organisations, Corresponding Societies, to discuss them. Although the advent of England's war with France led the authorities to suppress these Societies, Paines' ideas, Thompson maintains, went underground.

In the second part, Thompson turns to the industrial revolution. He argues that under the influence of *laissez-faire* dogma, the state gave the new forces of industrial capitalism free reign to exploit working people. As a consequence, common living standards dropped sharply. The novelty of the argument here is his view that assessments of living standards must be based on the concept that working people themselves had of their material welfare. Within these terms, he says, the workers who lost most from the rise of industrial capitalism were the communities of independent handloom weavers. They saw their whole way of life being destroyed by the rise of mechanised textile production. A subsidiary argument claims that Methodism did far less to foster working-class consciousness than the ethos of mutual aid that working class communities developed themselves.

In the third part, Thompson brings the themes of the other two parts together. He shows how from the end of the Napoleonic Wars to the 1830s working people, stimulated by the newly implanted radical ideas, responded to their increased exploitation by organising wave upon wave of political protest. Spearheading much of it were self-educated artisans. Although most of the movements were outlawed and suppressed, the working class was made by 1832; it had become the most important political presence in England.

A key feature of Thompson's methodology is that it self-consciously operates within the hermeneutic genre. Though he resorts to causal explanations much more frequently than his admirers think he does, he nonetheless aspires to explain events by referring to the motives, reasoning, meanings and intentions of the actors (or what he calls their 'experience'). As his subjects are the whole of the working class, the methodology requires him to engage in microhistory on a vast scale. And herein lies one of the problems of the text: its acute ambivalence towards generalisation. On the one hand, the fact that he seeks to engage in micro-history on a vast scale obliges him to go inordinate lengths to detail the particularity and diversity of working class experience. Most of the variations he specifies are occupational and regional/local; some are religious (where he says that the Methodist creed prevented Methodists from developing a political consciousness); and ethnic (where he says that the immigrant Irish were difficult to organise into formal protest groups). On the other hand, however, Thompson implicitly recognises that if he goes too far in emphasising particularity and diversity of experience, he will negate his overall argument that the working class developed a *common* identity. The problem of particularity and diversity is acknowledged towards the beginning of part two but is not resolved. He answers it with the undemonstrated assertion that:

> Nevertheless, when every caution has been made, the outstanding fact of the period between 1790 and 1830 is the formation of the 'working class'. This is revealed, first, in the growth of class-consciousness: the

consciousness of an identity of interests as between all these diverse groups of working people and as against the interests of other classes. And, second, in the growth of corresponding forms of political and industrial organisation. By 1832 there were strongly-based and self-conscious working-class institutions – trade unions, friendly societies, educational and religious movements, political organisations, period-icals – working-class intellectual traditions, working-class community-patterns, and a working-class structure of feeling.[9]

Thompson, not surprisingly, is unable to reproduce every recorded nuance of the experience of exploitation and protest felt by every social category in the whole working class. But given that his methodology commits him to do this, the text invites criticism that it has left out or neglected this or that category of people and this or that particular experience. In recent years, most of the criticism along these lines has come from feminist historians who claim that the text gives insufficient attention to gender differences.

We will now examine the criticisms leveled by one such critic, Catherine Hall.[10] Her central claim is that women played a 'very' different role in working-class radical culture from that of men. It was a culture, she says, that 'placed men and women differently and the highlighting of these forms of sexual division can give us some access to the gendered nature of popular culture in the early nineteenth century. Men and women experienced that culture *very differently*.'[11] To make her case, she starts off by closely comparing the respective roles played by a working-class leader, Samuel Bamford, and his wife, Jemima, in a procession and the great demonstration that preceded the infamous 'Peterloo Massacre' in Manchester in 1819. The analysis, based on Samuel's autobiography, leads Hall to conclude that whereas Samuel (typifying the male participants) entered the fray as an independent political being, Jemima (like the majority of female reformers) took part as 'a wife and mother supporting the cause of working men'.[12] Hall then explains these differences. She says that in part they were the product of the separate spheres doctrine. Working-class radicals picked the doctrine up from many enlightenment writers and also assimilated it, though adapting it to their own purposes, from the middle classes. In part, too, the differences sprang from changes in the organisation of protest. Up to the eighteenth century rioting was the main form of protest and was open to all, includ-ing women. But after the late eighteenth century protest was increasingly mobilised by formal institutions which women, having lower levels of literacy and schooling, found less accessible.

The purpose of Hall's critique cannot be to contradict Thompson's description of the place of women in radical culture since his description basically agrees with hers.[13] Rather it seems that the underlying objective is to show that a class analysis – and Thompson's by implication – cannot explain the gender differences in radical culture and working-class life as a whole.[14] As I said before, Thompson's commitment to microhistory on a vast scale makes the text inherently vulnerable to this sort of criticism. Moreover, the criticism is useful since, if plausible, it indicates that in one particular area the explanatory power of Thompson's thesis is limited.

Yet the criticism does not threaten the plausibility and explanatory power of the major parts of Thompson's thesis. If Hall had claimed that the domestic subordination of women prevented most of them from developing class consciousness or rendered them less class conscious than most men, this would have fundamentally challenged Thompson's thesis. So would the argument that by 1832 women's identification of themselves as women was greater than their working-class identity, or that antagonisms between working-class men and women were stronger than their sense of antagonism to the other classes. But she does not make this argument.

Another problem with Hall's case is that it is reflexive. It is as imprisoned in as monolithic a system of categorisation as it says *The Making* is. It claims that a class analysis cannot encompass the 'complexities' of the relation between gender and culture.[15] But in singling out only this area of complexity and refusing to consider others it exposes itself to the self-same criticism – of failing to encompass complexity. A class analysis of radical culture is gender blind; but a gender analysis ignores the possibility there may have been important (perhaps more important) differences in the experiences of people in other terms, by age, religion, ethnicity, locality and so forth.

Moreover, Hall does not consider the possibility that the differences in the experiences between men and women were less than they were within each gender. Women are simply assumed to have uniform experiences as are men. There is no *prima facie* reason to believe this assumption is true.

Finally, there is a problem in the critique with the meaning of 'difference'. Hall offers no criteria by which we can judge the significance of the gender differences she is talking about. She relies instead on the details of her evidence to verify her emphatic statement that women experienced radical culture 'very differently' from men. But the details do not clearly bear this out.

She claims that Samuel went to Manchester because he was politically committed while 'Her anxiety to go to Manchester stemmed from her fears for him'. This is difficult to reconcile with Hall's description of the procession. At its head were two hundred women supporters, 'including Bamford's wife, some of whom were singing and dancing to the music. The demonstrators had as their keywords "cleanliness", "sobriety", "order" and peace and the women symbolised these virtues.'[16]

Hall says that Samuel's preoccupations on the day were related to the organisation of the protest while Jemima's preoccupations were with the family. She organised the child-minder before the protest; after the massacre 'her anxieties and fears were focussed on her husband's safety'; and 'her first concern, once she knew that her husband was safe, was to get back to the child.' Yet Hall also says that Samuel was certainly not devoid of concern for his family. Immediately after the killings, Bamford 'began to worry as to where his wife was'; he 'blamed himself that he had allowed her to come at all'; and 'after much anxiety' he met up with her.[17]

Hall says that like all reform demonstrations, that which preceded Peterloo was 'predominantly' a male occasion. Yet Hall also points out that over a hundred women were wounded and two were killed at Peterloo; and that Mary Fildes, President of Manchester's Female Reform Society, shared the platform. She says in addition that women participated in many working-class political institutions: 'they were there, in considerable number and with considerable strength'.[18]

The case of Fernand Braudel's *The Mediterranean and the Mediterranean World in the Age of Philip II*

Braudel's *Mediterranean* is probably social history's most celebrated work if not its most monumental. A leading example of the highly prestigious French *Annales* school of history, the book is massive in scale.[19] The term *Annales* comes from the title of the journal which the leaders of the movement founded in 1929, *Annales d'histoire sociale et économique*. It is now called *Annales: économies, sociétés, civilisations*. The book was the product of two decades of prodigious scholarship based on research in nineteen archives in eleven cities of five countries, and the English translation of the text, published in 1966, is 1237 pages in length. The work originated as a Sorbonne thesis on the Mediterranean policy of Philip II (king of Spain from 1556 to 1598). But becoming dissatisfied with the narrow political scope of the thesis, Braudel turned it into all-encompassing study of the geographical, material, social and political character of the whole Mediterranean area. As such it represents what Lucien Febvre, Braudel's mentor and one of the founders of the *Annales* movement, had called *histoire totale*. The term does not literally mean the inclusion of every event that happened in the past, but the *holistic* study of the past. Instead of dwelling on a specific aspect of history or a society, the objective of works written in the vein of *histoire totale* is to deal in an interrelated fashion with all four dimensions of human existence: the material, the social, the cultural and the political. To its followers, *histoire totale* is a scientific approach to history, for it requires a systematic investigation of the past that draws upon and integrates the concepts and techniques of all the human sciences: economics, sociology, psychology, geography and anthropology.

In addition to the sheer scale of its scholarship, the fame of *The Mediterranean* stems from the brilliance and boldness with which Braudel took Febvre's notion of *histoire totale* and fitted it to his own revolutionary concept of historical time. Before Braudel's work, it was the convention of historians to think and write of historical time mainly as something that operated on just one level, as a rapid succession of unique events generated by the decisions of the members of the political elite. Braudel accepted the reality of this level of time which he conceived as the short-term wave, the surface event: *courte durée* or *histoire événementielle*. But, he claimed, the surface event, the stuff of traditional political and diplomatic history, was the least important unit of time. Underlying it were two others. These had much greater influence on human affairs and the actors were largely unconscious of their operation. Interacting with *courte durée* was medium-range time, the *conjoncture* or *moyenne durée*. At this level historians investigated the slower-moving time of social forces and of economic systems and cycles. Knowledge of these drew upon the disciplines of sociology and economics. The third level of time was the very slow moving history of the physical environment, *histoire structurale* or the *longue durée*, a level of time which historians had rarely if ever considered before. Taking hundreds of years to complete, *histoire structurale* was the most important unit of time of all since it consisted of the structures that limited the possibilities of human action. Studying *histoire structurale* required a knowledge of geography and associated disciplines such as climatology.

The Mediterranean is divided into three parts, each dealing with one of the *dureés*. The first is concerned with *histoire structurale*. Here Braudel detailed the Mediterranean's physical environment and its impact on human geography (the location of urban centres, the main transport routes and so forth). The second examines the Mediterranean's social and economic systems, the *conjoncture*. Here his erudition takes the reader through a dazzling array of topics including population trends, the rise in prices, an estimate of the size of the Mediterranean economy, an assessment of the role of cities on economic development, the effect of distance on the Mediterranean economy, forms of shipping, vagabondage and banditry, forms of war, the resources and weaknesses of the Spanish and Turkish empires, the place of ethnic minorities (the Jews, the Bulgars and the Moors) within these empires, and so on. The third part focuses on *histoire événementielle*. Here Braudel gives a very detailed (and much less readable) narrative of the events associated with the conflict between the Spanish and the Turkish Empires during Philip II's reign (interestingly enough, all of this part has been omitted from the 1992 abridged edition of the English translation of the text).

There are many problems with the methodology of *The Mediterranean*. The more serious of these arise from Braudel's ambition to produce *histoire totale*. Although the concept is somewhat vague it has a very strong resemblance to the convention of avoiding absences. The notion that a good account is a full one, that it should cover every social category, is little different from the objective of *histoire totale* to embrace the whole of human activity, every aspect of human existence. Indeed, the terms Febvre often used as synonyms for *histoire totale* – *histoire vraie* and *histoire à part entière* – are

very close in meaning to 'full account'. It is not surprising, therefore, that the problems that are inherent in the notion of the 'full
account' are very similiar to those in Braudel's version of *histoire
totale*.

To start with, given that there are an indefinite number of ways
in which human activity can be categorised, it was inevitable that
Braudel failed to include every conceivable social category or type
of human activity in his text. For example, he says nothing about
family and household structure and the place of women and children. Although there are pages of discussion about transport,
commerce and financial matters, he says very little about agriculture and by implication peasant society. Despite the notion that
histoire totale should draw on the techniques and concepts of all the
human sciences, the text bears almost no influence of anthropology: except for the discussion of vagrancy and banditry, it says
little or nothing about the relationship of ordinary people to the
law courts; popular beliefs, perceptions and values (*mentalités*);
religious institutions and practices; the everyday life of villagers;
and about guilds and other forms of community.

Moreover, in striving to produce *histoire totale*, to embrace all
the different aspects of human endeavour, Braudel inevitably created a text that lacked coherence. As one critic pointed out, 'The
parts of his "world" are all there, but they lie inert, unrelated, dis-
crete.'[20] Although the text is organised around the concept of the
three levels of time, it has no overarching theme. The huge body
of data which Braudel generated is not used to support an overarching causal explanation, to test a interconnected series of
hypotheses, to make a 'how-possibly' argument, to solve a large
problem connected to a turning point in politics or to the way contemporaries understood the world. There are no linkages
between the three levels of time and few within each level. To be
sure, a good many of the innumerable subsections of the first two
parts tackle interesting and important problems; but the problems have no overall connection; and most of the subsections
seem to have been devised simply to provide information for its
own sake. In other words, Braudel ended up with a text that failed
to hold together because it aimed to achieve the impossible: to say
everything and anything, to produce a full account.

Interestingly enough, the difficulties of *The Mediterranean* were
not lost on the next generation of *Annaliste* historians. Instead

of trying to follow the tradition of *histoire totale*, they increasingly turned to the study of large-scale historical questions, *histoire problème*.

■ Summary

This chapter has argued that there is a conflict between the basic subject-matter and the basic methodology that are conventionally prescribed for social history. On the one side, social history by definition is concerned with collectivities and the social categories that make up collectivities. On the other side, social historical accounts of past social life are expected to include all categories of people who lived there. These objectives are impossible to reconcile. Any one social category is not only indefinitely divisible but is also capable of being converted into an indefinite number of hybrids. When composing an account, it would be exceedingly difficult to conceive of all the categories that it could include. Even if we could conceive of the largest possible number, the inclusion of them all would render our accounts unintelligible. Although it is possible that the inclusionist convention means something else, that we should only include the most important categories, it does not provide any criteria for deciding what social categories are important. There is a solution to category selection, however, and this is to take a problem-led approach to social enquiry. Category selection basically looks after itself if we model our accounts on one or more of five modes of enquiry, each of which has a different objective. These modes are the hermeneutic, the intentional explanatory, the causal explanatory, the 'how possibly', and focused information-gathering.

■ *Chapter 2* ■

The Problem of Generalising from Fragmentary Evidence

A very common method in social history for supporting claims about a collectivity, is to generalise from fragmentary evidence – from a few supporting examples. The method gives rise to perhaps the best known of all the seven problems discussed in this book. The problem goes under a variety of names. They include the problem of typicality, the problem of using unrepresentative data, the problem of generalising from the particular, the problem of arguing from the particular to the general, the problem of demonstrating the unknown many by referring to the known few, the problem of inferring the whole from the part, the fallacy of extrapolating the unknown from the known, the induction problem, the problem of impressionistic or anecdotal evidence, and the problem of arguing or demonstrating by example.

In this chapter I want to start by suggesting why the method is so popular. I will then demonstrate that it is an unreliable method when used in isolation and that, in some contexts, its unreliability has serious consequences. I will then outline and assess some of the standard procedures and strategies practitioners have used to limit and control these weaknesses.

Let us begin, then, by discussing why social historians have a preference to demonstrate claims about large aggregates by citing *a few relevant examples*. Although there are many reasons why they adopt this technique, I will outline just a few. One is that the method is so simple to employ: of all the methods for confirming a claim, it is by far the easiest to apply. Another is that the method seems to make sense. If, after exhaustive research, we have found (say) twelve examples of people possessing a certain characteristic and none to the contrary, it seems reasonable to infer that most of the aggregate to which the twelve belonged also possessed the same characteristic. In addition, I suspect that many practitioners prefer the method believing as they do that the only alternative to it is **mass quantification,** a technique which they hold in disdain or which they find too abstruse or which they assume (often correctly) is inapplicable to their particular subject area. It is also likely that many are strongly attached to the method since they believe that the provision of a few well-chosen examples to confirm a major point can often give us more insight into the past and is certainly more readable than a book full of statistics. On top of this, many have probably carried the practice over from the 'old' history where it is the dominant method of confirmation – and seems to have worked well.

The main reason why practitioners use the method, however, probably stems from the fact that they feel, even if they have strong reservations about the method, that they have no choice. Most work in areas where the evidence about the large aggregate consists of nothing other than a fragment of the aggregate. The raw data are fragmentary either because the past society never systematically collected information on their particular subject area; or because the past society did collect systematic information on the area but preserved only fragments of it; or because the past society did collect systematic information but only fragments of it are accessible.

Perhaps the worst affected subject areas are the history of *mentalités*; most forms of 'history from below'; and most aspects of pre-industrial society. In very broad terms, the least affected subject areas are those related to elites (generally the best documented category in any given society); and those related to the industrialising societies of the nineteenth and early twentieth centuries since industrial development both impelled and permitted central governments to enumerate and investigate to an unparalleled degree the activities of their subordinate classes.

For the sake of accuracy, we should probably classify fragmentary evidence into three types: a complete or systematic fragment (one made up of all or the majority of the cases – e.g. all the people of a single village – belonging to a small sub-unit of a much larger population); a dispersed fragment (a pool of cases drawn from a disparate collection of sub-units of a much larger population);

and a mixed fragment (one which consists of complete fragment(s) and a dispersed fragment(s)).

Having discussed some of the reasons why the method is so commonly used by practitioners, let us now analyse the problems it gives rise to. The problems, it might be noted, are not unique to social history. They affect all fields of knowledge. They occur whenever all six of the following conditions come together. When we

1. study large aggregates of cases. (In social history these aggregates usually consist of all the individuals belonging to a collectivity, but they can also consist of other classes of entities e.g. households, localities, crimes, etc.);
2. know nothing about most of the cases making up the large aggregate. The known or knowable cases are a fragment of the aggregate;
4. use the fragment – the small number of cases within the large aggregate that are known about – as evidence for our claims about the whole aggregate;
5. do not demonstrate that the small number of cases making up the fragment have a reasonable likelihood of typifying the whole aggregate;
6. depend on the method to support our claims. Either the method is our sole confirmatory device or has been supplemented by another confirmatory method that is grossly defective.

Basing a claim on fragmentary evidence under these six conditions is one step better than basing it on no evidence at all, but it is only one step better. In essence, the problem with a claim made under these six conditions is that it has very shaky foundations. The foundations are insecure not because they are constructed from evidence that is wrong, but because the evidence is unreliable or *indeterminate*. The evidence does not necessarily support the claims since we have done nothing to demonstrate that the small number of supporting examples are typical of all the cases making up the large aggregate. The examples may well be typical of all the cases; but equally they may not be. Instead of being typical or fairly typical of all the cases, the examples could just as easily represent the exceptional cases; they might even represent the extremely exceptional cases. Unless the claim coheres with our background knowledge, there is no way of telling if the multitude of unknown cases are the same as our few examples or differ from them completely. It is quite possible that the multitude of unknown cases support our claims; but it is equally possible that the multitude of unknown cases contradict them. Thus generalising from a few supporting examples to a multitude of unknown cases, gives us no grounds for believing that the claims are true or even credible. The claims would only be true or credible if we had demonstrated that our few examples were definitely/probably typical of all the unknown cases, or if we had employed an additional method for confirming the claims (corroboration) that adequately supported them.

Let me spell out the implications of this problem of indeterminacy. Earlier I pointed to the temptation to believe that claims derived from the method of arguing by example must be true or credible if (a) the majority of the examples told the same story and (b) the examples were the fruit of exhaustive and painstaking research. But under condition 5 and 6 this belief is erroneous. By themselves both (a) and (b) do not make the claims credible let alone true. The crucial point is that we do not know if the pattern formed by the examples is purely fortuitous, *reflecting nothing more than the peculiarities in the ways the data were originally generated and/or were preserved subsequent to their generation*. Unless we can determine that the pattern is not fortuitous – and this means demonstrating that the distribution of the examples probably comes close to resembling the distribution of all the cases – the examples are not a reliable guide to the whole aggregate. We can no more depend on the examples to tell us about the whole aggregate than we can accurately predict tomorrow's general election by asking twelve people in the local pub about how they will vote.

Can the problem of fragmentary evidence be solved with a local case study approach? There has been a strong push behind this approach in recent years. The rationale behind it usually concerns research situations where data are fragmentary at the national level but are full or seem to be reasonably full at the local level. In such situations it is argued that practitioners should focus their efforts on local case studies. But I do not see how this approach can by itself solve the problem of fragmentary evidence. First, studying a few localities in depth may certainly tell us a great deal about these localities; but it still leaves us with the problem of generalising from the particular since we do not know if the few localities that have been investigated are typical of the many that have not. Second, even where historians have studied many localities belonging to the same society, their individualistic practices usually prevent them from generating a pool of standardised data – of comparable cases. With the notable exceptions of demographic historians and the practitioners in the *Annales* tradition, most historians investigating different localities in the same society in the same period seldom ask the same questions, adopt the same methods, possess the same theoretical orientations, use the same categories for presenting data. Sometimes they may even lack access to the same kinds of sources. Over the last two or three decades, for instance, there have been twenty-five studies of colonial New England towns and each has produced a different model of what a typical New England local community should look like![1]

I should stress that there are many circumstances in which the problem of demonstrating by example is either not serious, scarcely worth bothering about or does not occur. These circumstances cover the claims that are self-evidently true; that are trivial (i.e. commonplace, clichés); that are minor or inessential components in an overall argument; that do not pretend to be anything other than conjectures; and that are crucial to an overall argument but that are implicitly well-established in that they are consistent with the evidence produced by other, uncontested, studies (in most circumstances, such claims will be trivial, but in others they may be bold especially if they synthesise claims in a original way).

We become hostages to fortune, however, if we rely on the method to support contentions that are not only crucial to the overall argument but also bold, ambitious, interesting (meaning that they are original or challenge the orthodoxies or both). In these situations arguing by example is a positive liability for two interrelated reasons. The first, of course, is that the evidence we have used to support the contentions is inherently indeterminate. The second is that the method is such a weak one that it leaves our contentions practically defenceless. It is seldom difficult for assiduous defenders of the orthodoxies to find a few **counter-examples** in the primary sources. If these counter-examples outnumber (or are close in number to) our few confirming instances the defenders could justifiably argue that they had undermined or refuted our claims within our terms, on the basis of our chosen method. The criticisms might also imply that our research and scholarship had been shoddy since we had failed to examine all the relevant sources. Given that the fate of interesting ideas often turns on the thrust and cut of debate, it is thus foolhardy to depend on the method to support such ideas, since it can so easily be turned against them, jeopardising their chances of replacing the ortho-doxies. To repeat the point I made in the introduction, we ignore issues of method at our peril: there is no point in advancing a bold claim only to see it being cheaply dismissed because our strategy or procedure for defending it was inherently feeble.

I now want to illustrate the problem by examining a key section of a landmark book on the interaction of class and gender by two British historians, L. Davidoff and C. Hall, *Family Fortunes: Men and Women of the English Middle Class, 1780–1850*.[2] A case study based on an industrial area, Birmingham, and two rural counties, Essex and Suffolk, the book claims its contentions are applicable to the rest of England. The overall argument effectively falls into two parts. The first part contends that the rapid growth of capital-ism during the English industrial revolution was based on the activities of the middle-class family business, and that the resources mobilised by the wives and daughters 'underpinned' the efforts and ambitions of male middle-class entrepreneurs. The second part maintains that as these family businesses prospered and matured, new cultural patterns emerged. As they grew in wealth and economic security, middle-class families were able to engage in greater consumption. Their modes of consumption, however, were shaped by the ideals associated with the Evangelical revival. The ideals, amongst other things, stated that a truly religious life required the separation of the home from the business world. They also stated that women were naturally more religious than men, and had a special duty to maintain the spiritual purity of the home. The ideals impelled families to express their higher living standards by moving to the seclusion of the suburbs, to separate the home from the place of production. At the same time, the higher living standards allowed families to take women out of the busi-ness world and give them the leisure they needed to fulfil their new prescriptive roles as the moral guardians of the home. Thus the growth of capitalism in conjunction with the Evangelical revival were responsible for the marginalisation of middle-class women.

The key section I want to examine to illustrate the problem of typicality is in Chapter 6, '"The Hidden Investment": Women and the Enterprise'. The section is a central component of the first part of the overall argument and advances a bold claim.

To some extent, the boldness stems from the strength with which it is formulated. The authors write that female kin played a *'vital'* part in small enterprise; that 'middle-class men ... were, in fact, *embedded* in networks of familial and female support which *underpinned* their rise to public prominence'; and that the study 'argues for the *centrality* of the sexual division of labour within families for the development of capitalist enterprise.'[3] Couched in these terms, the claim implicitly challenges an historiographical orthodoxy. Before Davidoff and Hall's investigation, the generality of historical studies explaining the upward mobility of middle-class families had largely or wholly ignored the role played by female kin, implying that the characteristics of female kin had little or no capacity to explain middle-class success.

But there is another factor that makes their claim a bold one. The authors make seven propositions about how female kin contributed to middle-class family success. Some of these propositions are original; taken together, all the propositions are thought-provoking and imaginatively conceived. Women, the authors say, were 'vital' to the growth of family enterprise, 'underpinned' the upward mobility of men because they, (i) provided unpaid child rearing and training; (ii) were a source of unpaid work in the family enterprise; (iii) engaged in subsistence production and sideline occupations (dressmaking, sewing etc); (iv) gave unpaid care to live-in employees; (v) were direct suppliers of financial capital; (vi) brought business contacts and specialised skills to the family enterprise; and (vii) enacted displays of respectability that maintained the family's creditworthiness.

To support all seven contentions, the authors depend almost entirely on the method of demonstration by example, a method which is neither discussed nor defended in this section of the book or in the book's introductory chapter on methodology. Although the examples (a dispersed fragment) they cite are the result of prodigious research, the prodigiousness of the research by itself does not make the propositions credible since the authors do nothing to demonstrate that the examples are representative.

To be sure, the weakness of the method is not serious for some of the propositions since the propositions are either self-evidently true or implicitly consistent with our own background knowledge. Thus we can accept proposition number (i) on the ground that it is self-evidently true, perhaps trivial; and we can accept propositions (ii) and (iii) and perhaps (iv) on the grounds that they implicitly cohere with our background knowledge. But the same cannot be said about the other propositions, namely (v), (vi) and (vii). None is a truism, coheres with our background knowledge, is trivial, or purports to be pure speculation. So *if* the authors regard propositions (v), (vi) and (vii) as crucial to their claim, if, that is, the whole claim stands and falls on these three particular propositions, they need a far stronger method for persuading us of the credibility of the propositions.[4] The supporting framework of evidence for the three propositions is very weak in relation to the demanding job it must perform. Relying on a few positive examples to substantiate these three challenging and (perhaps) crucial propositions is hardly an effective way of leading us to accept the propositions, let alone their associated claim. In other words, the inherent indeterminacy of the evidence does not help to overcome the doubts we can reasonably entertain towards the authors' bold and strongly phrased ideas.

I must emphasise that all this does not mean that the three propositions and the associated claim are wrong. Rather it means that the propositions and their associated claim are weakly founded and that they could, in their own terms, be easily refuted. Since the authors are generalising about a large number of family enterprises (all the successful enterprises of Birmingham, Essex and Suffolk from 1780 to 1850) and are generalising from these parts of England to the whole of England, there is a reasonable chance that a dogged researcher could find a few examples that are incompatible with each proposition, that is, counterexamples.[5]

Many practitioners who are dependent on the method of demonstrating by example, but obviously feel uncomfortable with it, have tried to strengthen it in a variety of ways.

▌ Methods by which demonstration by example can be strengthened

☐ *Appealing to the testimony of experts*

One such strengthening devices is to cite examples that consist of the observations of contemporary 'expert' witnesses, that is, the testimony of professional or knowledgable people of a past society who had a close and specialised knowledge about any given aspect of the aggregate we happen to be studying.

To defend the notion that the modification to the method renders fragmentary evidence more credible, less indeterminate, the following argument could be offered. Experts by definition are people who have the training and/or the first-hand experience to make reliable and informed observations about the fields in which they work or are professionally engaged. By extension, therefore, if past experts have studied or are very familiar with a given collectivity, their testimonies about the values, actions and beliefs of the collectivity can be taken by social historians to be superior sources of evidence. Certainly, not all expert testimonies are dependable: expert witnesses can be wrong and do disagree amongst themselves. But expert testimonies can be regarded as reasonably trustworthy, even authoritative, as long as we critically evaluate them and they pass the normal tests of what is called internal textual criticism. These tests require us to 'interrogate' the sources, asking the following questions:

- Are there internal contradictions in the observations of each expert?
- Does the expert have a record of making erroneous observations or a record of making reliable ones?
- How close was the expert to the situation he/she was observing?
- Do the values and interests of the expert cut against or run with the grain of his/her observations? If the values and interests cut against the grain of the observations we can rule out the possibility that the observations were biased by the observer's values and interests; if the values and interests run with the observations, we cannot rule out that possibility and hence must treat the reliability of the source as suspect.

- Did other experts make similar observations despite the differences in their values and beliefs?
- Are the observations inherently plausible?

There are two additional arguments that can be advanced in favour of such evidence. One has come from Gertrude Himmelfarb, a highly respected practitioner of the 'old' history. Himmelfarb acknowledges that experts cannot be presumed to speak for anonymous masses of people. But, she maintains, the historian is no better placed; and, what is more, the historian 'cannot afford to ignore the considered judgments of these contemporaries'.[6]

The second argument is to say that when historians use expert testimonies they are, in a sense, employing the fieldwork practice of the anthropologist. There is little difference in principle between the social historian who goes to expert testimonies for data about large aggregates and the anthropologist in the field who depends on a few knowledgeable 'native informants' to provide data about the customs of the entire tribe.

But how good is this modified version of the method of demonstration by example? To answer this question we will now examine its application by one particular text. Published in 1967, the book is a pioneering study of crime in nineteenth-century England by a British historian, J.J. Tobias: *Crime and Industrial Society in the 19th Century*.[7] Although not as influential as the other texts we have discussed and although its views are now outmoded, Tobias's study nonetheless marked a turning point in the history of crime. Its courageous and novel treatment of fundamental methodological problems generated considerable discussion, stimulating its critics to become some of the most methodologically conscious and innovative practitioners of social history.

The book's central claim is that 'crime' in nineteenth-century England went through two distinct stages. In the first half of the century, crime levels (especially juvenile crime levels) soared. Driving them upwards was the 'social breakdown' brought about by the industrial revolution. The primary factors here were the high birth rate and the comparatively high death rates of parents: these produced a large and growing population of children devoid of parental supervision. In addition, migration into the towns severed the younger generation from traditional community systems of support and control. On top of this, the excessive growth of urban

populations created burgeoning slums where few civilising institutions existed and where criminal gangs provided the chief means
of association and support for the young.

In the second half of the century, Tobias argues, crime levels
subsided as society became more settled. The rates of population
and urban growth diminished, reducing the proportion of ju-
veniles inherently 'at risk' of offending. Moreover, society now
had sufficient resources to tackle social problems. It was able to
develop better policing and thus more effective mechanisms of
criminal deterrence, and to organise charitable and educational
institutions which provided greatly improved means of support
and supervision for the young.

What is of greatest methodological interest about the text is not
its explanation of the trends in crime (the 'social breakdown' theory
is a causal not an intentional explanation), but the particular strategy it employs to support its contentions about the trends. When
the book was published, mass quantification was at the peak of its
influence in the social sciences, and was making big in-roads into
the practice of history, especially in the United States. Tobias must
have felt considerable pressure to conform to this fashion. He
went to much trouble in the text to discuss criminal statistics as a
source, to highlight their problems, and to justify his decision not
to use them in his own study.

Tobias argued that the crime figures produced in nineteenth-
century England were completely unreliable. They bore no relation
to the actual levels of crime since an unknown number of crimes at
any given point were undetected and unrecorded. Moreover, all
kinds of factors had a major impact on the trends in crime figures
over time, preventing them from accurately reflecting the trends
in actual crime. These factors included changes in the law, changes
in court procedures, changes in public reporting habits, changes
in the effectiveness of the police, and even changes in police leadership at the borough and county level.

A much more reliable strategy for finding out about the offending population, Tobias went on to say, was to consult the testimonies of the experts of the period. Those professionally involved in
the prevention of crime and the treatment of offenders – prison
and reformatory officials, committees and commissions of enquiry
into policing, the criminal law and so on – were 'powerful authorities' on such matters, Tobias declared.[8] Thus to support all his

claims, including the claim that there was a massive crime wave in the first half of the century followed by a fall in crime in the second half, Tobias completely relied on the opinions of these 'powerful authorities'. His strategy, unfortunately, had several defects, and these I will now examine.

To some extent, the defects in the strategy arose from his particular application of it. To start with, he acknowledged that some of the 'powerful authorities' had derived their opinions about trends in crime not from first-hand observation but by consulting the very crime statistics which he himself had condemned! In addition, he made no apparent attempt to employ the traditional techniques of textual scholarship to establish the veracity of the observations of his sources. He 'interrogates' none of his sources. What is more, he found that on a good many issues the experts disagreed and that he could not tell which of them were right. For example, to support his contention that the first half of the century was hit by a real crime wave, he cited the authority of the Under-Sheriff of London and Middlesex, the Rev. W.L. Clay (the son of a prison chaplain), and of several witnesses before parliamentary committees of enquiry. But, he admitted, these views were at odds with those of Alderman Wood, Francis Place, the Superintendent of the Hulks, a Select Committee on Police (1816), and Edwin Chadwick. And then he added, 'This game of matching quotation to quotation could go on for a long time. . . .Enough has been said, however, to show the difficulty of reaching any conclusion.'![9]

This brings us to the defects that are inherent in the strategy. The reliability of the expert's information about a large aggregate is critically dependent on at least three variables. The first is how the expert obtained the information. Information based on a few examples of unknown typicality is obviously suspect. So is information which is not based on direct observation but is second-hand or comes from an unspecified source.

The second is the size of the aggregate and how widely it is dispersed. We can readily believe that an anthropologist's native informants belonging to a tribe of 300 people living in a confined area will have a very good chance of accurately knowing how many of these people infringed a certain tribal custom. By contrast, it is ludicrous to imagine that Tobias's 'powerful authorities' were ever in a position to know at first hand how many of the millions of people living in nineteenth-century England violated the criminal law.

The third – and weightiest – problem is that experts can be biased. Consciously or unconsciously, their observations can be distorted and filtered by ideology, values, vested interests, and so forth.

Where all these three inherent defects exist, are they capable of being minimised to an acceptable level? In most research situations, I tend to think not. The principal problem is that the social historian generally studies aggregates containing so many cases that the expert would only have been familiar with a few: most experts generalise from a few examples and probably have no way of telling if these are the exceptional cases. Although in some situations this problem will not exist because the aggregate will be relatively small, other problems will come to the fore. The problems here concern the soundness of the expert's observations. In theory, it is certainly possible to apply the techniques of textual analysis to check whether expert testimonies were based on good information and were biased. But in practice there are not many occasions where we can apply these techniques. Usually we do not have enough information about our experts to determine with reasonable certainty that their testimonies drew on good information and whether and how far they were biased. And there are even fewer occasions where, after running all these checks and eliminating the unsound testimonies, we are left with sound testimonies.

☐ *Appeals to the principle of common sense*

Another method for strengthening the method of demonstrating by example is to appeal to common sense or what philosophers have otherwise called 'folk psychology', 'folk opinion', 'folk theories', 'everyday reasoning'.

Common sense can be defined as widely shared *unreflective knowledge*. It consists of ideas about the world that seem to have universal application and that we take for granted, do not question. We trust common sense ideas because they appear to fit our everyday experiences of the world and because they seem to work when we call on them to help us in our daily activities. We presuppose that they are not the product of dogma or blind tradition or ideology but are firmly rooted in reality. Although we usually learn our common-sense beliefs secondhand, as a body of lore, these beliefs originally grew out of a process of trial and error and have had to stand the test of time ('the wisdom of the ages'). Common sense (or 'folk psychology' or 'everyday reasoning' and so on) is different from the notion of background knowledge I referred to earlier. Background knowledge (in the sense I am using the term) is derived from scholarly research or from scientific experimentation; it is the product of an institutionalised process of reflection, observation and calculation; and is subject to peer review. For the most part, common-sense 'knowledge' has none of these qualities: it is neither formalised nor subject to critical scrutiny.

> Common sense is best seen as a mix of *folk theories* or, if talk of theories seems too pretentious here, *folk opinions*. These, like scientific theories, help people better understand and explain the phenomena that confront them.... Folk theories differ from scientific ones in being immature: they are less precise, systematic and explicit; they lack a methodology for development. More seriously, they differ in being believed uncritically.[10]

Very often common sense 'knowledge' is trivial. But it is not always so. As common sense 'knowledge' is unreflective and unquestioned, it may contain ideas about the world which are interesting once we make them explicit and elaborate them.

Social historians seldom make overt appeals to common sense in order to support their claims. For example, they do not blatantly say, 'The evidence for my explanation about so and so is based on common sense'. Nonetheless, it seems that, especially when using fragmentary evidence, they often make these appeals in a fashion that is unstated, without necessarily being fully aware they are doing so. In these circumstances they presume or believe, perhaps without thinking too much about the matter, that an area of common sense lore provides tacit corroboration of the claim. Although they overtly support the claim with a few examples, they may unconsciously or semi-consciously tell themselves, 'we do not need to worry that much about the quality of our evidence: surely the claim is defensible or unexceptional because it makes good sense anyway'.

But if such appeals are unstated and by their very nature leave no traces, how do we know when they occur? One possible sign (and I certainly do not think it is an infallible one) is when the text is obviously struggling with fragmentary evidence and tries to supplement the evidence with an explicit statement that the claim fits a particular area of *modern-day* experience shared by everyone.

In this section I will illustrate the point by examining a text which, I suspect, relies on the principle, at least in part. A fine example of the history of *mentalités*, the text is Keith Thomas's *Man and the Natural World* (1983).[11] I will then briefly discuss some of the strengths of common sense appeals but also their weaknesses. The discussion will include an assessment of the attacks that have been levelled at common-sense 'knowledge' by certain groups of modern thinkers who argue that common sense is relative and has no truth or grounding in 'reality'.

Thomas's subject is the changing attitudes towards nature in England between the sixteenth and the early nineteenth century. The argument maintains that in the early sixteenth century the natural world was generally regarded as alien to humankind. The woods were perceived as wild and hostile; animals as non-sentient beings; and uncultivated nature as disorderly and crude. Largely shaped by medieval theology, the dominant idea was that despite the Fall, humans had ascendancy over nature, and that the sole purpose of nature was to be conquered and exploited by them.

In the seventeenth and eighteenth centuries, however, major shifts in sensibility occurred, laying the foundations of modern attitudes. According to Thomas, a wide range of factors, both cultural and material, underpinned the changes, though he does not specify whether each of these is crucial to his overall claim. One was the growing interest in natural history. By fostering new principles of taxonomy based on the anatomical structures of plants and animals, natural history led the educated classes to abandon the habit of seeing the natural world purely in anthropocentric terms. Another factor, the rise of pet-keeping, moved humans to attribute intelligence and character to certain animals, weakening the human sense of uniqueness. In addition, the emphasis in seventeenth-century Puritanism that God intended man to take care of His creation, and the lessening dependence on animals for production in the towns, stimulated the development of the concept of animal rights and the awareness of animal suffering. On top of this, the rapid expansion of land under crops helped to unleash a romantic yearning and taste for trees, woods and flowers; and urbanisation fed a nostalgia for country life. Lastly, the rapid sub-jugation of nature, the influence of landscape painting, and the extinction of many species of plants and animals, induced the educated to see the wilderness as a place of wonderment, aesthetic inspiration and spiritual renewal, in need of conservation.

Although there is very little methodological discussion in the text, Thomas endeavours to substantiate his claims by using the method of demonstrating by example. The material for all his examples is taken from a very wide range of literary sources. Now Thomas is very careful to point out where appropriate that his sources do not speak for ordinary people but only for the educated (the elite for the most part). As circumspect as he is, however, he constantly (and inevitably) begs questions about the typicality of his examples. A case in point is his argument that urbanisation underpinned a nostalgia for country life, a nostalgia, he seems to be saying, that affected not just the elite but tradesmen and shop-keepers as well.[12]

His argument, which is framed around a causal explanation, has the following structure. First, he postulates the causes of the nostalgia, and the three main causes are: (i) in the eighteenth cen-tury England urbanised rapidly and by 1800 was the most urban-ised country in Europe (apart from the Netherlands); (ii) the larger towns (especially London) became overcrowded, highly polluted and unhealthy; and (iii) the strong tendency of the litera-ture of the period was to portray the town as morally corrupt and the country as morally pure. Second, he deduces that these causes produced the nostalgia for country life. And third, he supports the inference that the causes had this effect by quoting four or so writers of the period whose statements (more or less) reflect the postulated cause and effect relationship. To be sure, this is not his only method of demonstration: it is supplemented with circum-stantial evidence, some of which relates to the growing popularity for writing about country matters during the period, and some of which concerns the trend in the period for townspeople to make short excursions to the countryside or to retreat to country houses in the summer. But the circumstantial evidence is weak. None of it specifically indicates that the reasons people liked read-ing books about the country and had country excursions and country houses correspond to the postulated cause and effect relationship. For example, as evidence of the growing interest in country matters, he shows there was a big and increasing demand for books on angling. Although this is an acceptable claim, he gives no evidence at all that what drove the large number of people to read angling books had anything to do with rapid urbanisation, urban pollution and the pastoral theme in literature. As a consequence, Thomas's claim is left vitally dependent on the four or so supporting examples.

Then towards the end of this section of the book the argument struggles. Thomas completely negates the authority of his four or so positive examples by pitting against them three counter-examples; and instead of discrediting these counter-examples, explaining them away, he ignores them and recapitulates the argument. A few paragraphs later, in the last sentence or so of the section, Thomas suddenly shifts the discussion to the modern world, hinting, I think, that his claim is buttressed by an appeal to common sense. The appeal refers to a sort of general principle that urban civilisation makes urban dwellers sentimentalise rural life.[13]

☐ *The strengths and weaknesses of common sense appeals*

There are two grounds for arguing that common sense appeals can enhance the plausibility of claims based on fragmentary evidence. The first is that common-sense 'knowledge' often furnishes us with the best explanations for human beliefs, actions and desires. Many philosophers of social science maintain that the theories of the social sciences and even the laws of economics, the most advanced of the social sciences, are either founded on 'folk psychology' or where not founded on it, are no better than it.[14] The second is that a multitude of our folk beliefs do work and do not seem to be wrong, or least not completely. If they did not work they would not have stood the test of time and have been discredited as superstitions, 'old wives' tales'.

But various arguments have been advanced against commonsense 'knowledge' and these are very strong. One argument is that it is unreliable. At any given point, much of it may be right; but, since none of it has been subject to systematic and rigorous testing, much of it may be wrong and we do not know which parts are right and which are wrong. Interestingly enough, Thomas himself implicitly recognises this problem. In an earlier section of the text, he discusses the knowledge about the natural world held by agricultural workers in the early modern period. He points out that they had a natural incentive to develop an accurate lore about wild plants, animals and birds since these were a major source of their medicines, food, shelter, heating, lighting and so forth. He then says that a great deal of this lore was nonetheless wrong or spurious and gives a host of interesting stories to illustrate the point (such as the beliefs that toads had jewels in their heads, that hares slept with one eye open, that cuckoo's spit was poisonous, that women stepping over the cyclamen plant would miscarry, hens should sit on an odd number of eggs and so on.)[15] There is a multitude of similar examples we could draw from our own modern society such as the widespread beliefs in 'the stars', lucky numbers, palmistry, good-luck charms and so forth.

Perhaps the more compelling argument, however, is that common-sense beliefs have a strong tendency to be culturally specific, that they vary substantially from society to society.[16] Hence a historian bringing common sense into the study of a past society, could well end up with a complete misunderstanding of the mindset of the people who lived there. The things that the historian takes for granted about the ways the world works, and assumes that the people in the other society also take for granted, will probably not be shared by the people belonging to that society.

■ Summary

In this chapter we have noted that in social history the most common method for supporting a claim is to cite fragmentary evidence, to adduce positive examples. We have also noted that lack of data usually force social historians to rely on this method, but that the method, if used in isolation, is not a good tool for making a claim credible, well founded. Fragmentary evidence is highly indeterminate if the typicality of the examples is unknown. Moreover, it is seldom that difficult to find a few counter-examples to undermine a claim based on a few positive examples. The problem is not serious or may not arise if the claim is a self-evident truth, only purports to be conjecture, is trivial, a minor or inessential part of an overall argument, or if the claim is crucial but is implicitly supported by background knowledge. The problem is serious, however, if the claim is bold as well as crucial. Sometimes we think we can overcome this problem by strengthening our fragmentary evidence. One strengthening device is to draw the fragmentary evidence from the testimony of experts. The other strengthening device is to supplement fragmentary evidence with an implicit appeal to common-sense beliefs. But the devices are unreliable and do not lessen the problems residing in the method of demonstration by example.

■ *Chapter 3* ■

Some Solutions for the Problem of Fragmentary Evidence

The objective of this chapter is to outline five solutions to the problem of fragmentary evidence. There is no guarantee, it needs to be emphasised, that the solutions will allow us to create truthful accounts – ones that comprehensively correspond to reality. They will, however, give us the capacity (all things being equal) to produce accounts that are more reliable than those based solely on fragmentary evidence or on fragmentary evidence used in conjunction with the testimonies of contemporary experts and/or our own common-sense beliefs. Although I have distinguished the solutions for the purposes of discussion and clarity, they can in fact by employed in whatever combination the practitioner finds appropriate.

(It may be as well to note that with accounts in the explanatory modes, other things are required for reliability; see Chapter 9.)

■ 1. The *crucial case*

A crucial case is a systematic fragment that, by virtue of its known characteristics, is inherently *biased against* the confirmation of a preferred hypothesis. Hence, if we can demonstrate that despite the bias the case lends support to the preferred hypothesis, then considerable weight must be given to the hypothesis. Although the crucial case may represent only a tiny fraction of the population of cases, it will circumvent the problem of typicality as long as we have good reason to expect it to confound the preferred hypothesis. In a sense, then, a crucial case is like the white racist who testifies in court that his West Indian neighbour accused of theft was at home at the time the offence took place.

By their very nature, good – clear-cut – crucial cases are not easy to find. Even assuming the primary sources provide us with what appears to be a crucial case, it is often difficult to demonstrate that its negative characteristics are necessarily biased against the preferred hypothesis. This problem, however, can be lessened by selecting the best possible crucial case, or better still, by confirming the hypothesis with many crucial cases each of which is strongly biased against the hypothesis in a different way. The last chapter will illustrate the possibilities of the method by referring to an explanatory account that relies almost solely on the evidence of three different crucial cases to verify a particularly bold thesis.

2. Extrapolating from comparable cases

Very often, social historians have to use fragmentary evidence to substantiate causal explanations. They might, for example, rely only on two or so positive cases to substantiate a causal explanation that generalises about a myriad unknown cases. The method of extrapolating from comparable cases is designed to supplement the evidence of those few cases. Essentially, the method depends upon the assumption, underlying causal explanation as a mode, that in every case where the same preconditions exist, the same outcomes will occur, or vice versa (constant conjunction). Accordingly, the method seeks to expand the evidence for an explanation based on a few cases, by looking for well-documented studies of comparable cases where the same preconditions coexist with the same outcomes.

The studies could be of cases taken from the same society or from different societies, past and present. Particularly useful to social historians of the pre-modern world has been the studies by social anthropologists on tribal societies in the twentieth century. A salient example of how the method can be applied is Alan Macfarlane's book on witchcraft in late sixteenth- and early seventeenth-century England, a book which attempted to generalise about the causes of witchcraft accusations from 460 indictments of witches in Essex.[1] By systematically examining the relationships between male accusers and female accused in these cases, Macfarlane found that in most instances the accuser and accused, were neighbours in a close-knit village, that the accuser was of higher status than the accused, who depended on community charity, and that prior to the event the accuser had violated customary obligation by denying her assistance. Macfarlane's explanation for the pattern was that witchcraft accusations were a device for relieving social strain: by labelling the women as witches, the accusers were able to justify their deviation from custom. To give the argument more evidential weight, Macfarlane showed how it fitted the first-hand investigations by anthropologists – notably E.E. Evans-Pritchard – of African witchcraft.

There are obvious limitations with the method. One is exceptions – what do we do if we find comparable cases that do not fit the causal hypothesis? Moreover, even if we do not find exceptional comparable cases, there is no way of telling whether the structure of the known comparable cases is typical of that of all the unknown cases. But these problems are not inevitable. We might be fortunate enough to be dealing with a class of phenomena where all the comparable cases are few in number and are known to fit the same structure. In addition, where there are multitudes of unknown cases in the same of class of phenomena, we can gain a fair idea about the representativeness of the known cases by taking a large number of them from contrasting social contexts (for example, rural/urban). If most of these known cases have the same structures in each context, some weight can be given to the typicality of all the cases.

Another way of supplementing evidence by extrapolating from comparable cases, is to draw on the relevant experimental and survey data on parallel phenomena generated by the modern social sciences. An example of the technique is in *Ordinary Men*, Christopher Browning's study of a group of ordinary German policemen involved in the Holocaust, a study based on their subsequent testimonies when prosecuted for war crimes. Browning argued that peer-pressure within the group was the primary factor that made the men into willing killers. As evidence, Browning cited a few of the testimonies; to supplement it, he drew on the results of the famous laboratory experiments on the nature of conformity and obedience conducted by Stanley Milgram in the 1960s.

The virtue of the method is that survey or experimental data can be replicated under tightly controlled circumstances. But whether these circumstances are always parallel to real life experiences (especially of people living in the past), is something that can never be taken for granted – as we shall see in Chapter 9, when we discuss Browning's study in more detail. When the case in question is a settler-colony of the metropolitan society we can also, under appropriate circumstances, supplement data for the former by drawing on data taken from the latter. Examples of the method are in David Fischer's mammoth work *Albion's Seed*, a study of how the cultures of four regions in Britain over the seventeenth and eighteenth centuries, had a determining influence on four corresponding regions in the United States. The success of the method depends, of course, on demonstrating that the culture of the metropolis was imported into the settler-colony without significant change (see discussion in Chapter 5).

3. Maximising the weight and variety of observations

This method of confirmation can take all manner of forms and is perhaps the best known to social historians and historians, though they do not give it any particular name. Indeed, it is the standard confirmatory procedure of the social sciences and the sciences where generalisations about a large unknown population are inferred from a small sample – or fragment – of that population. In essence, the method rests on the assumption that although the citation of all the known supporting instances does not prove that a claim is true, its probability of being true increases in proportion to the weight and variety of the supporting instances. Take the fictional case of Jim, the burglar: we could not be certain that it was he who broke into the building if three people independently of each other saw him in the vicinity at the time of the break-in *and* the break-in bore some of the marks of his *modus operandi and* some of the stolen goods were found in the possession of one of his friends *and* he had a poor alibi. But the probability that he did commit the burglary would be greater under those conditions than if the only incriminating evidence against him was that the break-in bore some of the signs of his *modus operandi*.

Excellent texts have been written on the range of ways the method can be applied to fragmentary evidence; so I do not need to replicate their advice here.[2] Instead I will discuss at length an unusual technique that has a particularly powerful capacity to generate a large variety and number of observations. An elaborate but exciting technique, it demands more abstract thinking than is generally associated with the historical craft and comes into its own when we want to tackle big questions.

Underlying the technique is a holistic notion of society. Very similar to that held by the earliest generations of *Annales* historians, the notion is that people belonging to a collectivity or category have multiple dimensions or attributes – material, social, demographic, cultural, political and so forth – and that the attributes are inextricably interconnected so that each interacts with all the others, a change in one having knock-on effects on all the others. In other words, the technique presupposes that a cause/effect relationship concerning one dimension of the collectivity or category will influence all the other dimensions and be reflected in their behaviour and structures.

On the basis of this holistic **ontology**, the technique proceeds along the following lines. It starts by advancing an overall hypothesis about the collectivity or category that is posited on a fundamental premise (we will call the overall hypothesis and its fundamental premise the *core theory*). The fundamental premise could take the form of a **covering law** (a well established scientific theory that some aspect of human behaviour always occurs under the same conditions), or an **explanation sketch** (Carl Hempel's term for a generalisation about human behaviour which is not scientifically established and which does not purport to be invariant).[3]

The technique then proceeds by inferentially deducing from the core theory a large number (as many as possible) of *auxiliary hypotheses* about the collectivity or category. Although the auxiliary hypotheses as a group should cover the whole spectrum of dimensions, each hypothesis can either refer to a specific dimension or to any combination of dimensions. If possible, the process of inferential deduction should produce not just one belt of auxiliary hypotheses but successive belts: the second belt being inferentially deduced from the first, the third being inferentially deduced from a mixture of the first and second, the fourth from those in previous belts, and so forth. The resulting network of conjectures generated by the process of inferential deduction should look something like this diagram:

Core theory → *First belt of auxiliary hypotheses about the material, social, ideological, cultural, demographic dimensions* → *Second belt of auxiliary hypotheses deduced from first belt of auxiliary hypotheses* → etc

Lastly, having mapped out all the possible logical inferences of the core theory, the researcher then proceeds to test them. The testing involves two procedures.

With the first, the investigator rigorously looks for and eliminates auxiliary hypotheses that are logically incompatible with other auxiliary hypotheses. By this I mean that their terms contradict the terms of another hypothesis. The aim of this procedure is to ensure that all the auxiliary hypotheses converge on the same conclusion. With the second, the investigator must comb the sources systematically for supporting examples for each auxiliary hypothesis. During the search for supporting examples, the investigator has to be prepared to reject or modify an auxiliary hypothesis if it is *empirically indefensible*. By empirically indefensible, I mean either that no positive examples can be found to support the auxiliary hypothesis or that counter-examples are found which cannot be satisfactorily explained. During this informal testing process, many hypotheses may have to be rejected and modified; indeed so many might have to be rejected and modified that the core theory itself may have to be modified or, at worst, abandoned and replaced by a better one. When modifying or reformulating the core theory, the objective should always be to come up with one that can generate more empirically defensible auxiliary hypotheses than were generated by the old core theory. (This should not be the only objective when altering the core theory. As I will indicate in Chapter 9, the other objective should be to prevent losses in its explanatory power.)

The advantages of the strategy are simple and plain enough. Firstly, the strategy is a very powerful device for extracting supporting examples. By generating the belts of auxiliary hypotheses, we effectively organise for ourselves a complete programme of research. The auxiliary hypotheses constituting this 'research programme' give us a multitude of precise cues about the sorts of evidence that need to be looked for if the core theory bears a reasonable approximation to reality. The auxiliary hypotheses, in other words, are of great help for doing research, for they tell us exactly what evidence we have to find, with the result that they minimise the risks of collecting irrelevant information and of overlooking the relevant (which, of course, is usually scarce by virtue of its fragmentary nature). Having a precise idea of what the relevant evidence should look like, we maximise the chances of finding it if it exists. We can go to the sources that are most likely to contain it, and we can spot bits of it straight away even when these are buried in or obscured by a mass of other data. To put this more simply, it is far harder finding something if we have no or little idea what we are searching for than if we do: seek and ye shall find.

The strategy, however, does not just help us amass evidence in depth. It also helps us mobilise a wide range, a broad base, of evidence. To be more precise, it enables us to discover unusual or surprising types of evidence, to turn what appear to be irrelevant facts into material that greatly extends our evidential range. And this is very important since a claim based on a variety of evidence is, as we noted at the outset, better founded than one based on a narrow base of evidence. A diagnosis which fits a wide variety of symptoms is likely to be more reliable (all things being equal) than one which based on one or two symptoms.

To understand how the strategy allows us to extend the evidential range, to turn stone into gold, we must remember that the strategy rests on a holistic ontology: it assumes that everything is connected, that cause and effect relationships in one human dimension have ramifications for and manifestations in all the other human spheres. This being the case, the strategy permits us, at least potentially, to take our evidence from anywhere within the whole spectrum of human activity, including the most unexpected, provided (of course) we have auxiliary hypotheses that enable us to argue how these different activities are connected. If, for example, the core theory is trying to explain why, say, the people of a certain village were especially prone to riotous behaviour, we do not have to restrict our evidence to their political beliefs (which might be very scanty). We could also support the claim by referring to evidence about their drinking habits and their wedding rituals (which might be far more plentiful), employing the appropriate auxiliary hypotheses to argue how drinking and weddings were connected to rioting.

The second advantage of the strategy is that it produces very persuasive theories that are difficult to refute. We can be confident that the core theory is well founded if we have formulated a large number and variety of auxiliary hypotheses and have found them to be empirically defensible and logically compatible. The strategy thus leads us to amass a variety of *different* types of evidence which converge on a conclusion, so producing a well-confirmed theory. What makes it difficult to refute is that it is protected by the thick belts of auxiliary hypotheses. If we disagree with the core theory and want to refute it on evidential grounds (there are other grounds on which we must appraise it, but I will deal with these in Chapter 9), we cannot do so by finding counter-evidence for just a few of the protective auxiliary hypotheses. We have to find counter-evidence for all or the vast majority of the auxiliary hypotheses, which is a daunting and very arduous task, since there are so many of them covering such a wide range of evidence.

Having spelt out the advantages of the strategy, let me now discuss the disadvantages. The first is that the implementation of the strategy is extremely demanding. The generation of all the auxiliary hypotheses requires considerable powers of imagination and abstract reasoning, and their empirical testing, a close familiarity with a huge range of source material. The second disadvantage is that the strategy cannot do much if the fragmentary evidence is unusually poor. There is not much point in generating a large array of brilliant auxiliary hypotheses if we cannot find any supporting examples for them.

The third disadvantage with the strategy relates to the problem of counter-examples. In the process of empirically testing auxiliary hypotheses, the investigator should, in principle, look for exceptions to each auxiliary hypothesis and, if they seem to be serious anomalies, reject the auxiliary hypothesis in question. All this is quite consistent with the long-standing scholarly convention that we should always look for counter-examples and declare them if we find them.

I will discuss the problem of counter-examples at greater length in the next section. For the moment, I will just note that the manner in which the research programme deals with counter-examples makes me uneasy. As I pointed out earlier, the research programme which effectively arises from the generation of the auxiliary hypotheses, is a powerful evidence-detecting device. As such, it enables us to see the positive examples but not the negative ones. The programme tells us what evidence we need to look for if the core theory has a reasonable approximation to reality. It does not tell us what evidence we should look for if the core theory is wrong or a bad approximation to reality. To be sure, the strategy enjoins us to look for the negative examples when we come to test the auxiliary hypotheses empirically. But I very much doubt if this injunction has the same power as the research programme itself. On balance, the strategy is slanted more toward the mobilising of positive examples than the negative.

The account I have given of the strategy is an adaptation of a famous model about how scientific knowledge grows which was advanced by a philosopher of science, Imre Lakatos, in a book called *The Methodology of Scientific Research Programmes*.[4] Lakatos had little idea about how many scientists actually followed his methodology; I confess that (apart from myself) I do not know of any social historians who have claimed to have followed my adapted version of it or something like it either. As far as I can tell, most social historians do not seem to start a research project with a clearly worked-out core theory, nor do they plan their research so as to find evidence for a whole series of auxiliary hypotheses formulated through a deliberate process of deductive reasoning. If practitioners were surveyed about how they arrived at their conclusions, most would say, I suspect, that it was by collecting facts, by following the cues in their sources and by engaging in an exhaustive and painstaking examination of all the appropriate documentary material.

An example of the methodology in use: Lawrence Stone's The Crisis of the Aristocracy

Be that as it may, some texts are organised in a way that, at least coincidentally, bears a remarkable resemblance to the strategy.

Even if their authors had not heard of Lakatos's scientific research programme, their books read as if they had! To my mind, the text which has the strongest resemblance is Lawrence Stone's *The Crisis of the Aristocracy*.[5] Interestingly enough, although in his introductory chapter Stone is not particularly informative about his overall methodological strategy, he does state that 'many of the ideas behind this study are derived from the French [*Annales*] school of historiography', and then comes very close to saying that he has taken on board the holistic ontology of society adopted by the *Annalistes*. 'This book', he writes, 'sets out to do two things: firstly to describe the total environment of an *élite*, material and economic, ideological and cultural, educational and moral; and secondly to demonstrate, to explain, and to chart the course of a crisis in the affairs of this *élite* that was to have a profound effect upon the evolution of English political institutions.'[6]

The subject of the book is the decline of the English aristocracy between 1558 and 1641. It was a decline, Stone postulates, that was one of the three major causes of the English civil war of the 1640s, the other two major causes being the conflict over religion and the decline in the respect for the monarchy.[7] Very little of the book, however, is taken up with demonstrating how the decline of the aristocracy actually caused the Civil War. The whole book is in the mode of causal explanation.

Although Stone does not explicitly invoke the concepts we have used – a 'core theory' made up of an 'overall hypothesis' based on a 'fundamental premise' – these concepts can be usefully applied to his methodology. His overall hypothesis is that the English aristocracy experienced a decline in this period but that the key area in which they declined was in status: the critical cause of aristocratic decline was that they lost the respect of the other categories in society, the most important being the gentry, the category immediately below the aristocracy in rank. The emphasis he places on the decline of the aristocracy in terms of status is often overlooked by his critics. But it is clearly signalled in asides throughout the book and quite unequivocally stated in the conclusion: 'During the reign of Elizabeth the gentry certainly regarded the peerage with some apprehension. ... By the early seventeenth century this attitude of respectful subservience was breaking down'.[8] His fundamental premise is that the whole society was dominated by conceptions of status – status was fundamental to power and wealth. In other words, status is the master variable of the society in this period. Although he does not invoke it, there is a 'covering law' (or 'explanation sketch') that he might have employed to explain why status was so important in this period, namely, that because in pre-industrial societies material resources are few, great weight is attached to personal standing since personal standing is the only resource which everyone can possess and provide a common standard by which everyone can be judged and categorised. Alternatively, we could say that his 'explanation sketch' is that the decline in status of elites is crucial for the occurrence of revolutions.[9]

But in order to establish his overall hypothesis, Stone had to overcome a fundamental problem: fragmentary evidence. How could he show that the other categories in the society, especially the gentry, had much less respect for the aristocracy by 1640 than in 1550? How, that is to say, could he confirm that the attitudes of very large aggregates of people changed, especially in relation towards something as intangible as status? His researches certainly enabled him to find a few positive examples to support his overall thesis. These include observations by contemporaries (expert witnesses?) that the standing of the aristocracy had diminished over the period, and stories ('significant little incidents') culled from the end of the period about individual members of the gentry treating aristocrats with disdain.[10] By themselves, however, these supporting examples are incapable of providing substantial confirmation of his overall hypothesis. To overcome this evidential problem, the text is filled with multitudes of what are *in effect* auxiliary hypotheses, inferentially deduced from the overall hypothesis. (I say, 'in effect', since there is no evidence that Stone employed them consciously.) Each auxiliary hypothesis takes the form of a direct or indirect cause of aristocratic status decline. As the hypothetical causes cover so many aspects of each human dimension, they enable Stone to trawl through his sources with nets of all shapes and sizes, catching a staggering range of positive examples in support of the overall thesis.

I will now outline how he organises these auxiliary hypotheses, and then look more closely at his discussion of one particular area of them. The order of the material in his text, I should emphasise, follows a rather different pattern from that which will be outlined here. The first belt are what we may call the broader auxiliary hypotheses. These spell out the more general causes of the aristocracy's declining prestige. Ten such causes are postulated, covering practically every aspect of the aristocracy's world.[11]

☐ *Belt 1: broader auxiliary hypotheses*

1.i.   Their ownership of wealth fell relative to that of the gentry. This was not a comparatively important cause of status decline: contemporaries placed a much greater value on aristocratic hospitality and conspicuous spending than on ownership itself as a token of prestige. But it was important as an indirect cause, in that it led the aristocracy to take certain compensatory measures which directly damaged their prestige (e.g. raising the rents of their tenants).

1.ii.   The proportion of people owing them deference fell because of the relative and absolute shrinkage in the size of their tenantry, historically their largest source of deference.

1.iii. They went down in the eyes of their remaining tenants by raising their rents, attempting to make good the effects of increased extravagance and the contraction in their landed assets.

1.iv.   Their general capacity to be held in awe through violence and intimidation contracted because their sources of military power shrank.

1.v.   Their group esteem was damaged when the Crown created a large number of new peerage titles in return for money.

1.vi.   Their prestige was injured when religious and political issues weakened their ability to influence parliamentary elections.

1.vii. They undermined their reputation for generosity and liberality in the countryside by cutting down on their rural hospitality, switching more of their expenditure to conspicuous consumption in London.

1.viii. The social esteem traditionally connected with high birth was damaged in this period by the spread of education and the rise of new ideas of meritocracy.

1.ix.   The capacity to exact customary forms of obedience in this period was being eroded by the rise of new ideologies – specifically individualism, Calvinism and puritanism.

1.x.   The increasing unpopularity of the Court tarnished the popularity of the aristocracy itself since with diminishing landed wealth the aristocracy attached themselves to the Court to find alternative sources of income.

Now it is very difficult for Stone to substantiate each of these ten broad hypothetical explanations of status decline. The available evidence is inadequate. So, to overcome this problem, he postulates that each of these broad causes was the outcome of a large range of more specific factors. He inferentially deduces what these sub-causes were, and, where possible, supports each sub-cause with whatever supporting examples he can find. These sub-causes thus comprise a *second belt* of auxiliary hypotheses. Where he cannot find supporting examples for a sub-cause, he repeats the process of inferential deduction. He assumes that a sub-cause was in its turn the outcome of a large variety of causal mechanisms. He inferentially deduces these mechanisms, and tries to find positive examples that support their existence. In effect, these causal mechanisms are the causes of the sub-causes. They comprise a *third belt of* auxiliary hypotheses.

To illustrate how these additional hypothetical causal chains are constructed, let us examine the architecture of one of them, hypothesis 1. iv, that the diminishing military power of the aristocracy undermined the respect which they had traditionally commanded.

This part of his thesis has often been noted by critics, quite rightly in my view, as the most brilliant section of the book.[12] Stone starts it by demonstrating why, at the beginning of his period, the prestige of the aristocracy was so tightly bound up with military power. The explanation, he says, is that in the fifteenth and early sixteenth centuries England was gripped in a sub-culture of violence. Underlying the violence, he states, was a wide range of factors. They included a general irritability resulting from bad diet and chronic indigestion; the high value placed on status which rendered people highly sensitive to slights to their honour; the fact that people in this age were not taught to restrain their impulses and passions; the strong personal ties between landlords and tenants; the custom whereby the gentry entered the households of the aristocracy and became their armed retainers; the widespread practice of carrying arms; the high frequency of rebellion by unruly magnates which habituated people to use violence to solve personal problems; the Crown's reliance on the aristocracy to fight its wars; and the lack of rules about the conduct of quarrels.

As violence was so prevalent, it follows, Stone argues, that notions of status would be dominated by it. The militarily powerful were held in awe and fear. Being an extremely valuable resource, military might was highly esteemed. The weak, having to rely on the strong for military protection, admired their protectors. All this benefited the aristocracy, earned them the highest status, because they, along with the Crown, had the greatest military power, defined in terms of fighting men, castles, arms and fighting spirit.

Having set up this logical linkage between a highly violent society and the high status of the aristocracy which existed at the beginning of his period, Stone is then in position to demonstrate his auxiliary hypothesis 1.iv, that during his period the diminishing military power of the aristocracy undermined their high standing. By my count, eleven causal explanations are advanced. If sufficiently precise, each is supported with a few positive examples. Although most of these are inferential deductions from auxiliary hypothesis 1. iv, some have also been generated from the other hypotheses in the first belt. Irrespective of how they are generated, all eleven hypotheses/explanations form part of the second belt of auxiliary hypotheses. For convenience sake we will label them sub-hypotheses of hypothesis 1.iv. The majority of the explanations, as can be seen in the list below, locate the cause of shrinking aristocratic status in the decline of social violence. In large measure, what Stone is saying is that just as the high levels of social violence at the start of his period was the cause of aristocratic high standing, so the reduction in social violence during his period helped to erode this high standing. In other words, what contributed to the aristocracy's decline in status was growing social pacification; this meant that the society had less demand for the aristocracy's military services, and, feeling more secure, people had less reason to kowtow to their former protectors.

☐ *Belt 2: Sub-hypotheses of hypothesis 1.iv*

The society became less violent because:

1.iv.1   of the success of the Crown's long-term programme, pursued from the late fifteenth century to the end of the sixteenth, of controlling and destroying unruly magnates;

1.iv.2   one monarch, Elizabeth 1, was conspicuously successful in personally settling disputes between members of the aristocracy;

1.iv.3   some of the over-mighty aristocratic families died out over the sixteenth century through natural causes;

1.iv.4   the aristocracy themselves lost much of their taste for warfare and physical aggression as a consequence of the rise of different outlets for their energies, talents, and competitive instincts (life at Court, the pursuit of wealth, conspicuous consumption, the cultivation of the arts, civil litigation);

1.iv.5   the aristocracy's military skills waned through lack of use, England enjoying long periods of external peace (1562–88, 1604–24);

1.iv.6   the aristocracy became less interested in warfare following the development of new ideals of service i.e. in government and at Court;

1.iv.7   of the introduction of the rapier which, because it was so lethal, made the aristocracy less inclined to pick quarrels and produced a code for conducting quarrels without violence;

1.iv.8   the aristocracy were less able to call upon their tenants to provide them with armed support, having weakened their loyalty by increasing their rents and reduced their number through substantial sales of land to the gentry;

1.iv.9   the aristocracy, under the influence of puritan doctrine, learnt habits of self-restraint and were thus less likely to fly into rages, precipitating casual violence;

1.iv.10 the medieval code of honour, which previously had contributed to the aristocracy's hyper-sensitivity towards insults and slights, was increasingly displaced by book-learning;

1.iv.11 the gentry, driven by the new fashions for privacy and formal education, were less willing to serve as armed re-tainers in aristocratic households.

Stone is able to support some of these sub-hypotheses with posit-ive examples. But some he cannot. Where he cannot support them, he inferentially deduces a large range of causal mechanisms that would have produced them, and then cites examples to sup-port these causal mechanisms. For example, to explain the entan-glement of the aristocracy in civil litigation, a component in 1.iv.4, Stone argues that the entanglement was the product of the follow-ing factors: massive sales of land by the aristocracy, the growing tendency of the aristocracy to receive a legal education, the lack of a central land registry system, the confused state of land law, the practice of making secret encumbrances of title, the existence of a host of court systems with overlapping jurisdictions, and so on. Most of these causes of litigation are supported by a handful of positive examples.

☐ Limitations and advantage of the methodology as seen in Stone

Let us now appraise Stone's methodology. What are its limitations and advantages? It should be noted that Stone's methodology does not allow him to 'prove' in any absolute sense that the aristo-cracy declined in status. The evidence he cites does not 'prove' that the ten broad causes of decline existed since it is mainly indirect and based on positive examples of unknown typicality. Moreover, the logic of his methodology does not 'prove' that the ten broad causes were sufficient (in the sense of being sufficient conditions) to produce the decline since, in terms of strict logic, the analysis of a single case cannot ascertain causal sufficiency; only the comparat-ive analysis of a multitude of cases can do that (I will not elucidate this point for the moment but leave it to the next chapter). What his methodology does allow him to achieve, however, is three things.

Firstly, it enables him to set up an almost impregnable claim, one which is extremely difficult to refute, since it is based on so many supporting arguments. To attack the core theory we would have to demolish all of his auxiliary hypotheses. In practical terms, this would require us (a) to chip away at all of the ten broad auxiliary hypotheses, and to succeed in this we would have to (b) refute the vast number of arguments he gives in support of each. Such a task is most daunting, remembering that one of these broad auxiliary hypotheses (1.iv) is based on eleven supporting arguments alone, many of which in their turn are based on a further battery of arguments. The sources may well contain counter-examples that negate each of the arguments; but the job of digging them out would deter most scholars. Indeed, it seems to have done so: many seventeenth century experts have tried to falsify a few of Stone's broad auxiliary hypotheses by pitting counter-examples against each one; but no-one has yet found sufficient counter-examples to negate most of these broad hypotheses.[13]

The second advantage of the methodology is that it enables Stone to find an extraordinary variety of positive examples, a large range of different types of evidence, that converge on the same conclusion, thus making it well-founded, difficult to resist – reliable. Certainly, each of his causes of status decline is supported by only a few examples of unknown typicality. But taken as a whole, the examples are so wide-ranging that they greatly enhance the weight of the overall hypothesis. As I said before, a claim based on a broad base of evidence is, as a general rule, more reliable than one based on a narrow base of evidence. A diagnosis which fits a wide variety of symptoms is more likely to be accurate (all things being equal) than one which based on one or two symptoms.

The third advantage of the methodology is that it has produced a marvellous piece of history, one that wonderfully illuminates the whole environment of a social elite. The text is an excellent example of the point I made in the introduction, that the employment of a sophisticated and rigorous methodology is not just compatible with stimulating and readable history but can make it so.

4. Eliminating rival hypotheses (the hypothetico-deductive/argument to the best explanation)

This method is conventionally associated with 'scientising' social history – especially quantitative social history – and the construction of highly abstract and mechanical explanatory models, all of which were very modish in the 1970s and have now fallen into disrepute. These unfavourable associations, however, are most unfortunate because the method, when adapted to the problem of fragmentary evidence, is a very powerful tool. It can take us a long way in resolving the fragmentary evidence problem in every mode of social history: the causal explanatory, how-possibly explanation, focused description, intentional explanation, the hermeneutic. What is more, the method is the best possible device, the most rigorous available, for dealing with two side-problems of fragmentary evidence: the problem of abnormally thin evidence and the problem of exceptions.

Though intellectually demanding, the method is simple to design. Instead of trying to find supplementary evidence to corroborate the one claim, the method requires us to specify a series of the best possible rival claims; inferentially deduce the consequences of each claim; hunt for all the positive and counter-examples for each consequence for each claim; and then ruthlessly appraise the plausibility of every claim in relation to the others so as to determine which one (on the balance of probabilities) is the *most* plausible. In effect, the positive examples supporting each of these hypotheses provide the counter-examples for at least one of the competing hypotheses. I should hasten to add, by the way, that the critical appraisal process should never stop. Once we have determined the most plausible hypothesis, we certainly should not regard its most favoured status as permanent. We must always regard its most favoured status as provisional, and constantly search for better candidates.

How do we go about formulating the alternative hypotheses? From my own experience, I think it best that the candidate hypotheses be sketched out in a preliminary fashion before the research begins. By this means, we start the research having at least some idea about the different sorts of positive examples we should be looking for. It needs to be emphasised, however, that we should always be prepared to change the hypotheses during the course of research or after it in response to our encounters with the raw data. Thus as we work through the material we might find that it forces or stimulates us to think of new hypotheses, to modify others to make them more feasible, and drop those that appear to be completely wide off the mark. Reflection combined with a great deal of background reading are probably the best devices for working out the preliminary candidates.

Perhaps the greatest virtues of the method is its capacity to deal resolutely with exceptions. As the social world is so complex, it is a prolific generator of exceptions. (The technical term for this phenomenon is that all theories are **underdetermined**.)[14] Exceptions are great nuisances. They are easy to find and once found they are normally very difficult to deal with. If we do not declare them, while advancing a claim, and someone finds them later, they make our scholarship look careless. If we do declare them without comment while advancing a particular claim, we implicitly weaken our claim, inviting critics to say that our supporting arguments lack rigour. But if we declare them and try to explain them away, we face the danger of cluttering up the prose with complex arguments and details. And if we take the *ad hoc* approach, and try to accommodate them by putting up additional theories that are consistent with them, we may end up with a mess of mutually inconsistent arguments.

The big advantage of the method of confirming by eliminating rival hypotheses is that it minimises these difficulties. The very business of formulating rival hypotheses prevents us from overlooking negative evidence; indeed it programmes us to search for it. Moreover, in giving us a coherent framework for categorising incompatible examples, the method provides a very orderly system for talking about and thus for handling the messiness and contrariness of reality. Lastly, the method enables us to do all these things *and* provisionally resolve the evidential problems which are generated by the messiness and contrariness of reality.

But what do we do if, despite our best eliminationist efforts, we come to the conclusion that two or more of the hypotheses, though better than all the others, are equally well founded? Although this outcome creates ambiguity, it nonetheless is not an altogether bad outcome. As long as we can show they are equally well-founded and the others are worse, we have made some progress. We have at least reduced the range of possibilities. In doing so, we know exactly what we should be looking for if new raw data are discovered. Moreover, by reducing the range of possibilities, we identify the problem more sharply, and a sharply defined problem is more able than a vaguely defined problem to suggest techniques by which the problem can be solved through the generation of different kinds of information.

☐ *An example of the method of eliminating rival hypotheses*

Let us now see how the method works by examining an influential work of microhistory, one written by a founder of the genre. The work is Carlo Ginzburg's *The Cheese and the Worms: The Cosmos of a Sixteenth-century Miller*.[15] The book is a study of the thoughts of Menocchio (Domenico Scandella), a self-taught miller from Montereale, a hill village in the Friuli, northern Italy. Most of Ginzburg's source material on Menocchio comes from the verbatim records generated by the trials of Menocchio for heresy.

There were two separate trials, both in private, before a tiny tribunal officiated over by the Holy Office's provincial inquisitor, with a notary taking a transcript of the proceedings.[16] The first trial took place in 1584. It followed Menocchio's denunciation by the local priest (Menocchio's enemy) who complained that his parishioner had been spreading heretical opinions among the peasants of the village. Although not tortured during the trial, which lasted for three months, Menocchio eventually acknowledged his errors (largely out of expediency, Ginzburg maintains) and was punished with life imprisonment. After successfully petitioning for a commutation of his sentence, he was released after two years, but ordered to wear a penitential robe for the rest of his life and never to travel beyond his village. Undaunted, he began arguing with local peasants about his ideas again. Denounced once more, his second trial occurred in 1599. The tribunal this time was less forgiving. It tortured him to make him identify his accomplices (he had none, Ginzburg claims), then had him executed.

For evidence about the content of Menocchio's thoughts, Ginzburg makes some use of the statements made to the tribunal by the witnesses it called, most of whom were peasants from Menocchio's village. The bulk of the evidence, however, comes from Menocchio's responses to the probing questions put to him by the inquisitor in the first trial. These responses, Ginzburg insists, represent genuine self-testimony. They were not made under duress: the inquisitor was keen to draw Menocchio out and argue with him, confident (at least initially) that all that was required to lead a simple peasant to amend his thoughts was persuasion. For his part, Menocchio was all too eager 'to be questioned and listened to so attentively by such learned monks'.[17] In Ginzburg's view, Menocchio was exceedingly proud of the originality of his ideas, intoxicated by them; they had been fermenting in his mind for years but he had not been able to expound them properly, except in a highly simplified form to his fellow peasants. Indeed, he had dreamt of discussing them with a very elevated audience: '"if I had permission to go before the pope, or a king, or a prince who would listen to me, I would have a lot of things to say; and if he had me killed afterwards, I would not care"'.[18]

Menocchio's opinions, Ginzburg maintains, were extraordinarily heterodox. Amongst other things, Menocchio condemned the church hierarchy for oppressing the peasantry; stated that Scripture could be expressed in four words; claimed that love of thy neighbour was more important than love of God; denied the virgin birth, the divinity of Christ, the existence of hell, the immortality of the soul, and the possibility of the second coming; rejected all sacraments; sought the radical renewal of society; argued for the equality of all religions and religious tolerance; advocated a simple religion; thought that the body decomposed into the four elements after death; and, most striking of all, claimed that the universe was not created by God but that both God and universe emerged out of chaos: '"all was chaos...and out of that bulk a mass formed – just as cheese is made out of milk – and worms appeared in it, and these were the angels. The most holy majesty decreed that these should be God and the angels, and among that number of angels, there was also God, *he too having been created out of that mass at the same time* ...."'[19]

Ginzburg's overall objective is to highlight the possibility that there were was a reciprocating relationship and not a one way one between literate culture and oral culture in this period. His means of attaining this objective is to take Menocchio as a test case, to show that Menocchio's response to literate culture was preconditioned by oral tradition. Establishing the claim about Menocchio is exceedingly difficult since no firm evidence about the contents of such an oral tradition has survived. To deal with the evidential

problems, Ginzburg, who is a highly self-conscious methodo-
logist, employs several interwoven procedures.

Traditional historical scholarship often depends on a technique
called comparative textual analysis to trace the influences upon
the ideas in a text or as a confirmatory device. Ginzburg employs
it to work out how Menocchio made sense of the books he had
read. To prepare the way for this, Ginzburg establishes from the
internal evidence of the transcripts that Menocchio was familiar with at least eleven books including the Bible, certain works
of piety and versions of the scriptures, an almanac, Boccaccio's
Decameron, Mandeville's book of travels, and perhaps the Koran.
After determining what editions Menocchio must have had access
to, and reading these works himself, Ginzburg then carefully
combs the transcript to determine which portions of Menocchio's
testimony were obviously influenced by them. Having done all
this, Ginzburg's next step is to engage in his comparative textual
analysis. He matches the statements by Menocchio which were
influenced by the books with the relevant passages in the ori-
ginals, noting carefully all the similarities and the differences
between the two. The bulk of *The Cheese and the Worms* consists of
Ginzburg's detailed discussion of these similarities and differences.
What he tries to show us is that, although Menocchio's opinions
and conceptual language were strongly influenced by the texts,
there were also gaps, discrepancies and distortions in Menocchio's reading of the texts. Ginzburg's key inference is that these
gaps, discrepancies and distortions are vital clues about Menocchio's preconceptions, his world view.

But where did the biases in Menocchio's interpretations come
from? This brings us to Ginzburg's central claim, that although
Menocchio was an unusual representative of the peasantry, he
read his books through the 'interpretative filter' of ancient peasant beliefs and values; 'the roots of [Menocchio's] utterances and
of his aspirations were sunk in an obscure, almost unfathomable,
layer of remote peasant traditions.'[20] The central claim, in other
words, is that traditional peasant concepts strongly shaped Menocchio's ideas.

To demonstrate this central claim, Ginzburg invokes two confirmatory procedures. The first is to maximise the variety and
weight of supporting observations. In the *Cheese and the Worms*, a
small number of two varieties of observations are generated. One

variety consists of Menocchio's use of language. Here Ginzburg shows that Menocchio's vocabulary, although peppered with the jargon of learned culture (which helped Menocchio articulate his thoughts), also drew extensively on the phraseology of peasant everyday experience.[21] The other variety consists of references to parallel cases. Here Ginzburg shows that a couple of Menocchio's contemporaries – self-taught, northern Italians (one being a miller, also tried for heresy like Menocchio himself) – not only read several of the same texts that Menocchio did but also construed key passages and themes in these texts in a very similar manner.[22]

The second procedure is the eliminationist method. Ginzburg sets up four hypotheses which compete with his preferred hypothesis and shows how they are flawed. The first candidate is that Menocchio was mad. It is dismissed by Ginzburg on the ground that before the trial the inquisitor himself seriously considered the possibility but rejected it when witnesses testified that Menocchio spoke in earnest and was sane.[23] The second candidate is that Menocchio's 'interpretative filter' was the product of the Anabaptist movement, a clandestine sect that believed in a simple religion, the mortality of Christ, religious toleration and many other ideas which Menocchio also held. But Ginzburg rejects this hypothesis with the argument that many of Menocchio's other beliefs were fundamentally at variance with those of the Anababaptists (they claimed, for example, that Scripture was the only source of truth whereas for Menocchio it could come from a wide variety of texts; they condemned indulgences, whereas he did not).[24] The third hypothesis is that Menocchio's ways of reading texts were shaped by 'generic Lutheranism'. Arguing against this possibility, Ginzburg says that Menocchio did not understand key tenets of Lutheranism (justification by faith and predestination), and that the Reformation did not have the remotest connection with Menocchio's notion that the universe and God had emerged out of chaos.[25] The last possibility – that Menocchio's ideas came from direct contact with self-taught unorthodox heretics like himself – Ginzburg disputes, given all the other evidence that Menocchio 'didn't parrot the opinions or ideas of others. His way of dealing with books, his contorted and awkward statements, are the sure signs of an original approach'.[26]

How well does Ginzburg's overall argument stand up? Several questions hang over it. The most obvious is whether the thoughts of one peasant are capable of being representative of 'the' peasant oral tradition, even assuming there was a unitary peasant oral tradition. Another question relates to the reliability of the transcripts as a window on Menocchio's ideas; it is quite possible that the inquisitors might have asked leading questions of Menocchio and that his answers might have been misconstrued by the notaries (who generally wrote them down in the third person). Moreover, Ginzburg has no way of being able to tell *how far* Menocchio's ideas were derived from peasant culture, for he cannot determine the extent to which they were also the product of Menocchio's fertile imagination.

Even so, Ginzburg's methods produce a highly plausible account. The comparative textual analysis procedure clearly indicates that at least some differences in meaning existed between Menocchio's readings of the texts and what these texts actually say. The possibility that these readings were at least to some degree influenced by the peasant oral tradition, is established by maximising the variety and weight of the supporting evidence. Lastly, by demonstrating that the best possible competing explanations to the preferred hypothesis have serious flaws, Ginzburg reinforces the preferred hypothesis.

■ 5. Situational logic

As mentioned in an earlier chapter, intentional explanations attempt to explain the *rationale* behind the particular course of action taken by an actor. The object of the explanation is to recover the *conscious* reasons or intentions that led the actors to *choose* to act in the way she or he did. The problem with this approach is that reasons and intentions take place in the mind and are therefore not directly observable. In addition, as political historians have found, if actors record the reasons for acting after the event, they frequently give false accounts of these reasons either because their memories are faulty or for self-interested purposes. Besides, most of the actors whom social historians study are subordinate people who usually did not record their reasons for acting or whose reasons may only be obliquely apparent from their outward behaviour. How, then, can we find out what their reasons might have been?

A method for solving this problem is adapted from the situational logic model of the philosopher, Karl Popper. The model was not expressly developed to solve the evidential problems of intentional explanation, but as a way of explaining individual actions.[27]

Popper's model has two premises. Firstly, it assumes that the reasons which an actor has for acting are adequate (in this sense the actor has agency). Secondly, it looks at the specific situation confronting an individual actor entirely from that actor's point of view – in relation, that is, to the actor's own desired aims and assumptions about how the world works. On these premises, the model infers the particular reasons that led a particular actor to act from what a notional rational agent would have done in the same situation, *given the particular actor's desired aims and given the particular actor's beliefs about how the world works*. To put this another way, the inquirer works out the reasons by assuming that the actor's decision was appropriate, perhaps even the best possible, in the situation, considering the actor's own perception of all the elements comprising the actor's situation.

Although not its express purpose, Popper's model has a considerable capacity to organise circumstantial evidence about the likely reasons that lay behind the decisions taken by a tightly-knit group of actors or a single actor. Pivotal here is his idea of the subjective logic of the situation: if this can be reconstructed, if we can understand the values and the beliefs that the actor brought to the situation, we can obtain a good approximate idea about the particular reasons that led to the action. The key to obtaining this understanding is to know the culture of the surrounding society, for what the culture does is to provide rules that tell its members what values and beliefs they should have and ground rules about how they should apply these values and beliefs to particular situations. As actors are rule-followers, their actions in particular situations will often be guided by the wider society's rules about which values and which beliefs they should enact in predictable situations. From this it follows, that if we, the outsiders, know the rules of a society as well as its members do, then we too will know what sorts of values and beliefs a group of actors were enacting in predictable situations. A knowledge of the rules will certainly not allow us to predict the values and beliefs of the actors in every situation: some actors choose to break or bend rules, some situations are unpredictable and are not covered by the rules, and some societies have very loose or conflicting sets of rules. Even so, an understanding of another society's rules will often give us a fair idea about the sorts of beliefs and values – and therefore the conscious reasons – that motivated an action in a specific situation. Learning a society's rules, then, can provide us with good circumstantial evidence about the subjective reasoning that led an actor to act as he or she did; and can thus go some way in solving the evidential problems associated with intentional explanations, especially in regard to subordinate people.

But how do we, as social investigators, learn another society's alien rules? This question is now a central question in some of the social sciences, particularly anthropology, and has become intrinsic to what is called the hermeneutic approach to social enquiry. We will return to this question and its implications for social historians in Chapter 8.

■ Conclusion

In this chapter we have looked at five possible methods for handling the problem of fragmentary evidence. The first method – crucial cases – deals with the problem of fragmentary evidence by taking an amply documented case (or set of cases) which is slanted against the preferred hypothesis, and showing that it nevertheless is compatible with the hypothesis. The second method – extrapolating from comparable cases – gives evidential weight to a causal explanation that generalises from a few known cases to the unknown many. It does so by citing studies of parallel cases where the same preconditions demonstrably co-exist with the same outcomes. The third method – maximising the variety and weight of supporting evidence – is also a supplementation method. Its aim is to increase the probability of a claim by accumulating as many positive examples as possible representing the greatest possible range of types of evidence. The fourth method – confirmation by eliminating rival hypotheses – can be used for most modes of social history. It postulates a hypothesis that can fit each group of positive examples. It then requires us to evaluate all the competing hypotheses in a comparative fashion to determine the most plausible hypothesis, the one that on the balance of probabilities is supported by the best evidence. The fifth method – the situational logic method – is restricted to intentional explanations. The method reconstructs the reasons of actors in a particular situation by examining the social rules that might have governed the values and beliefs of the situation in question.

■ *Chapter 4* ■

The Problem of Establishing Important Causes

The problem of establishing important causes could also be called the problem of establishing major or significant causes. It commonly occurs when we are trying to explain such problems as *why* a collectivity or category changed or *how* it came to acquire a certain attribute and our research of the documents suggests the phenomenon was driven not just by a few but umpteen different causes. How do we establish which of all these causes were the major or important ones? We cannot assume they are equally important; therefore how do we find out which were the major ones and which were the minor? Are there any reliable and defensible criteria we can use in arriving at a decision or can the issue only be decided on a purely subjective basis?

The problem has in part been vividly depicted in an imaginary little story by E.H. Carr in his well-known book *What is History?*:

Jones, returning from a party at which he has consumed more than his usual ration of alcohol, in a car whose brakes turn out to have been defective, at a blind corner where visibility is notoriously poor, knocks down and kills Robinson, who was crossing the road to buy cigarettes at the shop on the corner. After the mess has been cleaned up, we meet – say, at local police headquarters – to inquire into the causes of the occurrence. Was it due to the driver's semi-intoxicated condition – in which case there might be criminal prosecution? Or was it due to the defective brakes – in which case something might be said to the garage which overhauled the car only the week before? Or was it due to the blind corner – in which case the road authorities might be invited to give the matter their attention? While we are discussing these practical questions, two distinguished gentlemen – I shall not attempt to identify them – burst into the room and begin to tell us, with great fluency and cogency, that, if Robinson had not happened to run out of cigarettes that evening, he would have not have been crossing the road and would not have been killed; that Robinson's desire for cigarettes was therefore the cause of his death; and that any inquiry which neglects this cause will be waste of time, and any conclusions drawn from it meaningless and futile. Well, what do we do? . . . what answer have we to the interrupters?[1]

In short, what was the major cause of the accident? The drinking of the driver? The bad road? The bad brakes? The desire of the pedestrian to buy a packet of cigarettes?

Carr does not argue that there are no methods for deciding these questions or that the decisions we come to are just a matter of taste and opinion. On the contrary, he argues that there is a defensible and objective method. The best way to answer such questions, Carr seems to say, is to establish which causes always or mostly occur in conjunction with the same outcomes and which ones do not. He implies that what distinguishes an important cause from an unimportant one is its *regularity,* its generalisability – its constant conjunction with the same outcome. An important cause will always or usually be found with the same outcome and is thus predictable; an unimportant cause, however, will be found only found once or some of the time in the context of the same outcomes. Thus, he says, we might consider the drinking of the driver to be a significant cause of the accident for this can be generalised to other accidents: a fall in drunken driving can be expected to reduce the overall road toll. But it makes no sense to regard smoking as a significant cause of the accident since smoking cannot be generalised to other accidents: it is hardly likely that a national smoking ban will lead to a decline in the road toll.

Although Carr was a traditional historian (his main works were on the history of the Russian Revolution and its aftermath), his way of looking at the problem of causal importance is modelled on a convention followed by the social sciences, which in turn derived it from the experimental method practised by the physical sciences. In social history, the approach is often called 'historical sociology', and its most notable practitioners are Theda Skocpol, Charles Tilly, Barrington Moore, Reinhard Bendix and Perry Anderson, amongst others.[2] Like Carr, historical sociologists assume that in order to establish whether a cause is important we must engage in *systematic comparisons of cases.* Like Carr, historical sociologists suppose that if the same cause can be found in all or most comparable circumstances, then it must be important; otherwise it is unimportant. They too equate important causes, in other words, with causal regularity or generalisability – the constant conjunction principle. By implication, an important cause has some semblance to a 'covering law' or an 'explanation sketch', concepts which we covered in the last chapter.

Before I continue let me dispose of two doubts that readers might entertain about what has been said so far. First of all, they might ask why it is necessary to go to the lengths of using systematic comparison as a means of distinguishing the important from the minor causes when the whole operation could be more simply and easily done by a process of deduction from a general theory. Surely, many readers might say, social science and social history literature have many general theories about the nature of human society; each theory gives primacy to some kinds of causes over other kinds; thus to find out what the important cause might be for any given case, all we need to do is to deduce it from the relevant general theory. The difficulty with this suggestion, however, is that it ignores the problem of theory choice. The social sciences and social history are filled with competing general theories about the nature of human society, including Marxist theory, functionalist theory, structuralist theory, gender theories about patriarchy, to name but a few. Given this plethora of general theories, how do we know how to select the right theory? If we took the one that best pleased our personal tastes and preconceptions, it would hardly provide a rational foundation from which to deduce important causes. The only rational way of making a decision would be to find out which theory gave primacy to a cause which was linked to the outcomes of all our cases or, at least, was linked to more outcomes than the causes postulated by the other theories. And that can only be done through systematic comparison. It provides a rational procedure for discriminating between competing theories.

The second doubt which readers might entertain concerns the equation that historical sociologists make between causal importance and causal regularity. Readers might be puzzled by this equation, saying that it is too narrow, that it does not necessarily hold, and that it needs to be qualified. To some extent, I think they are right, and I will state my reasons shortly. But for the moment, I will suggest that readers should not find it puzzling since we tend to employ a very similar rule-of-thumb practice when checking the veracity of an historical explanation which we have encountered for the first time. When mulling it over, do we not seek to satisfy ourselves that it works by seeing whether it fits comparable situations? Do we not try to think of similar cases to see whether they contained the same alleged causes and the same outcomes? If we can think of any cases where the alleged causes were different but the outcomes were the same, or where the alleged causes were the same but the outcomes were different, do we not reject the claim or at least regard it as tenuous? The reason we reject the claim or regard it as tenuous is that we expect that causes which are supposed to be major or important causes should be found in parallel cases. If we do not find them in parallel cases, then we assume that the causes are not major or important; perhaps we might even say that they cannot have been the causes.

Granted, then, that systematic comparison is an appropriate method for identifying important causes, how do we go about systematic comparison? The choice of method is highly dependent on the type of data that are available, whether they are **quantitative** (measurable) or **qualitative** (non-measurable). If we are fortunate enough to have access to good quantitative data for a large number of cases, we can identify important causes with various statistical techniques that measure the degree of strength in the association between postulated causes and their alleged outcomes across all the cases. The techniques vary from working out simple percentage distributions to sophisticated multivariate analyses. Amongst the advantages of the quantitative approach is that it allows us to deal with large numbers of cases and to define causal importance in a probablistic sense which accommodates exceptions. This approach will be discussed in Chapter 6. A quite different comparative approach, however, is needed if the only available data are qualitative. Although the best techniques for this approach are powerful, their range of applications is limited. Amongst other things, they are manageable only if applied to small numbers of cases and they do not tolerate exceptions at all easily. The rest of the chapter will discuss these qualitative techniques and then illustrate them by examining in detail how one particular work in historical sociology has used them.

The notion of causal importance we have discussed so far is rather vague and crude. To give it greater precision and sophistication we need to introduce the very useful concepts of **sufficient and necessary condition**. Historical sociologists often apply these, or variants of them, though not always calling them by the same names. Four concepts are involved. They are **sufficient condition**, **necessary condition**, **sufficient *and* necessary condition**, and **neither a sufficient nor a necessary condition**. I will now discuss these concepts, translating them as far as I can into our earlier but cruder language of 'causal importance'.

Sufficient conditions are conditions which wherever they occur are enough in themselves to produce the same outcome wherever the sufficient conditions. A cause is a sufficient condition if in every context where it occurs it is always succeeded by the same outcome. To put this abstractly, wherever x and y are present they are always succeeded by z. Thus whenever towns receive rain, their streets always get wet; rain is a sufficient condition of wet streets. Earthquakes are not a sufficient condition of wet streets: sometimes earthquakes rupture water-mains causing the water to flood the streets; but obviously earthquakes do not always have this effect. A sufficient condition for an outcome, however, does not mean that it is the only factor that will bring about that outcome. Another factor or set of factors could also be a sufficient condition. For example, although rain is a sufficient condition for wet streets, there are other sufficient conditions for wet streets: burst water-mains, firemen squirting hoses, the operation of street-cleaning machines, even communal ceremonies involving displays of mass urination, and so on.

This brings me to the concept of *necessary condition*. When a cause is a necessary condition for an outcome, the outcome is always linked to it. Wherever the outcome occurs, the same cause will be found in the same context as well. The test of a necessary condition is its absolute indispensability. Thus oxygen is a necessary condition for combustion, wings are a necessary condition for the flight of birds, and eyes are a necessary condition for sight. However, a necessary condition for an outcome, though essential to that outcome, will not by itself produce the outcome. For example, while violent death is essential to murder, a murder requires an additional condition for its occurrence: the murderous intent of an assailant. Compared with a sufficient condition, therefore, a necessary condition is a less important kind of cause. Whereas a sufficient condition declares 'wherever there is an *x* and a *y*, there is a *z* but that other things can also produce *z*; a necessary condition puts this the other way round: it declares that wherever there is *z*, we always find an *x* and a *y* but that the *x* and the *y* were not enough in themselves to produce the *z*.

The most important kind of cause is something which is both a necessary *and* a sufficient condition for the outcome. Consider one of the examples I used above of a necessary condition. Oxygen is a necessary condition for combustion. Without it, combustion cannot take place. But oxygen by itself will not produce combustion; hence oxygen is a necessary but not a sufficient condition for combustion. What would provide both the necessary and the sufficient conditions of combustion is the presence of oxygen *and* fuel *and* some device for igniting the fuel. Consider the other example: murder. Now violent death is a necessary condition of murder. But it is not a sufficient condition because suicide or accident can also produce violent deaths. What would provide both the sufficient and necessary conditions for a murder are violent death *and* the murderous intent of an assailant.

The weakest kind of condition is a factor which is *neither a necessary nor a sufficient condition* for an outcome. The outcome will occur without the factor and there will be an indeterminate number of occasions where the factor is present and the outcome is not. By implication, the factor will either have a purely accidental connection with the outcome or only occasionally be associated with it. An example is a loud voice and a good academic record. A person can have a good academic record without having a loud voice, and lots of people with loud voices do not have good academic records – as we well know. Another example is Carr's one of cigarette smoking and motor vehicle accidents: accidents can occur when the drivers are non-smokers, and a lot of smokers do not have accidents.

In summary, there is a hierarchy of criteria we can use to establish 'causal importance':

1. Conditions which are neither necessary nor sufficient have no causal role in relation to the outcome at all or may need to belong to a group of factors to be a necessary or sufficient condition for that outcome. They thus either

have nothing to do with the outcome or are of minor importance.

2. Causes which are necessary conditions are essential to an outcome but will not by themselves produce it. Hence they are of some importance.

3. Sufficient causes will always by themselves produce the outcome. They are therefore important causes and have completely predictable consequences.

4. Causes which are both necessary and sufficient to the outcome are supreme causes. They are perfect predictors of a class of outcomes since they always produce the outcome and nothing else will do so. In effect, if we claim that our causal models are both sufficient and necessary to an outcome, then we are claiming they are mono-causal.

Before we go on, we need to clarify several points. One is that the concepts of necessary and sufficient condition are precise technical terms; and my ways of labelling them by talking about their degrees of importance is quite irregular. Another is that the concepts are applicable to entities that are not causes. A related point is that when referring to a condition as sufficient or necessary in a causal sense, we should not, strictly speaking, refer to it as a 'cause' but as a 'postulated cause' or a 'hypothetical cause' or a 'pre-condition'. *The reason for this is that the concepts do not entail causality*; a constant conjunction between two things could be a complete coincidence. The last point is that necessary or sufficient conditions do not have to be single factors; a group of factors can as a group act as a necessary or sufficient condition. In the absence of one of more of the factors, however, the group is not a sufficient or necessary condition. A factor belonging to a group of factors is perhaps best called a contributing 'cause'. Such factors often constitute conditions which are neither necessary nor sufficient.

Having outlined the standard notion of causal importance, the concepts of necessary and sufficient condition, and how these things can be applied to qualitative data, let me now discuss many of the standard objections and problems that are associated with causal analysis and the systematic comparisons which are generally employed to test for causal regularity.

■ Standard objections to causal analysis

These can be lumped into two groups. In the first are the objections and problems which are conventionally associated with all systematic comparisons irrespective of whether they are qualitative or quantitative. There are four of them.

Ia. Comparisons are invalid if any of the cases contains an excessive amount of internal diversity. For example, if the cases are countries, one of these may have a region or place containing a small population which, because of quite exceptional circumstances, behaves in an extremely abnormal fashion. The behaviour of this unrepresentative region or place may have a disproportionately large effect on the history of the country as a whole and on the data recorded for the whole country. Hence when we come to make inter-country comparisons, our generalisations about this country in relation to the others will be distorted by the behaviour of one of its small but highly aberrant regions or places.

Ib. Systematic comparisons are wrong in principle because history is about unique entities and, as a consequence, nothing in the past can be compared with anything else.

Ic. The study of causation is wrong in principle because it emphasises structure and is deterministic. It grossly underestimates the capacity of actors to make choices and to shape their own situations to suit their own ends through the exercise of their own rationality (or agency as it is often called).

Id. The systematic comparison of cases will not allow us to pick up the important causes of *aberrant* cases. Obviously, there may be occasions where we might want to reconstruct the causal structure of a particular case which has no parallel in any general case. When this occurs, no amount of systematic comparison of the general case is going to tell us what were the important components in the causal structure of the aberrant case.

Although problem Ia will not always occur in a study, it is nonetheless a very real and obvious possibility. This being so, it is reasonable to expect every comparative study to anticipate the problem by showing that the internal variations within the cases are not excessive. Item 1b represents an extreme objection to the systematic comparative method which I do not agree with. If taken to its logical conclusion the objection would forbid us from using generalising concepts in history such as 'social class', 'monarchy', 'feudalism', 'the family', and force us to employ only particular terms, a restriction which would prevent us from talking about almost anything related to the past. Besides, although some things in past time may be unique, there is no evidence that everything is. Moreover, the objection begs questions about what constitutes uniqueness, a very difficult issue which I will take up in the next chapter on the problem of similarities and differences. Item 1c, the ontological objection to causation, has more substance. It represents the standard criticism of causation made by historians and theorists of an intentionalist and hermeneutic persuasion. I will say more about the criticism and the issues it raises in the later chapters on quantification and concept-presentism. For the moment, I will confine myself to the comment that we have every right to expect anyone engaging in a comparative study of causation to confront the criticism since it is such a well-known and prominent part of the social historical literature on the social 'bedrock'. Problem 1d is inherent in systematic comparison and nothing can be done about it as long we continue to define important causes in terms of causal regularity.

The second group of problems are those that are specific to the qualitative mode of systematic comparison. There are four:

2a. The qualitative mode of comparison is suitable only for topics involving a handful of cases. If we have more than about half a dozen cases, the method becomes very cumbersome. This immediately narrows the range of topics it can be applied to. It precludes us from studying classes of phenomena containing multitudes of cases. And we cannot study only a few of the cases of a multitudinous-case topic because we usually have no way of telling that the chosen few are typical of the unknown multitude. As a consequence, the qualitative mode of analysis restricts our choice of topics to those where the number of cases is 'naturally' or inherently small.

2b. Whether there are such topics is questionable. Social history topics deal with sets of socially defined categories and collectivities, and, unlike biological species, these sets are not obviously distinct. Very often the boundaries between one set of social categories/entities and other sets are hard to draw. Although we have to draw the line somewhere, the divisions can be arbitrary.

2c. Under the constraints of the qualitative method, *exceptional cases* are extremely difficult, perhaps impossible, to handle. Since we are comparing such a small number of cases, one exceptional case is a very big exception while two would comprise overwhelming exceptions. Moreover, given that we are using the analytical tools of necessary and sufficient condition to compare cases, we do not appear to have any conceptual room for exceptional cases. What do we do when we are comparing the causal structures of, say, six cases and we find that a particular cause is a necessary condition of five but not of the sixth? Properly speaking, such a cause cannot be called a necessary condition.

2d. The definition of 'important cause' is problematic. By equating an important cause with causal regularity, the definition takes no account of the *relative strength* of any given cause. In some cases, a cause may well be the largest and most powerful component in a causal structure. But in other cases, it is possible that a cause will be the smallest and weakest component of a causal structure, contributing, say, less than 1 per cent to the outcome. The problem with the definition is that in effect it will treat two such causes – one very powerful, the other very weak – as equally important. It is a very moot point whether a cause that plays a very minor role in a causal structure can be regarded as an important cause even though it may be a necessary condition or it may be a cause belonging to a set of causes which together constitute a sufficient condition.

Under the constraints of qualitative data, what can be done with all these four problems? I can think of no ways any study can limit problems 2a and 2c. Indeed any study that threw up problem 2c is probably beyond redemption, doomed, if it threw up exceptions and at the same time tried to claim causal regularity! However, there are ways of limiting problems 2b and 2d and the mark of a good study is that it will employ these techniques effectively. Thus, a good study should be able to minimise problem 2b by putting up a strong defence for the selection of cases, demonstrating that they belong to a distinct set. A good study should also be able to minimise problem 2d, with a close examination of the evidence, showing at the very least that the regular cause was *not* something that played a infinitesimal role in a causal structure.

Illustrating the problems: Theda Skocpol's *States and Social Revolutions*[3]

A former student of the prominent Harvard historian, Barrington Moore (himself an author of several famous works of historical sociology), Theda Skocpol is a brilliant practitioner of comparative social history (or historical sociology if you like). She has also won renown as a leading theorist on the subject, having edited a volume of essays on its methodology and written several essays (one co-authored).[4] These works should be consulted by everyone working or intending to work in comparative social history/ historical sociology, particularly if the work is in the qualitative mode since this mode is her speciality. (In Chapter 6 I will refer to useful texts specialising in the quantitative mode.)

States and Social Revolutions is a monumental work in many senses: in its sheer size, the resoluteness with which it tackles some fiendishly complex historical subjects, the breadth of its scope, the boldness and originality of its integrating theory, the explicitness of its methodological strategy, and the rigour with which it is argued. Broadly speaking, the book is in two parts. The first endeavours to establish the important/major causes of three revolutions: the French revolution of 1789, the Chinese revolution of 1911–49, the Russian revolution of 1917. It is quite clear from the text that Skocpol defines as important/major causes those that are *general* to all three cases. In the Introduction she says: 'I shall argue that these cases reveal similar causal patterns despite their many other differences'; 'Any valid explanation of revolution depends upon the analyst's "rising above" the viewpoints of participants to find important regularities across given historical instances'.[5] The object of the second part is to explain why the post-revolutionary histories of these three societies had certain fundamental features in common, namely, 'the emergence of more centralized, mass-incorporating, and bureaucratic states'. [6] In my discussion and appraisal of the text's methodology, I will, for the sake of simplicity, concentrate on the first part.

What is unusual (refreshingly so) about *States and Social Revolutions* is that its methodology is spelt out and defended in the Introduction. As a result, from the very beginning of the book, Skocpol directly confronts and anticipates many of the problems which I itemised above concerning the method of systematic comparison.

To start with, the Introduction discusses the rationale behind the choice of cases, vigorously defending the decision to confine the selection to China, Russia and France, thus anticipating problems 2a and 2b. Skocpol admits the choice may seem arbitrary since the three cases are not the only examples of revolutions; there are many others. Moreover, she concedes, her exclusion of rebellions from her analysis may also seem arbitrary since rebellions are close relations of revolutions in that they too are characterised by a great deal of social violence. But, she argues, her choice of cases is not arbitrary since the revolutions in China, Russia and France had several things in common which rendered them distinctive. That is to say, they were *social* revolutions: they were brought about by a confluence of internal class conflict and external political crises and they produced both class and political transformations. In these respects, they differ from rebellions in that rebellions may involve class conflict but do not lead to social or political transformations; and they differ in type from what she calls 'political revolutions'. Unlike social revolutions, political revolutions are not brought about by class conflict and while they lead to transformations in political structure they do not produce transformations in class relations. Lastly, she says that what made the French, Russian and the Chinese revolutions distinctive as social revolutions is that they occurred in countries that had possessed long histories of political independence, of sovereignty. Their 'state and class structures had not been recently created or basically altered under colonial domination'.[7]

In addition, the Introduction directly confronts the hermeneutic-intentionalist objection that causal explanation is deterministic and ignores the agency of the actors. In this way, she anticipates yet another problem with systematic comparison, 1c. Agency, she insists, cannot explain revolutions because revolutionary leaderships do not create the revolutionary situations they exploit; many revolutionary outcomes are unintended by revolutionary movements; and the motives of individuals belonging to revolutionary movements are extraordinarily diverse and often contradictory. Revolutions, she emphasises, implicitly taking a shot at the likes of E.P. Thompson, are not made by actors: they emerge from structures.

Another thing she spells out in the Introduction is the particular method she employs for making systematic comparison. A modification of the concept of necessary condition, the method is derived from John Stuart Mill's *A System of Logic* (1843). Two procedures are involved, one Mill called the 'method of agreement' and the other, the 'method of difference'. With the method of agreement, the investigator tests for causal regularity by taking all the cases that have the same outcomes (z) and seeing whether each case also contains the same hypothesised cause or set of causes (e.g. $x + y$). If each case does contain the same postulated cause or set of causes, the investigator can justifiably conclude that this cause or causal set ($x + y$) was indispensable to the outcome (z). Although Skocpol does not say so, the method of agreement is the concept of necessary condition but called by another name. With the method of difference, the investigator tries to confirm the results of the first method. The investigator takes another set of cases, which are as similar as possible to the first lot but for one thing: they do not possess the outcomes (z). The investigator then sees if these negative cases contained the same hypothesised cause or set of causes ($x + y$) as the first lot of cases. If they do not, the result reinforces the conclusions of the method of agreement. The hypothesised causes in the positive cases *must have produced the outcomes, since the negative cases contained neither the same outcomes nor the same postulated causes but were similar in every other respect.* Thus in a sense, the method of difference is a *negative necessary condition*: if something is postulated to be a necessary condition (i.e. the outcome cannot take place without it), it follows that whenever the outcome is absent, the postulated necessary condition should be

missing too. The method of difference is very close to what economic historians call a **counter-factual** hypothesis, except that a
counterfactual hypothesis refers to a fictional case not an actual one.
   The whole approach of the book is centred on these two methods. Skocpol applies the method of agreement to France, China
and Russia to test her hypothesis that their revolutions had common causes. Then she applies the method of difference to three
countries which experienced political transformations but not social
revolutions to see if they lacked the postulated common causes. The
three negative cases are Japan, England and Prussia. 'These cases
are suitable as contrasts', she says, 'because they were comparable
countries that underwent non-social-revolutionary political crises
and transformations in broadly similar times and circumstances to
France, Russia, and China.'[8] I will now discuss her argument in
detail before evaluating it, seeing how far it manages to deal with
the other problems associated with systematic comparison.
   As I mentioned before, Skocpol's hypothesis is that the revolutions in France, China and Russia had two sets of causes in common and that these causes acted in concert. (Note that by
implication she is not saying that the common causes were *sufficient conditions* of social revolution.) The first was the failure of the
states in each of these three societies to handle acute external crises. With Russia, the crisis took the form of the major military
defeats inflicted by Germany in 1915–17; with France, the crisis
was represented by the Bourbon regime's embroilment in a succession of three financially disastrous wars (the War of Austrian
Succession in 1740–8, the Seven Years' War of 1756–63 and the
American War of Independence, 1774–8); and the crisis affecting
the Manchu regime of imperial China was engendered when the
country was militarily defeated by Japan in the war of 1895–6.[9]
According to Skocpol, these three crises cannot be explained by
chance or inadequate leadership, but in terms of deep-seated
structural factors which were very similar in each country. For
geographical and historical reasons, the external security of each
country was inherently difficult to maintain. At the same time, the
capacity of their respective states to provide this security was
undermined by the *comparative* backwardness of each state's admin-
istrative/military apparatus and of each country's economy (back-
ward, that is to say, in relation to the countries threatening the
state's external security). As France was both a maritime and a

continental power in a zone of intense great power rivalry, its defence needs were intrinsically large; but the capacity of the Bourbon regime to sustain these needs was undermined by its archaic tax system and the low productivity of the bloated peasant sector. The imperial state of the Chinese empire in late nineteenth century had to face unparalleled threats from foreign powers, demanding that the empire be opened up to their economic influences. But undermining the imperial state's ability to withstand these threats were the increasing predations on its tax base by provincial and local gentry. A growing external threat to imperial Russia came from the growth of German power. Yet the Tsarist state's ability to deal with this military threat was greatly weakened by the comparative backwardness of the Russian economy, retarded by the inertness of peasant society.

According to Skocpol, the external crises of the three autocratic regimes acted as the triggers of peasant revolution. In each case, the crises did not directly drive peasant revolution but enabled it to take place by preventing the state from crushing it. In each case, what prevented the state from acting effectively was the breakdown of its military/administrative capacity. The process by which the breakdown occurred was very similar across the three countries. In response to the external crises, *the dominant classes* successfully challenged the power of the autocracy – engaged in political revolution – and constitutional chaos resulted. The chaos of the political revolution variously destroyed the morale of the bureaucracy and military, created acute divisions inside the dominant classes, and generally sowed great confusion within the structure of government. In France, it was the calling of the Estates-General in early 1789 that initiated the political revolution which paralysed the central government. In China, the constitutional chaos which led to the destruction of the central government was the overthrow of the Manchu dynasty in the political revolution of 1911. In the case of Russia, the constitutional chaos was brought about by the political revolution of February 1917 in which the Tsar was deposed.

The second important precondition of the social revolutions in France, China and Russia was class conflict of a particular kind. Skocpol argues that it was not class conflict *per se* that brought about the social revolutions but the specifically rural character of the class conflict. Moreover, she argues that the key factors that underpinned this rural class conflict were not chance, agency (in terms of leadership and ideology or whatever), relative deprivation or exploitation but two structural factors that the three countries had in common. One was the relative backwardness of the agrarian economy of each society which ensured that it contained a very large peasant sector. The other factor was the particular character of peasant social organisation. In each society, the peasantry enjoyed an unusually large degree either of solidarity or of social independence from the dominant class or of a mixture of both. These institutional arrangements, Skocpol argues, were highly conducive to peasant unrest since they lessened the power of vertical bonds in the countryside with the result that they diminished the capacity of the dominant class to exert personal influence over the peasantry, normally an important source of social control and stability in hierarchical agrarian societies. In the case of pre-revolutionary France, peasant social independence was derived from high rates of peasant proprietorship, and peasant solidary ties at the local level were fostered by the collective decision-making of village assemblies and by the control peasant communities exercised over the distribution and use of local common land. In imperial Russia, the peasantry had less economic independence but developed strong habits of mutuality through the village commune, the peasant-run institution that collectively owned and distributed local land. In China, however, the situation was rather different. The gentry dominated local rural communities, and peasant competition over land prevented peasant solidarity except amongst kin.[10] Hence the spirit of independence and of solidarity among the settled peasantry was much weaker in China than it was in France and Russia. But, she says, a growing number of Chinese peasants were dislodged from their local communities and obtained social independence by joining social bandit groups. Between the late nineteenth century and the 1930s the number of such groups increased as a consequence of growing population pressures on land supplies, natural disasters, civil war in the countryside, and the breakdown of the central government.

In sum, Skocpol's theory of social revolution has two fundamental causes. The first cause is the structural inefficiencies of the state. These make it vulnerable to external military defeat which in turn produce constitutional chaos – political revolution – which destroys the state's internal coercive capacities. The second is the economic independence and relative solidarity of the peasantry. These render the peasantry susceptible to insurrection. Thus when the first cause is activated, there is nothing to stop overt class conflict in the countryside, which is underpinned by the second cause. Seen as a process, the first cause leads to political revolution by the dominant classes which unleashes the second cause, the social dimension of social revolution which transforms class relationships, destroying the dominant classes (in the case of France, the dominant classes were not destroyed but their privileges greatly curbed).

By using the method of difference, Skocpol then tries to highlight by negation the significance of the two sets of interacting causes. As I said before, she takes her contrasting cases from England, Japan and Germany when these countries were in a similar condition to China, France and Russia. Thus she examines England during the parliamentary revolution of 1640–89, Germany during the 'failed' political revolution of 1848–50, and Japan during the Meiji Restoration of 1868–73. Like the positive cases, the negative cases consist of societies that were agrarian and were going through political transformations but did not experience social revolutions. What she finds is that none of the three negative cases witnessed a combination of *both* severe external crisis and rural class conflict. In England an independent peasantry had largely disappeared by 1640 and the rural subordinate classes were dependent upon the landed upper classes; in much of Germany (notably east of the Elbe) the same had occurred by 1848; in Japan, an economically independent peasantry still existed by 1868 but was under tight bureaucratic control and thus lacked institutional autonomy; in Germany and England, the state was not under intense external pressure; and although the state in Japan was under severe external pressure, it was sufficiently rationalised to cope with this pressure.

Assessing Skocpol's success in dealing with problems of systematic comparison

So far we have discussed the methodology of *States and Social Revolutions*, and the relation of the methodology to the theory. I will now appraise the methodology, seeing whether and how far Skocpol successfully deals with the problems that are inherent (or at least are seen to be inherent) in systematic comparison. The problems are those I listed above. I will not assess the factual adequacy of her claims since these are outside our purview.

1 a: Do any of the cases contain excessive internal diversity?

Not a few specialists on the history of the French and Russian revolutions have argued that a disproportionately large role – perhaps a decisive role – was played in the two revolutions by the events and the insurrectionary movements in just two cities: Paris in the case of the French revolution and Petrograd in the case of the Russian.[11] Skocpol anticipates this problem by including in her narrative of both revolutions accounts of the events and the insurrections by urban workers in Paris and Petrograd. More than that, she directly confronts the problem by arguing that widespread peasant revolts have been the crucial ingredient in virtually all successful social revolutions, not only in Russia, China and France but also in those that have taken place in newly independent societies. 'This is not surprising', she says, 'given that social revolutions have occurred in agrarian countries where peasants are the major producing class.' Rebellious peasants have the power of numbers and are sufficiently widespread to bring about social revolutions in agrarian societies; rebellious urban workers in the same societies do not have the power of numbers and the geographical dispersion to weaken the state and the class structure of old regimes to the same extent.

> Without peasant revolts, urban radicalism in predominantly agrarian societies has not in the end been able to accomplish social-revolutionary transformations. The cases of the English and the German (1848) Revolutions... help to demonstrate this assertion. Both of these contrast cases had vigorous urban-popular revolutionary movements. Yet they failed as social revolutions in part for want of peasant insurrections against landed upper classes.[12]

1b: Systematic comparisons are wrong in principle because history is about unique entities

This problem is not applicable to Skocpol since it is, as I argued earlier, a non-problem.

1c: The search for causal regularity ignores the role of human agency

In her Introduction, Skocpol offers some effective theoretical arguments demonstrating why it is entirely appropriate to devalue the role of agency in revolutions. But in her analysis of one particular case, China, agency plays a much larger part in producing peasant revolution – the social part of social revolution – than her overall theory allows.

Skocpol concedes that her theory about the structural causes of peasant revolution (i.e. the social part of social revolution) does not really fit the Chinese peasantry. Unless they were bandits, Chinese peasants lacked both the solidarity and the institutional autonomy to rebel against large land owners; the gentry, she says, dominated the local peasant community.[13] To be sure, she says that large numbers of Chinese peasants had snapped their ties with gentry by joining social bandit groups between the late nineteenth century and the 1930s. But she admits that there was nothing exceptional about the existence of such groups; they had always proliferated in the bad times throughout Chinese history. Moreover, she more or less says that by the 1930s these peasant-social bandits were incapable of organising rebellion, let alone a successful social revolution, by themselves. Historically, 'all of the more sustained forms of peasant-based revolt were sooner or later led or infiltrated by nonpeasants', and by the 1930s 'the basic structural changes' which permitted this had not 'fundamentally altered'.[14]

To explain why the peasant-social bandits did become social revolutionaries, Skocpol emphasises the role of agency, of purposive human action. She says that what was essential to peasant revolution in China was the activity of the Chinese Communist Party after 1927; it mobilised peasant revolt; without the Party's initiatives, organisation and leadership, peasant revolt would probably never have occurred. A 'new kind of national political leadership, the Chinese Communist Party, operating in the context of political-military fragmentation, ultimately found it necessary to attempt to fuse its efforts with the forces of peasant-based social banditry in order to build a Red army capable of taking and holding regions to administer.' Under the protection of the Red army, the peasantry in North China took over local politics, and from this base revolted violently against the gentry in the 1940s. 'Thus,' she concludes, 'the peasant contribution to the Chinese Revolution resembled much more a mobilized response to the revolutionary elite's initiatives than did the peasant contributions in France and Russia.'[15]

In short, although in her Introduction Skocpol advances some effective general arguments about why structure is more important than agency in creating social revolutions, some of her own evidence subsequently weakens these arguments. She tacitly admits that with one of her three cases the relative importance of agency and structure is reversed: with the Chinese social revolution, agency is more important than structure. By implication, she has not dealt adequately with a major objection – the intentionalist objection – to the method of systematic comparison. As we will see in a moment, this problem spills over into another: if China is an exception to the general pattern, has Skocpol failed to establish causal regularity and, by implication, the important causes of social revolutions?

☐ 1d: Systematic comparisons do not allow us to pick up important causes of aberrant cases

This problem would be relevant to *States and Social Revolutions* if it could be shown that one or more of the cases is aberrant, by which I mean, is an exception in kind. Skocpol assumes that all her three positive cases fit her general model; but whether her own evidence shows that is another question which we will examine in a moment.

☐ 2a: The qualitative mode of comparison is suitable only for topics involving a handful of cases

Skocpol overcomes this problem very elegantly by applying the method of agreement to three cases and the method of difference to another three.

☐ 2b: How can the choice of cases be justified?

It will be remembered that in her Introduction, Skocpol defends her choice of positive cases on two broad grounds. Firstly, she says that the revolutions of China, France and Russia can be distinguished from rebellions and a good many other revolutions by the fact that they were social revolutions: they both were caused by class conflict and caused transformations in the class structure. Secondly, she says that what made these revolutions distinctive is that they took place in countries that were long-established sovereign states and not colonial or newly-independent societies.

In her Conclusion, the second ground is clarified and elaborated to some extent. There she says that many other countries have gone through social revolutions – Algeria, Mexico, Yugoslavia, Angola, Vietnam, Cuba and so on – but claims that what makes these social revolutions different from those of China, France and Russia, is that virtually all occurred in former colonial territories. To be more precise, the key feature that puts them in a different category is their causal structure. The causes of social revolutions in France, China and Russia were the product of historical situations which were quite dissimilar from those in newly independent societies. Hence, the causes of one type of social revolution are not generalisable to the social revolutions in the other type. Whereas the social revolutions in her study were caused partly by agrarian class conflict and partly by confrontations with foreign military competitors, nearly all the other social revolutions were caused partly by agrarian class conflict and partly *by international disruptions of colonial controls*'.[16] Although she does not spell out what she means by this, she suggests that the states of newly-independent territories are weakened by the past experience of colonialism. An example she gives is Vietnam which emerged 'after French colonialism, which had itself displaced the previously existing indigenous imperial regime, was disrupted by Japan's conquests and subsequent defeat during World War II.'[17]

Is this distinction plausible? Skocpol is attempting to distinguish between two types of social revolution in terms of their causal structures, and there seems to be little difference *in essence* between the causal structures of each type of social revolution. With the French-Russian-Chinese type, the external crisis triggered by foreign military competition helps to cause social revolution since it disorganises the state, thus preventing the state from suppressing peasant unrest. With all the other social revolutions, she seems to be saying that the legacy of colonialism undermines (in unspecified ways) the power of the state, preventing it from crushing peasant unrest as well. Although the source of the state's incapacities in one type of social revolution is different from the source of the incapacities in the other type, it has the same effect: it stops the state from crushing peasant insurrection. Both types of social revolutions have the same essential components in their causal structures: disorganised states and rural class conflict.

If my interpretation of what Skocpol is saying about the 'international disruption of colonial controls' is right, then she has fundamental difficulty in trying to justify her decision to limit her positive cases in her book to just France, China and Russia. Her study excludes many cases which, given their causal structures, seem to be essentially of the same type as the few which she includes. In other words, her choice of cases seems to be arbitrary and indefensible. Ultimately, she has not effectively dealt with another problem which is inherent in systematic comparison as a method for ascertaining causal regularity and, by implication, causal importance. This in turn raises a further question: to what extent is her theory for the three cases she studies applicable to the many cases she leaves out?

☐ *2c: Under the constraints of qualitative data, exceptional cases are extremely difficult, perhaps impossible, to handle*

To test Skocpol's claim that she has discovered the common causes and thus the important causes of social revolutions we need to demonstrate that only one of her three positive cases is a distinct exception, fundamentally different in type. By this I mean that its causal structure was markedly different from that of the other two cases. If it turned out that her explanation of social revolution did not fit France, China or Russia then her attempt to discover causal regularity would have failed as would, by extension, her objective of trying to distinguish the important causes of social revolutions from the minor causes. As I have kept on hinting, the case which is most likely to be the exception, the disconfirming instance that falsifies her theory, is China. I will examine closely her own analysis of the causal structure of the Chinese revolution and determine how far it diverges from her analyses of the other two revolutions.

It will be remembered that social revolutions had two core causes, the disorganisation of the state and agrarian class conflict. Now, I think we would be very hard pressed to show that, within the constraints of her own evidence, Skocpol fails to show that China somehow deviated from that basic pattern. To that extent, China is not an exception. But if we were to break each of the core causes into its constituent parts, would we find sufficient evidence for exceptionalism?

By formalising Skocpol's general model of the first core cause – state disorganisation – we find that it has six constituent parts which are strung together in a causal chain. The sequence of the parts in the chain can be seen in the flow diagram in Figure 1.

GENERAL MODEL OF CAUSE 1

1. Acute military pressures from outside are imposed on the state
   +
2. The relative backwardness of the state and the economy
   $\longrightarrow$
3. The state suffers a severe external crisis
   $\longrightarrow$
4. The dominant classes successfully challenge the regime
   $\longrightarrow$
5. A political revolution and constitutional crisis ensue
   $\longrightarrow$
6. The state becomes disorganised

Figure 1

As I see it, Skocpol's account of China follows this general model of the first cause very closely.

However, it is when we break the second cause – agrarian class conflict – into its constituent parts, that we find that the Chinese case does not fit. To highlight the point, we only need to compare a flow diagram of the four constituent parts of the general model with a flow diagram of Skocpol's account of the equivalent parts of the Chinese variant (Figure 2). As we can see, every constituent part of the Chinese variant is different. Firstly, the institutional structures in the countryside are quite different. Whereas in the general model, the peasantry have community autonomy and/or economic independence, in the Chinese case the settled peasantry lack community autonomy and solidarity. As a consequence, secondly, the social relationships in the countryside are different. In the general model, the dominant classes exercise little hegemony over the peasants, but in the Chinese case the landlord or gentry class exercise tight control over the settled peasantry. Therefore, thirdly, while the peasantry as a whole have a potential for insurrection in the general model, the settled peasantry do not have this potential in the Chinese variant. Although the Chinese peasantry do have a potential for insurrection, the structures that produce this are idiosyncratic (civil war, natural disaster etc); the composition of incipient peasant rebels is idiosyncratic (the uprooted poorer peasants who join social-bandit groups); and most important of all, the mechanisms that mobilise the peasantry into revolutionary action are idiosyncratic (a centrally organized vanguard party). As I said before, Skocpol concedes that without the intervention – the agency and by implication the propaganda, the leadership, the beliefs and values and so forth – of the Chinese Communist Party after 1927, peasant revolt would probably never have occurred in China.

Given all these circumstances, can we say that China is a distinct case? Does the causal structure of the Chinese revolution diverge sufficiently from the causal structure of the general model to indicate that the Chinese causal structure is different in kind (type) from that of the general model? If we think it does diverge sufficiently, Skocpol has failed to demonstrate causal regularity. As she has based her claim about causal regularity on only three positive cases, it only requires us to show that one of these cases is different in kind, for her entire claim to collapse. In coming to a decision on

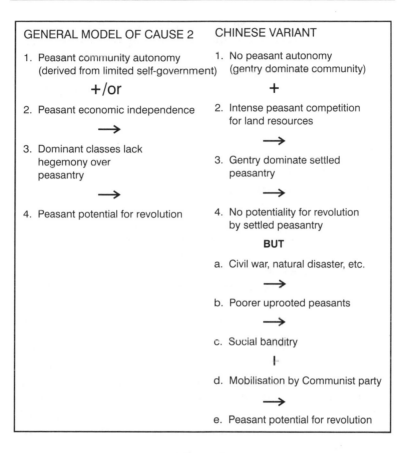

Figure 2

this matter, we have to consider, on the one hand, that China has the same two core causes, that one of its core causes has the same constituent parts as the matching cause in the general model, and that the outcomes are the same for China as for the other two cases; but, on the other hand, that the constituent parts of China's second core cause differ markedly from the equivalent constituent parts in the matching cause of the general model. My inclination is to conclude – most tentatively I must add – that China's causal structure belongs not to a fundamentally different type but to a different sub-type.

A more pertinent moral that can be drawn from this whole exercise is that it is very difficult, when testing for causal regularity under the constraints of qualitative evidence, to decide which cases are exceptions and which are not. Unfortunately, this vexing problem is neglected in the methodological literature; we will come back to it in Chapter 5.

> *2d: The definition of 'important cause' becomes problematic if a common cause plays only a minor part in a causal structure*

Skocpol anticipates this problem in an indirect way by showing that rival theories of revolution have less explanatory power than hers. (This device is a variant of the method of eliminating rival hypotheses.) Skocpol critically examines many alternative theories throughout the book but the main ones are of three types. They are what she calls aggregate-psychological theory, systems/value consensus theory, and political-conflict theory. T.R. Gurr's theory of relative deprivation is discussed as a representative of the first type; Chalmers Johnson's theory of the dis-synchronisation between values and environment is used as an exemplar of the second; and Charles Tilly's theory of mobilisation is taken as a paradigm case of the third. Much of the Introduction is given over to theoretical arguments demonstrating the explanatory weaknesses of these alternative views; and arguments of a more concrete nature are advanced where appropriate in the case studies.

To be sure, the procedure does not eliminate the possibility that her preferred explanation refers to very minor causes. But it does lessen that possibility provided we accept that the rival theories are very good ones and the best available. Whether Skocpol's rival theories meet these conditions is an evidential question which can only be answered by studying the literature of each of the revolutions in question.

■ Conclusion

In this chapter we have seen that the standard method for demonstrating which of a myriad causes of an outcome were important and which were minor, is to refer to parallel situations. This requires us to engage in systematic comparison. The assumption here is that causes that are postulated to be major or important are regular causes: they will always (or usually) be found wherever the same outcomes occur.

The method for determining important causes depends on whether the data are qualitative or quantitative. If the data are qualitative (non-measurable), the most powerful tools for ascertaining causal regularity are the concepts (or derivatives) of necessary and sufficient condition.

There are many possible objections to the use of systematic comparison as a method for ascertaining causal regularity. While many of these objections are of little foundation, some are not. These objections must be anticipated and confronted. They include the possibilities that one of the cases is excessively internally diverse; that agency plays a stronger role in the outcomes than causal structures; that the cases are not a distinct set of entities; that the causal structure in at least one of the cases is an exception in kind; and that a common cause played only a minor role in a causal structure.

■ *Chapter 5* ■

The Problem of Establishing Similarities and Differences – of Lumping and Splitting

Few social phenomena are absolutely identical. How, then, can we tell when they are similar enough to be regarded as members of the same class of objects or dissimilar enough to be put into different classes? How, that is to say, do we draw justifiable boundaries around social phenomena which are not exactly the same?

The problem overlaps into all the other six problems discussed in this book, especially the first problem, that of absent categories. But although very closely related, the absent categories problem and the problem of similarities and differences have different emphases. The absent categories problem is centrally concerned with whether in the first instance we have chosen the right/best categories (gender, ethnicity, locality and so on) for a social analysis. For its part, the similarities and differences problem gives more priority to the question about how we should *distribute* the cases once we have the categories to put them in – about whether, in other words, our allocation of particular cases across a given set of categories is justifiable. Hence when we encounter the differences and similarities problem we typically ask 'should this case belong to that class of social phenomena or this one?'

Another way of talking about the problem of similarities and differences is to refer to it as the 'lumping' and 'splitting' problem, a term used by J.H. Hexter, though in a different context.[1] An example of 'lumping' in social history is the claim by many Marxist historians that the French Revolution of 1789 and the English Civil War of the 1640s are both 'bourgeois revolutions'. According to such historians, these events are not unique entities, each in a class of its own; nor are they entities that belong to different classes of upheavals. Instead, so Marxist historians say, the two events should be lumped into the same overarching class of objects, namely, 'bourgeois revolutions'. When we split, however, we do the opposite. We refuse to see entities as members of a large aggregate. We either break the aggregate up and divide its members into a larger number of classes of objects; or we go to more extreme measures and fragment the aggregate into its individual components, putting each into a class of its own (*sui generis* as it is called in Latin); or we put most entities into one or more classes and define the remainder as exceptions; or engage in some other disaggregationist strategy. An example of 'splitting' is the claim by many American labour historians, led by Werner Sombart in 1906, that America in the late nineteenth and early twentieth centuries should be regarded as an exceptional case in relation to all the other western democracies because it alone did not produce a socialist working class. The implication is that although America seems to belong to a class of societies – collectivities – we call western democracies, it nonetheless should not be lumped with the others since its failure to produce the social foundations of a powerful socialist party renders it fundamentally unique.[2] Another example of a splitting decision is the claim by many early modern European historians that England should be treated as different from other societies in western Europe in the late seventeenth and eighteenth centuries since it was more urbanised, had a more productive system of agriculture, achieved greater political stability, possessed a parliamentary system of government, and so on.[3] Splitting also comes into the criticism levelled by many feminist historians at E.P. Thompson's famous theory of the rise of the English working-class in the early nineteenth century. They argue (as we saw earlier, pp. 32ff) that where Thompson's theory goes wrong is that, apart from neglecting women, it fails to recognise that the 'experience' of exploitation and struggle by working-class women was different (in kind, they appear to imply) from that of working-class men: men and women, they seem to say, should be treated as two distinct types, not submerged into the one generic type: 'the working class'.

There are several typical situations in social historical enquiry where the problem of establishing differences and similarities arises. The first is in situations where *comparative standards* are

applied. Social historians very often attempt variously to demonstrate, highlight, assess the significance of social phenomena in
one place and time, by relating them to what are taken to be comparable social phenomena (cases) in another place and time (or
several). Thus to give an idea of, say, the scale of crime or migration in one place or period, practitioners will often compare it
with the level of crime or migration in other places and/or periods. By definition, the assumption which underlies the procedure
is that the phenomena being compared belong to the same class.
But do they? It is common practice to condemn the procedure
where it is applied in particular instances on the ground that the
comparative standards are 'too distant' or 'remote' from the phenomena being compared – that apples have been compared with
oranges. How can the objection be anticipated? More generally
speaking, how can we decide when the assumption underlying
the procedure is justified? These thorny questions are functions
of the similarities and differences problem.

The second area where the problem is troublesome is where we
employ comparison as a *method of supplementing evidence* for causal
explanations based on a few known examples. In Chapter 3, we
called the method 'extrapolating from comparable cases', and saw
that it works by looking for well-documented studies of all other
cases where the same preconditions co-exist with the same outcomes. The reason why the problem is a great nuisance here is
that it burdens us with the obligation to show that the preconditions as well as the outcomes in the two sets of cases belong to the
same class.

This brings us to the third and related area where the problem is
especially vexing, namely, where *empirical evidence is cited either for
or against particular instances of causal, probablistic and statistical varieties of explanation*. In broad terms, we can say that the role of positive cases in these explanations is to provide empirical support for
them; while the role of counter-examples is to provide empirical
evidence against them. In these circumstances we obviously need
to select our cases accurately, ensuring that the cases belong to the
appropriate class. For example, if we wanted to explain why villagers in eighteenth-century Germany engaged in riots, we would
have to take as our supporting evidence (positive cases) eighteenth-century Germans that belonged to the village class. If we
wanted to confirm or disconfirm the explanation by taking as our

cases late twentieth-century New Zealand city-dwellers, we would obviously be selecting the cases from the wrong class, making what Gilbert Ryle, the philosopher, calls a 'category mistake'. With the similarities and differences problem, however, it is very often impossible to be certain whether the cases have been selected accurately, come from the right class – that is, whether they definitely confirm or disconfirm an explanatory theory. Usually, the appropriateness or otherwise of the cases is ambiguous and open to question, except when they consist of blatant category mistakes. It is partly for this reason that disputes over the appropriateness of cases feature so frequently in debates and criticisms concerning individual causal/statistical/probablistic explanations. Typically, such disputes are taken up with claims and counter-claims about whether the characteristics attributed to the cases have been properly interpreted, whether the cases possess contra-indicative characteristics which outweigh the indicative, and whether in consequence the cases fit the theory or are inconsistent with it. An apt illustration of the point was our critical discussion in the last chapter of Theda Skocpol's *States and Social Revolutions*. Here we argued that a key weakness in her theory is that her own evidence shows that many of the characteristics of the Chinese case diverge in major respects from those of the French and Russian cases; to be precise, there were key elements in the causal structure of the Chinese case that differed markedly from those in the Russian and French cases. Yet we also noted that it was extremely difficult to decide whether these divergences meant that the Chinese case was in a different class from the other cases. Although many of the elements in the causal structure of the Chinese case were distinctive, there were others which resembled those in the Russian and French cases. The discussion, in other words, exemplifies how the indefinite particularity of any given part of social life makes its identity highly problematic: we are bound to find some particulars that justify lumping it in such-and-such a class, and other particulars that suggest otherwise, that it really belongs to a different class altogether.

Another typical situation where the problem exists is also one involving comparison, and that is *where we discuss change and continuity*, one of the social historian's most favoured topics. When we want to know if something – a society, an institution or state of affairs or whatever – changed over time, we are essentially comparing its condition at the beginning with that at the end of a given period. Thus if we conclude that the thing had been 'transformed' by the end of the period, we are saying in effect that it had become so dissimilar that it belonged to a different class; and if we conclude that the thing had experienced continuity over the period, we are effectively saying that it still belonged to the same class of objects at the end of the period as it did in the beginning. The difficulty with these sorts of conclusions is the question they beg. How do we tell when change is slow enough to constitute continuity and things are sufficiently unstable to be justifiably defined as change?

The last typical situation where the problem manifests itself is with claims *that a certain category of people within a past society was a distinct entity and should be split from a broader category* – put into a class of its own. A key example – though certainly not the only one – is the insistence by feminist historians that female subjects in the past were different from male subjects and thus should be distinguished in social historical accounts. In specific instances where the categories in question are blatantly different, such claims do not need defending. In other circumstances, however, indefinite particularity (discussed below) may render the claim questionable: although the category could be distinctive in regard to some particulars, there could be others that indicate it belongs to the broader category and should not be split from it. In these circumstances, how do we know when our decisions to split off the category are warrantable?

The problem of similarities and differences disappears or diminishes if the phenomena in question are or can be satisfactorily expressed in quantifiable terms. When this happens we can apply one or more of various statistical tests – such as Chi squares – to see how closely related the cases are in a mathematical sense. The problem, however, is very difficult to overcome when the data are qualitative – impressionistic – and cannot be satisfactorily expressed quantifiably. Moreover, where the data are largely or entirely impressionistic and unquantifiable, they severely limit the range of comparative studies that can be undertaken: very often but not always, such data prevent the study of differences of degree and only permit the study of differences of kind.

The object of the rest of this chapter is to sketch out some strategies for tackling the problem under the constraints of qualitative evidence. The first section analyses the causes of the problem and makes a series of suggestions about how it can be managed. The succeeding sections describe and appraise the actual attempts of several practising social historians to overcome the problem.

▌ The causes of the problem and strategies for managing it

Difficulties with lumping and splitting generally arise from one or more of four causes, apart from, that is, the inadequacy of our conventions or rules on the matter.[4]

☐ *1. Unquantified class terms*

The most basic cause comes from the failure, when using unquantified class terms, to define them explicitly or to apply them in a manner which makes their sense clear. Often practitioners use unquantified class terms such as 'similar', 'comparable', 'different', 'exceptional', 'unique', 'very different', 'distinct' without explication as if these terms have some sort of definite, transparent and intrinsic meaning. This is far from the case; they do not mean anything in themselves. The meaning of class terms is highly context-sensitive. What people understand by them vitally depends on the particular yardsticks, norms, markers, measures and so on of difference and similarity they take as their standards of comparison, and these standards vary enormously from setting to setting. In the context of high-precision engineering, a difference of one millimetre might be considered intolerable since the standard of difference in this context is extremely fine; in the context of taking a stroll down to the shops, a one millimetre difference between two alternative routes is unnoticeable since the standard of what would constitute a difference in this particular context is far larger in scale. In the context of geological time, a difference of 40,000 years between eras is relatively slight; in the context of human history, it is enormous. To be sure, each community of language-users such as our own has a body of shared understandings, usually more implicit than explicit, about what some of these standards are. Even so, many shared understandings are far looser and refer to a much larger range of standards than others, without us being aware of it. In these circumstances, we run the risk when we casually assert that one case is 'different from', or 'very different from' or 'similar to' another case, not only of being seriously misunderstood but of giving rise to a wide variety of misunderstandings. While an author could have in mind a standard of fifty feet (15 metres) when saying a couple of roads were different in length, the readers could have in mind a range varying from a hundred yards (91 metres) to ten miles (16 km). Class terms, in short, tend to be highly ambiguous in their unquantified state. As a consequence, propositions about similarities and differences are very difficult to test unless the class terms refer to explicit standards.

To make the standards explicit, several procedures are available, all involving the use of controls. One is to base the standards of difference or similarity – the controls – on a theoretical model of the phenomenon drawn from a relevant field of the social sciences. Thus if we wanted to test whether a case was in the same class as other cases, we would construct a model, adapted from a reputable theory in the social sciences, about what either a typical or an atypical case would look like given the logic of the situation, and then see how far the real case in question resembled the model. An example of this will be given in the next section. Another procedure, more appealing to historians, is to base the controls on actual social phenomena. Alternatively, if we wanted to demonstrate that a group of cases had little in common, we could ask if the differences between them were at least as great as those between a group of control cases which were as different as chalk is from cheese according to the consensus of opinion held either by 'insiders' at the time or by the modern historical community. Often, of course, there will be no obvious consensus – then or now – about which group of cases would provide an adequate standard. In these situations, we have to rely on reasoning and analysis to demonstrate that a certain group was an appropriate control, spelling out the major respects in which each case in the control group was very different from the others.

Greater rigour and precision can be added to the definition of similarities and differences by distinguishing between two levels of differences: *those of degree* (which in effect are relatively minor) and *those of kind* (which in effect are radical differences). With little or no quantifiable data, it is very difficult to demarcate the control cases along these lines, but it can be done. For example, we could classify two control cases as different in kind if: (a) in objective terms each had defining characteristics which were the polar opposite of the other (and not just different); (b) the historical development of one diverged in major ways from that of the other (for instance, while one society urbanised and industrialised, the other did not); (c) the people in one case were extremely different from the people in the other case in terms of language, customs, beliefs, values, and sensibility (the classic example is the huge gulf between aborigines and white settlers in New South Wales in the late eighteenth and early nineteenth centuries); and (d), given physical contact between the peoples making up the two cases, the people in one case thought their culture was incompatible with the culture of the people in the other case. We could refer to the testimony of contemporary experts as evidence of (c); but it is not an empirically adequate procedure, for the reasons I spelt out in Chapter 3. It would be far preferable to use the broadest possible variety of indicators of incompatibility, such as evidence of strong taboos against intermarriage, patterns of residential segregation, discriminatory legislation and practices, outbursts of collective violence, the structure of victim–offender relationships in crime cases, and so on.

□ 2. *Level of abstraction in describing phenomena*

Often a great deal of confusion about whether things should be lumped or split stems from the failure to appreciate a truism, that our sense of whether things are similar or different depends on the level of abstraction of our prior descriptions of them. Detailed descriptions tend to make things look different, while generalised – broad-brush – descriptions blur and mask differences. Hence, a classification process that starts with a fine-grained description of the phenomena, is inherently biased towards producing evidence of the uniqueness of the phenomena; whereas a classification process that starts with a far more abstract description of the phenomena, has an in-built bias towards producing evidence that they are not distinctive but belong to a class of related objects. The best, perhaps only, solution to this problem is to base lumping and splitting decisions on explicit comparative standards.

☐ 3. Indefinite particularity

A less obvious cause of the lumping and splitting problem is what I shall call indefinite particularity. As each given part of social life can be decomposed into an indefinite variety and number of particulars, no restriction is placed on our ability to say when it is comparable or incomparable with another part. Although we could take some particulars as our criteria for saying it belonged to a certain class of objects, we could take other particulars as our criteria for putting it into an altogether different class of objects. Consider the example of two households. We could justifiably say they resembled each other, belonged to the same class, if they both contained two parents and two children. We could reinforce this claim if we found they occupied the same part of town, belonged to the same income bracket, distributed their outlays on goods and services in the same proportions, lived in houses of the same size, had moved to the area in the same year, and had similar age structures. But the particulars we have selected are not exhaustive. We could, in addition to all these criteria, decide if they were similar or different by taking account of a multitude of other particulars, for example, the marital histories of the parents, the schools the children attended, the age of the dwellings of the two households, the gender mix of the children, the medical histories of the mothers, the recreational patterns of the two families, the occupations of the fathers, their religious faiths and so on and so forth. In this context, could we still say the two households belonged to the same class if the parents in one had been married before and the others had not, or the children went to different schools, or one mother had broken her leg badly when she was twenty and the other mother had never had broken a leg let alone any limb?[5]

The solution to the indefinite particularity problem lies in constraining the number of particulars (characteristics) which can be attributed to an object. Several constraining mechanisms can be employed here either separately or in conjunction. In essence, they reduce the number of characteristics by assuming that some characteristics of an object are more important than others and that these define the object.

One such constraining mechanism distinguishes between *necessary* particulars and *accompanying* particulars. Necessary particulars are vital to the existence of the object; without any one of them the object would not be what it is. Thus, having a certain atomic weight and molecular structure are some of the necessary characteristics of gold. Accompanying characteristics, for their part, are those which are accidental to the existence of the object; their association with the object is a coincidence, a matter of chance. Thus, being wet is not a necessary characteristic of gold nor is its ownership by me: these are its accompanying characteristics. Given that accompanying characteristics are by implication minor or unimportant, we can disregard them, reducing the overall number of particulars. A variant of this procedure goes further by distinguishing between the accompanying characteristics and those that *are both sufficient and necessary* to the object.

Another mechanism is to discriminate between particulars according to their capacity to explain important phenomena in the surrounding society. For example, if we happen to be investigating a collection of people living in a society dominated by religious values, we could categorise these people by selecting only those particulars which had the strongest connection with these values and their manifestations. We would ignore a multitude of other particulars that had no bearing on religiosity, for example, those related to dental care and chimney-cleaning – unless, of course, teeth-flossing and soot somehow or other played a part in the society's religious ceremonies.

A completely different strategy for constraining the number of particulars is the internalist approach. As this strategy comes into Chapter 8 on the avoidance of presentism, we only need to describe and assess it briefly here. In essence, the strategy is based on the general principle that historians should, as far as possible, examine the past within the terms of the people who lived there. The principle is frequently applied by practitioners to classificatory problems and comes down to the simple rule: that when in Rome we should do as the Romans do. The key assumption behind the strategy, in other words, is that any classification of the entities and processes of a past culture should always follow the practices of that culture. For example, if we want to know whether to put certain members of fourteenth century Genoese society into this category or that one, we should determine, as far as possible, how they understood the ways their classification system worked and then distribute them according to their criteria, using their terminology.

An advantage claimed for the strategy is that it neatly circumvents the controversies which ensue when historians devise sweeping abstractions – like 'bastard feudalism', 'class conflict' – to designate social phenomena that take no account of temporal and spatial variations. In addition, it prevents us from making lumping and splitting decisions which are ethnocentric, presentist.

Amongst the drawbacks of the internalist approach is that it is only suitable for simple and tight-knit societies: we cannot put past people into 'their' categories if they belong to a highly divided society where one group classifies people one way and its opponents classifies them according to a different schema. Moreover, a common objection to the strategy is that insider ways of splitting and lumping simply reflect the values and interests of dominant groups and thus leave powerless people – like homosexuals, women and ethnic minorities – invisible or inadequately represented. In addition, as the strategy implies that we should only categorise the phenomena which the insiders were conscious of, it would lead us to ignore all the phenomena of which they were unconscious even though these affected their lives (a prime example here is the inequality of women).

☐ 4. Internal variability

The last cause of the lumping and splitting problem stems from the internal variability of a case. How do we tell if an object belongs to a certain class if some of its characteristics belong to another class? The answer to this problem is simple enough: it lies in establishing whether the combined weight of one set of characteristics (or particulars) belonging to the object is greater or smaller than the combined weight of the other set of characteristics (particulars). The method will not work, of course, unless the problem of indefinite particularity is dealt with first. So, before the method is applied, it is essential to use some constraining mechanism to limit the number of particulars that will be taken into consideration. Rigour can be added to the weighing-up process, by demonstrating that the categories of particulars in both sets have different intrinsic values and then building these different intrinsic values into the weighing-up process

The method has a crucial implication for a fashionable view held by many social historians about the social world and how it should be studied. The view is that any given large population of social entities is bound to contain large internal variations, and that accordingly it should never be treated as a single unit of analysis. Instead, they say, it should be divided into many distinct categories and each should be taken as a separate case. The influence of this disaggregationist view is manifested in such popular injunctions as 'we should only study the locality or the region in social history and not generalise about the whole country using national data', or 'we should distinguish men from women when talking about a population and not lump them together', and so on. Where the fashion has led practitioners to adopt this disaggregationist strategy, we can assess their claims within their own terms with a very simple test: by determining whether the differences within each case (category) are greater than the overall differences between this case and any other case. Thus, we can say a disaggregationist strategy has been successful if the variations within each case is smaller than the differences between any two of the cases; and we can regard it as a failure where the opposite true, where the diversity within each case is greater than the differences between any two cases.

Having discussed the main causes of the similarities and differences problem, and sketched some of the solutions, we will now critically examine three social historical works which have endeavoured to deal with the problem. Before we do so, however, one thing must be emphasised: that although the problem is pervasive in social history, we should only expect it to be addressed at length when the practitioner is advancing a major argument about the division and composition of the social world – that *this* case is an exception, or that *this* collectivity should be disaggregated into these distinct categories, or that *this* category of people has a unique culture, or that *these* cases belong to the same class. All three works to be discussed below are of this type.

▮ The case of David Fischer's *Albion's Seed: Four Folkways in America*[6]

The overarching thesis of Fischer's massive volume (it runs to nearly 900 pages) is made up of the following propositions: that America has always been not a unitary society but a highly region-alised one; that four distinctive regional cultures have always dominated American society and have a great deal of capacity to explain important aspects of American history; that these four dominant cultural regions were off-shoots of four early colonial settlements ('cultural hearths', 'cultural seedbeds') founded in America in the seventeenth and early eighteenth centuries; that each cultural hearth was comprised of a unique set of 'folkways'; that the folkways of each founding settlement were brought directly from a particular cultural region of Britain by a key group of immigrants; and that the transplantation and reproduction of each set of folkways was not unintended but represented 'the will and purpose' of the elite of each migrant group.

The first such cultural hearth, the Puritan colony of Massachu-setts, was transplanted from the East Anglia cultural region in Britain in 1629–40. The second seedbed, the 'cavalier' colony of Virginia, was reproduced by the gentry migrants from south-west England in 1642–75. The third, the Quaker colony of Delaware, was a replication of the Quaker culture of the north Midlands of England from 1675 to 1725. The fourth, the 'back-country' cul-tural hearth of the Appalachians or southern highlands, was brought by immigrants, primarily Presbyterians, from the bor-derlands of northern England, the Scottish lowlands and north-ern Ireland between 1717 and 1775.

From what has been said so far, it will be apparent that Fischer believes not just in the primacy of culture but in the uniqueness and profound stability of the culture of any given society. As Fischer sees it, each of the four cultures which America inherited from the four parent regions of Britain (the 'Albion's seed' in the book's title), persisted for many generations, even up to the mod-ern era in some respects, and played a far greater part in Amer-ica's development than any other factor or collection of factors (such as frontier, class relations, the subsequent influence of the metropolitan society, relations with the Indians, the coming of other immigrant groups and so on). Indeed, he believes so strongly in the durability of culture, that he goes to considerable lengths to show that many of the elements in the four parent British regional cultures of the seventeenth century were implanted before the Norman invasion and had been reproduced since then with little change! Although it has now become a well-established practice for anthropologists to stress the diversity of human cultures, Fischer perhaps gives more weight than they would to the stability of culture, the profound resistance of a society to cultural change.[7] He also goes far further than his fellow American historians have gone in disaggregating the notion of a 'British' migration to America.

The book is organised in four sections, each on one of the cultural hearths. The discussion in every section follows the same sequence: the historical background and cultural traits of the British parent region are sketched, details are given of how the settlement was founded and of the formative influences in its early history, the social composition of the key migrant group is discussed, and then the contents of the settlement's 'folkways' are spelt out and compared with those of the other settlements.

Fischer spends comparatively little of the book demonstrating the first proposition since his intention is to leave this to later volumes. The little he does say comes towards the end. Here he claims that the hegemony of the four regions on American life is reflected in the familial lineage of nearly every president which, up to the 1850s, was specific to one or another of these regions; and in the fact that each region is the site of each of modern America's four main dialects. The four regions in modern America, he goes on to say, have greatly different homicide rates, rates of duration of schooling, and levels of local government spending, and the best explanation for these things is the persisting influence of the folkways which each region inherited from its cultural hearth.

Fischer's principal proposition, however, is his claim that the folkways of each of these four cultural hearths were 'very different' from those of the other hearths.[8] Fischer has a shorthand definition of a folkway: 'the normative structure of values, customs and meanings that exist in any culture' and that tend to be exhibited in its artifacts.[9] But he also has a long definition of a folkway. A folkway, he implies, is made up of twenty-four categories of distinguishing characteristics – or types of traits or sets of particulars (Fischer calls them 'ways'). These categories consist of speech, architecture, family life, marriage, gender, sex, child-rearing, ways of naming, age, death, religion, magic and superstition, learning, food, dress, sport, work, time, wealth-distribution, rank, transience and social interaction, order, power, and freedom. The principal claim takes up most of his book, and it will be our main focus of attention from here on.

Fischer's procedure for confirming the principal claim is plainly a version of the method of generating the maximum variety and weight of evidence, though he does not label it as such or discuss his procedure explicitly. When he spells out the contents of each settlement's folkways, he systematically takes us through *all twenty-four* categories of characteristics making up a folkway, and presents a vast range of evidence showing that *in regard to every single one of these twenty-four categories* the hearth differed from the three other hearths. The cumulative effect of this is quite dazzling; by the end of the discussion of each hearth, we feel practically overwhelmed by the massive number and diversity of the supporting examples that each hearth was 'very different'. The supporting evidence, what is more, is not just qualitative but quantitative, consisting of imaginatively conceived indicators, many based on quite novel source materials.

But how well does he handle the four problems of lumping and splitting?

□ 1. Unquantified class terms

Fischer's concept of 'very different' plays a the central role in his proposition and, indeed, his overarching thesis, yet it is quite elusive. For a start, Fischer never offers an explicit definition of 'very different' or of any of the large variety of terms he uses as synonyms (and near synonyms) for 'very different' – such as 'distinct', 'distinctly different', 'differed profoundly', 'important differences', 'fundamentally unlike', 'special', 'differed very much', 'a world apart', 'strong differences', 'deep differences', 'striking contrast', 'distinctive', 'unique' and so on.[10] In addition, he does not think of elucidating the term by telling us how he would distinguish a folkway which was 'very different' from one which was just 'different', let alone by talking about the idea of difference in a wider theoretical/methodological discussion on the lumping and splitting problem (the book has almost no methodological discussion). Furthermore, he does not convey his notion of 'very different' through more indirect means, for example, by telling us what a folkway would look like if it were in the same class as another; by stating what would persuade him to agree that one or more of the folkways was similar to the others (technically, such a statement is known as a **potential falsifier**); and by acknowledging the possibility that some of the hearths were closer together than others (he seems to imply the opposite – that they were *equally* 'very different'). He seems to assume, in short, that the notion of 'very different' is quite unproblematic. As a consequence, during the whole of his monumental efforts to document his primary claim, we are never sure how different his notion of 'very different' is – whether he takes 'very different' to mean different in kind (type) or different in major degree or something else. The imprecision in turn makes his primary claim very difficult to test.

The difficulty of understanding what he means by 'very different' is compounded by another factor. As I mentioned before, the ideas of 'similarity' and 'difference' mean nothing in themselves but are context-dependent. Hence, when we say that a particular entity is 'very different' from something else, other people will not have a clear idea about how large that difference is unless they know what our standard (yardstick or reference point or norm) of 'very different' is. Fischer, however, does not specify what sort of standard he has in mind; he fails to put his claim that each folkway was 'very different' in an explicit comparative context, whether that be a theoretical model or actual cases. There are, it should be said, a few hints in the book that he may have had a particular standard in mind. On two occasions he says that the differences between the four hearths as revealed in every 'decennial census' were greater than the differences between 'European nations'. But these statements are nothing more than fleeting, undemonstrated and vague asides: he does not tell us anything about which categories of differences, which 'European nations', and which period of European history he is talking about.[11] Thus the statements are so open to interpretation they do not help us determine what his standard of 'very different' is.

To be sure, Fischer implicitly delimits the concept in one particular respect: he qualifies his primary thesis with the reluctant
concession that the four cultures did have some common characteristics:

> Nearly all spoke the English language, lived by British laws, and cher-
> ished their ancestral liberties. Most dwelled in nuclear households, and
> had broadly similar patterns of marital fertility. Their prevailing reli-
> gion was Christian and Protestant. Their lands were privately owned
> according to peculiar British ideas of property which were adopted
> throughout much of the United States. But in other ways these four
> British cultures were very different from one another.[12]

To me, the qualification is substantial, implying that on balance
the differences between the four cultures were not differences in
kind, they were not radical differences as it were, but differences
of a lesser sort – of major degree: after all, the things which he says
the four have in common – language, religion, legal systems – are
fundamental. But whether Fischer intends us to draw this inference is not clear; the point, made in passing in two quick sentences
in two places, is undeveloped. Overall, then, Fischer does not give
us a clear sense about what he means by 'very different'; perhaps
because he assumes that it will be obvious from the massive range
and number of positive examples he cites.

☐ 2. Level of abstraction in describing phenomena

As a rule, the finer the detail of a description, the more distinctive
something will seem (and vice versa). Fischer does not discuss this
problem, or appear to recognise its existence. Yet his description
of the characteristics is often highly detailed. This creates the very
real possibility, which he does not anticipate, that what helps to
make the four hearths appear 'very different' is an artifact of the
low level of abstraction of the description. To take an example,
when he discusses each colony's category of 'order-ways', he
divides the category into four sub-categories (ideas of order,
ordering institutions, forms of disorder, and treatment of the disorderly); breaks these sub-categories down into finer categories (the
'forms of disorder' sub-category, for instance, is broken down into
five sub-sub-categories each consisting of a type of crime: crimes

of conscience, crimes of morality, crimes of authority, crimes of theft, and crimes of violence); and then presents data under each of the sub-sub-categories showing how the colony in question differed from the other colonies. At that level of specificity, it is hard to think of any place in the modern world that would have exactly the same 'order-ways' as any other place. The level of abstraction is so low it virtually guarantees uniqueness.

☐ *3. Indefinite particularity*

As we have frequently noted, Fischer's strategy for demonstrating that each hearth was very different is to point to the myriads of particulars which the hearth *did not share* with the other three hearths across all of the twenty-four categories of characteristics. The strategy is contaminated by the problem of indefinite particularity in two respects.

First, if we look closely enough at some of Fischer's 'ways', it is not difficult to think of characteristics which we can expect a hearth to have shared with the other three hearths. Take the category which Fischer calls 'speech ways' ('conventional patterns of written and spoken language'): under the sub-category of vocabulary, he lists all the dialect words and phrases which were unique to each hearth; thus in the case of Virginia, he lists 48 such words and phrases. But what about all the other expressions which were not regional dialect? Although Virginia had 48 dialect expressions, it surely had a much larger number of expressions which were standard English and thus spoken in the other three settlements.

Second, although the four hearths might well have varied across the twenty-four categories of characteristics which Fischer does mention, we do not know whether they varied across the categories *which he conspicuously fails to mention*. At first sight, Fischer's long definition of a folkway seems impressively comprehensive, given that the 'ways' consist of twenty-four types (categories) of particulars (characteristics). But it only takes a moment's reflection to think of any number of other types (categories) of particulars (characteristics) which the long definition excludes. A prominent example which sprang to my mind is what we might call 'knowledge ways', epistemological rules about how the world should be studied, and how false beliefs can be distinguished from true ones – an exclusion which is most odd since the content of such rules is a sensitive indicator of a society's capacity for science. But he also excludes what we might call 'aesthetic ways', notions of what constitutes beauty as opposed to ugliness; 'nature-valuing ways', attitudes towards the natural world and the human relationship to it; 'grooming ways', attitudes towards personal appearance and how it should be enhanced; 'etiquette ways', notions of what constitutes correct conduct in specific social contexts; 'technology ways', the value placed on technological innovation and the practices which either encourage or discourage it; to mention but a few.

Of course, after doing some research on the matter we might find that in relation to all these excluded categories, the four hearths had quite different characteristics – thus reinforcing Fischer's claim. But what say we kept on thinking up additional categories until we found some with characteristics which were similar in all four hearths – a situation which is quite possible under indefinite particularity? What would happen to Fischer's primary claim then? How could we tell if these apparently anomalous cases invalidated the claim? Unfortunately, Fischer does not anticipate these questions either directly or indirectly. His book contains no implicit or explicit discussion of the question of indefinite particularity; he fails to recognise the possibility that a folkway might be made up of more than twenty-four categories of characteristics; he does not tell us why he selected these twenty-four categories and not others (his assertion that all cultures include the twenty-four 'ways' does not necessarily imply that a culture will have no other sorts of 'ways'); he does not tell us anything about the rationale he used to select the twenty-four categories; and he does not suggest that some categories might be more important to a folkway than others let alone attempt to lay out the reasons why he thinks they are more important. Fischer's silence on these matters makes his primary claim virtually untestable. It leaves him far too much room, far too many options, to deny the validity of an anomalous case in an *post hoc* fashion every time one seems to be found. Suppose for example we found that the four hearths had very similar 'knowledge ways' – one of the 'ways' excluded from Fischer's list. Fischer could deny the validity of this finding by saying a folkway by definition does not include 'knowledge ways'. Or suppose we found that all four hearths had the same 'chicken-plucking ways' – another way excluded from the long definition. Fischer could deprecate the validity of this by saying, 'Yes, this might considered a "way" but surely it is a very trivial one, much less important than any on my list of twenty-four, such as "freedom ways", "sports ways", and "naming ways".' Or imagine we discovered that the hearths had the same 'pet-keeping ways' – which also are excluded from the long definition. Fischer could deny the validity of this apparent anomalous case by stating that, although he agrees 'pet-keeping' ways are as important as any of his twenty-four categories, the significance of this counter example is outweighed by the combined weight of all the positive cases. Or say that we discovered that the four colonies had the same 'winking ways', another category omitted by the long definition. Fischer could deny the validity of this case on the ground that the long definition takes into account the meanings people attributed to their actions and that the people living in the four hearths were not conscious of winking. And so on and so on.

☐ 4. Internal variability

We saw in the earlier theory section that (especially for a disaggregationist) it does not make much sense to state that a case belongs to a different class than another case if the differences within each case are greater that the differences between them. How far does this problem affect Fischer's insistence that each hearth was 'very different'?

The first point to note here is that the text itself keeps on turning up evidence that in certain respects some hearths were not culturally homogenous but heterogenous. When referring to Virginia, Fischer says in respect of 'learning ways' that levels of literacy varied greatly according to gender, race and class;[13] that in connection with 'sport ways', the gentry reserved horse-riding and gambling to themselves while the lower classes engaged in blood sports;[14] that apropos of 'time ways', the gentry had leisure while the subordinate classes had no time of their own;[15] that in regard to 'wealth ways', there were geographical variations in the structure of wealth distribution;[16] and that in relation to 'rank ways', the elite had internal differences about how to classify society.[17] In his discussion of the Quaker colony of Delaware,

Fischer admits that in ethnic terms it was highly diverse and this diversity made itself felt in 'family ways',[18] 'gender ways',[19] and in 'power ways'.[20] In his description of the 'borderlands' hearth, Fischer explicitly emphasises that its 'North British' colonists had very mixed religious and ethnic backgrounds,[21] that they settled not just in the southern highland but in other regions of North America as well,[22] and that a large minority of the southern highland colonists came not from North Britain but other parts of Europe.[23]

The second point to note is that most – but certainly not all – of the book's supporting evidence for the primary claim is drawn from source materials – statutes, personal reminiscences, descriptive accounts and so on – generated by each colony's educated elite. As each elite was small and relatively homogenous, Fischer's inferences from the sources to the whole population of a colony are inevitably biased towards conclusions that the entire population of a colony was culturally homogenous. Moreover, many of the customs described by Fischer are inherently subject to marked internal variation. A salient example are 'food ways': Fischer advances a most intriguing generalisation in respect of cooking, that the puritans of Massachusetts mainly baked, the Quakers of Delaware mainly boiled, the Cavaliers of Virginia mainly fried and grilled and roasted, while the border people boiled. Is this generalisation inherently plausible given the large size of the populations it refers to, the lack of institutional regulation over food preparation, the frequency of daily meal-times and the sheer variation in personal/family circumstances?

Nothing advanced so far proves that the internal differences within each of Fischer's hearths were greater than the differences between any two of them. Even so, it is a distinct possibility which, we could argue, Fischer might have anticipated.

The case of Ian Carter's *Farmlife in Northeast Scotland 1840–1914; The Poor Man's Country*[24]

The overarching object of this work is to question the standard modernisation model of rural transformation favoured by economic historians, that the penetration of British agriculture by the capitalist mode of production inevitably created a three-tier class structure consisting of large landlords, tenant farmers, and a permanent class of propertyless wage-workers. The book takes a particular case – the Scottish northeast from the 1840s to 1914, the centre of a thriving cattle industry – and attempts to demonstrate that it does not fit the standard model. Carter argues that although the capitalist mode of production dominated the agricultural sector in this region by 1840, it produced a far more complex class structure than the standard model allows. Certainly, it created the three classes of improving landlords, capitalist large farmers and wage-earners. But it also sustained the land-holding peasantry – a pre-capitalist social formation which was large (by late century its membership was six times larger than the numbers of capitalist large farmers) and did not decline until about the turn of the century despite the advent of economic depression from the 1880s. Moreover, contrary to the standard model, a significant proportion of the wage-earners employed by the capitalist farmers were not permanent proletarians but sons of peasant farmers who later in life returned to their class by taking over the family small-holding or by becoming a small-scale pioneer on undeveloped land leased out by the large landlords.

Carter claims that what enabled this large pre-capitalist peasant 'fraction' to reproduce itself was that they were indispensable to the capitalist sectors of the economy. They supplied a substantial proportion of three crucial inputs: the hired labour required by tenant farmers; the store cattle which tenant farmers fattened for the London market (the cornerstone of farmer prosperity); and the pioneering tenants who developed waste land for the large landlords which they later leased to capitalist farmers. However, the depression in cattle prices brought about by competition with Irish and Canadian suppliers eventually prevented the peasantry from reproducing itself. The depression cut land prices and so discouraged landlords from renting out waste land to the peasantry for development; and, by squeezing the returns which peasant farmers received from raising store cattle, it deterred their adult children from staying on the farm, inducing them to seek better opportunities in the town or the colonies. Thus rural northeast Scotland came to an end as 'the poor man's country'.[25]

In sum, Carter's whole thesis is based on the arresting paradox that the domination of the capitalist mode of production was compatible with a large and thriving peasantry. Pivotal to the thesis, in other words, is the claim that a social category in rural northeast Scotland in the late nineteenth century, which he repeatedly calls the *peasantry* (or 'peasant farmers', 'peasant fraction'), did actually exist, was quite different from nearly all the other categories in the rural social world, and formed a prominent part of this world until 1914. The claim raises a rock-bottom splitting and lumping issue. What does he mean when he talks about the 'peasantry' and what criteria does he use to differentiate the peasantry? The nub of the issue here is how he manages to distinguish the peasantry from that other category he talks about: capitalist farmers. Carter insists that the two categories are distinct, that justifiable boundaries can be drawn around each – in his language, they are *different 'fractions'*. At the same time, he wants to maintain that they are different fractions *of the same social class*, that they had several key things in common: both fractions held and farmed land, both leased their land from large landlords, and both produced for the market (large numbers of store cattle in the case of peasants, fat cattle in the case of capitalist farmers). In other words, Carter seems to be engaging in a subtle exercise of lumping at one level but splitting at another. But it is a risky exercise since, from what has been said so far, the characteristics which the two 'fractions' had in common seem to be fundamental. The rest of this section will mainly be concerned with assessing how well he manages to justify his splitting – disaggregation – of the two 'fractions' given that they overlap in apparently fundamental respects.

☐ *1. Unquantified class terms*

How is the peasant 'class fraction' defined? Carter goes to considerable effort to define 'peasantry' in relation to 'capitalist farmer'. Although his text keeps on indicating that contemporaries did employ the concepts 'crofter' and 'muckle farmer' to distinguish between two grades of land-holders, one small scale, the other large, his definition does not rely on the consciousness of insiders: for he argues that that they 'usually' failed to see class as 'a major organising principle of social life.'[26]

Instead, his definition refers to two 'objective' standards, drawn not from actual cases – from studies of peasants in other societies – but from Marxist theory.[27] Both are closely interconnected. The first theoretical standard is the relation of each land-holding fraction to the labour market. By this standard, the essential feature that distinguishes the peasantry is that they 'always sought to work their holdings with family labour, and hired labour only when absolutely forced to do so'; and the key criterion that distinguishes capitalist farmers is that they 'always had to draw from the market a high proportion of the labour power needed to work their holdings.'[28] He also invokes the same standard to split the peasantry into two sub-fractions: 'poor' peasants who must work for wages off the family farm in order to make ends meet since the holding is too small to support them, and 'middle' peasants who do not have to work off-farm.

His second theoretical standard is the relation of each fraction to the cash crop market. By this standard, what distinguishes the peasantry, he says, is that they endeavour to be as self-sufficient as possible, although they have to sell some produce on the market to obtain the cash to pay rent, rates and purchase worn-out equipment. By the same standard, what distinguishes capitalist farmers is that they purchase a much larger proportion of the goods and services they consume, and hence are much more dependent on the cash crop market. In Carter's words, the peasant's 'dependence on the [cash crop] market was much slighter than in the case of the large farmer'.[29]

These two standards are plain enough. But how clear are the boundaries he extrapolates from them to demarcate peasantry from capitalist farmers? The first standard seems to draw a dividing line between peasants and capitalist farmers by saying that the latter hire a 'high proportion' of their labour power, while the former do not. This begs the question about how high a 'high proportion' is, and how we would recognise all the landholders who hire a 'high proportion' of their labour power as opposed to all those who do not. Is the boundary 50 per cent, or less than that? If more, would 60 per cent be the boundary line, or 80 per cent or what? The second standard begs the question about how 'slight' a landholder's dependence on the cash crop market would have to be before the landholder could be deemed a peasant as opposed to a capitalist farmer. What precisely does Carter mean when he says that the peasant's dependence on cash crops was 'much slighter' than the capitalist farmer's? How would we know what a 'much slighter' dependence looked like if we saw one in the primary source materials? Would our notion of 'much slighter' be the same as Carter's? Would your notion be the same as mine? The boundary lines, to put it bluntly, are not precise enough to make the compatibility thesis testable.

To be sure, in the rest of the book these definitions are not used as working definitions. In their place, Carter employs a proxy variable – a quantifiable indicator – of poor peasants, middle peasants and capitalist farmers. The proxy variable is size of landholding. In his discussion of the proxy variable, which occurs just after the discussion of the two standards, Carter states: 'we may assume that any farm of 100 tilled acres or more would rely on hired labour and hence be worked on the capitalist mode of production'; and that we can 'assume' that the cut-off point between middle and poor peasant would be fifty tilled acres.[30]

It is quite legitimate for Carter to base the proxy on various assumptions. But he is obligated to clarify and justify the capacity of the proxy variable to act as an indicator of poor peasant, middle peasant, and capitalist farmer. Although Carter goes some way to oblige us, the question is whether he goes far enough. During his discussion of the proxy, which takes up less than half a page, he admits that farm size in this period and (by implication) in general is a rough guide to farm incomes and productivity since it takes no account of the quality of the soil of a landholding, and the stage of a landholder's life cycle. (The roughness would not matter if Carter attempted to estimate the degree to which these factors affect the reliability of his proxy variable, or to assure us that the factors do not unduly distort the conclusions he reaches by using the proxy variable – but he does neither.) In addition, he offers no arguments to justify the 50 acre cut-off point between middle peasant and poor peasant; and the sole argument he advances in support of the 100 acre cut-off point between middle peasant and capitalist farmer consists of an undocumented assertion, three lines in length, that a farm of 100 tilled acres required two pairs of horses which was beyond the labour resources of the average farm family.[31]

To be sure, definitional problems often disappear when the things they refer to are placed in their empirical context. But do Carter's definitions of peasant and capitalist farmer and the proxy become clearer and justify themselves when considered in the light of the data he presents later in the book? I am not sure they do. For example, if we take his claim that peasant landholders were six times more numerous than capitalistic farmers in the northeast, and if we relate it to his notion that peasant landholding families always do their utmost to avoid spending money on hired labour, then we would expect that in the northeast there would have been far more unpaid family members than paid agricultural workers working on all the farms and crofts put together. But Carter's Table 4.2 shows the opposite: the aggregate of hired agricultural workers was greater than the aggregate of relatives on farms and crofts assisting without pay in nearly every census over the 1841–1911 period.[32] We would also expect the proportion of all male wage labourers working on landholdings of less than 100 acres (Carter's indicator of peasantry) to be appreciably less than the proportion working on landholdings of 100 acres and over (his indicator of capitalist farmers); instead his Table 4.7 shows that the proportions were not very far apart at all, being 46.7 and 53.3 per cent respectively[33] Furthermore, although Carter leads us to believe that the 'poor peasant' fraction were not capitalists because they did not have enough land or surplus to hire workers, his Table 4.6 does not demonstrate the point as unambiguously as he thinks; from it we can infer that for every three landholders of less than 50 acres in the region there was one hired hand (male or female) working for landholders in this category.[34] The table suggests, in other words, that in terms of his own definition up to one third of 'poor peasant' landholders were 'capitalists'.

In sum, Carter's thesis that a large and thriving peasantry was compatible with a capitalist mode of agricultural production is very difficult to test since his concepts of peasant (poor and middle) and capitalist farmer are so ill defined.

☐ *2. Level of abstraction in defining phenomena*

☐ *3. Indefinite particularity*

Carter's compatibility thesis does not display either of these problems. He preempts them through his attempt to specify in advance the two defining characteristics of a landholding peasantry: its low dependence on the cash-crop market and on hired-labour.

□ *4. Internal variability*

The work often points to variations within the case, especially
the differences between the sand-stone districts and the 'central
wedge' of the region, which had different concentrations of
capitalist farmers. But what about other variations? Towards
the beginning of the study, Carter says the strong demand for
dairy produce and vegetables generated by the city of Aberdeen
was a powerful stimulus in the neighbouring rural districts for
the establishment of capitalist farming on a small scale: 'The
acreage of each market garden seems to have been rather small,
but the intensity of production – using spade cultivation –
meant that many market gardeners were capitalists, relying on
hired labour to work the holding.'[35] In a later part of the book,
it transpires that the *county* of Aberdeen contained 62 per cent
of the northeast's crofts and farms.[36] Taken together, these two
pieces of information suggest that Aberdeen is an important
exception to Carter's compatibility thesis. At the very least it
could be used to argue that Carter could have done more to
acknowledge that in addition to the sandstone/central wedge
distinction, there is another, within the central wedge itself,
and that the 'wedge' has two quite distinct social structures: one
in the rural districts around Aberdeen, the other in all the other
rural districts. At the very most, the importance of the Aberdeen exception could be used to argue that the compatibility
thesis is relevant only for a minor component of the social structure of the northeast.

The case of Alan Macfarlane's *The Origins of English Individualism: The Family, Property and Social Transition*[37]

The main question which Macfarlane, an anthropologist of
Nepal and a social historian of early modern England, addresses
in this work is a bold one: did England ever have a peasantry
from the thirteenth to the eighteenth century? The answer which

Macfarlane gives is an emphatic 'no', and he goes on to use this to explain why England was the first country to industrialise:

> The hypothesis…is that the majority of ordinary people in England from at least the thirteenth century were rampant individualists, highly mobile both geographically and socially, economically 'rational,' market-oriented and acquisitive, ego-centred in kinship and social life.[38]

Macfarlane, however, directly acknowledges that the answer he arrives at depends entirely on how 'peasantry' is defined, on the characteristics with which it is attributed. Accordingly, the book, which is highly reflective about methodological matters, devotes a considerable amount of attention to clarifying and justifying the concept of 'peasantry' it favours. We will now examine its handling of definitional problems, leaving aside the argument of the thesis, for the argument largely turns on some highly technical points of detail, principally legal in nature, which only an expert in the field can assess.

☐ *1. Unquantified class terms*

Macfarlane starts his study by systematically laying out and assessing the alternative concepts of peasantry commonly found in the theoretical literature on the subject (sociological and anthropological) and in historical works on English society. The common-sense definition of peasantry – 'people who live on the land and work as farmers or labourers' – and the concept used by many historians – 'small holders and cultivators of the land' – he rejects, on the grounds that they are far too broad, lacking in discriminating power. A tighter definition intended to exclude tribal societies – 'small holders and cultivators in a pre-industrial society that has a state and urban markets' – he also finds unacceptable, saying that it is insufficient, that it excludes the nature of land ownership and the mode of consumption and production. This leads him to his preferred definition. The necessary characteristics of 'peasantry', he says, are small holders and cultivators in pre-industrial societies with urban markets and states. But, he says, to be *necessary and sufficient*, another characteristic must also be present, something which in the rest of the work he keeps on referring to as the 'central feature', namely, a situation where law or custom prescribes that the productive resources of the holding are owned by the peasant family *as a whole* (by parents and children as a collective body) and cannot be alienated from that family but must be passed down to and distributed amongst the next generation. In essence, then, the crucial factor that distinguishes a peasant holding from a capitalist small holding is the nature of property rights: an individual owns the capitalistic holding and has the ultimate and exclusive right to dispose of it at will, whereas the family jointly owns the right to the peasant holding and cannot alienate it from the family.

Macfarlane goes on to say that where these necessary and sufficient characteristics exist, we should expect to find other characteristics in a peasant society, though not necessarily all of them. His long list includes the right of each family member to be supported by the holding; inheritance through equal partibility as opposed to primogeniture; the absence of wills (for these admit the possibility that children can be disinherited); a minimal labour market (since the family provides all the labour required); the lack of a marketable surplus; a very limited division of labour at the local level (because each household is maximally self-sufficient); a values system where land is not regarded as a commodity and the family attaches intense symbolic importance to the land; the relative independence of peasants from market forces; very limited geographical mobility and thus a high concentration of kin within a locality; comparatively large household sizes (since equal partibility inheritance practices encourage women to marry at a comparatively young age); patriarchal and highly authoritarian households (since children have little scope to pursue careers outside the household); and small inequalities in the distribution of wealth (because hired labourers are few and because of equal partibility).

Macfarlane states quite explicitly that this model of what an English peasantry should look like (if there was one), is closely based on the famous study of the Polish peasantry by Thomas and Znaniecki *(The Polish Peasant,* 1918) and on modern studies of the nineteenth Russian peasantry by T. Shanin. Macfarlane, in other words, takes the actual case of the east European peasantry as his yardstick for judging whether England had a peasantry.

Now, we can agree that a major strength of the model is its crispness and clarity. It spells out explicitly what the necessary and sufficient characteristics of a peasantry are; it commits itself to claiming that one of these characteristics (the 'central feature') is the key distinguishing mark of a peasantry; and its description of this central feature seems precise and definite, not subject to different interpretations.[39] All this makes Macfarlane's thesis testable. But clarity of definition is one thing, its justification is another: why take this model as the standard and not some other model? Given that England from the thirteenth to the eighteenth centuries was quite a different place from eastern Europe in the late nineteenth and early twentieth centuries, is it possible that Macfarlane has taken a definition of peasantry which is virtually guaranteed to exclude the English case? Why not take the example of the peasantry in certain parts of western Europe such as France as the standard?

In the methodological chapter, Macfarlane attempts to anticipate these questions by providing four reasons for his choice of the east European model. But none is persuasive. It is really beside the point, for example, to chose this model as the standard of comparison on the ground that studies of the Eastern European peasantry are original![40] More important still, right at the end of the methodology chapter, Macfarlane makes a surprising admission – that the model does not fit western Europe. He says that the eastern European model of the peasantry is the 'classical' model of the peasantry; that west European peasantries had moved a long way from the 'classical' model well before the twentieth century; and in fact there may have been 'perennial and basic differences' between the peasantries of eastern and western Europe. He then ends up saying that one of these differences was that the western peasantry did not have the 'central feature' of the eastern peasantry:

> In relation to the present work, the difference [between east and west European peasantries] is most important in relation to the unit of ownership. The nature of the contrast between 'classical' and 'west European' peasant ownership is most easily illustrated by a diagram. In the former, all the members of the family are joint-owners; in areas of single-heir inheritance in western Europe, only one son is a joint-holder with his father.[41]

The obvious question he begs here is why, given there are alternative models of peasantry, one with the 'central feature', one without it, did he prefer one over the other as his standard of what a peasantry should look like? As we noted in the theory section, lumping decisions always invite question as to whether apples are being compared with oranges. In this instance, it is self-evident that if England was an orange and not an apple, eastern Europe would be more like the apple, and western Europe more like the orange. So when trying to determine if England had a peasantry, why take the eastern peasantry as the standard of comparison instead of the western peasantry? Why, in other words, take the less relevant standard of comparison than the more relevant one? Earlier in the methodology chapter, Macfarlane says that the reason he did not take the Asian peasantry as his standard of comparison was because 'There are many who may recoil at comparison of England and, for example, Asia, alleging that there are too many other cultural and historical variables to make it worthwhile.'[42] By the same token, many would recoil over his decision to use eastern Europe instead of western Europe. The only argument Macfarlane offers for this preference is that 'If we are trying to discuss why industrialisation occurred first in England and the degree to which England is different from, say France or Italy, it is clearly inappropriate to construct the indexes by which to measure the societies from one of the nations we are trying to compare.'[43] But in this immediate context, we are not trying to discuss the question about why England industrialised first but the prior question: whether it had a peasantry. Besides, if, as he finds later in the book, English small farm holders and cultivators lacked the 'central feature', and given that the 'west European peasantry' also lacked the 'central feature', then how can Macfarlane claim that the absence in England of the 'central feature', allowed it to industrialise before other west European countries?

What, however, saves the day for Macfarlane's standard is the next chapter. The subject of this is the historiography on the 'peasantry' in England from the medieval period to the industrial revolution. Here Macfarlane is able to show, successfully in most instances, that from Marx to the present day the prevailing tendency within the historiography has been to assume that joint family ownership – the 'central feature' – characterised the English 'peasantry' before it was extinguished by the advent of capitalism.[44] In effect, then, the standard which Macfarlane uses to judge whether England ever had a peasantry is based on a common interpretation by historians. In the rest of the book, furthermore, he provides additional documentation of this standard interpretation, mostly in relation to the works by medieval historians.[45]

☐ *2. Level of description in describing phenomena*

☐ *3. Indefinite particularity*

These problems do not affect Macfarlane's argument. The reason they do not do so is that right at the start he recognises that the argument pivots on definitional matters, and accordingly he is very careful to lay out the criteria which a class of people must meet before they can be called 'peasantry'.

☐ *4. Internal variability*

This does not affect his argument either, since it is empirically supported by data from a small range of local case studies.

■ Conclusion

The chapter has dealt with the four problems that face us when we have to decide whether the social phenomena we are studying should be put in the same class or different classes, given that few social phenomena are exactly the same. The chapter pointed out that the problems permeate our work as social historians because so much of our work in one way or another is concerned with distinguishing and comparing social phenomena. The first problem is that class terms like 'difference', 'exception', 'unique', 'distinctive' and 'similarity' have no intrinsic meaning. It was suggested that the best way to manage this problem, was to clarify the specific meaning of the class terms in each situation by explicitly taking theoretical models or actual cases as standards of comparison – as controls. The second problem is that the level of abstraction at which phenomena are described can substantially affect the extent to which they resemble each other. The chapter suggested that this problem solves itself when we elucidate our use of class terms by putting them in the context of comparative standards. The third problem arises from indefinite particularity – our capacity to attribute an indefinite range of characteristics to an object – for this capacity allows us to find whatever characteristics we like to justify our classificatory decisions. The chapter suggested that to solve this problem we needed to constrain the proliferation of characteristics, for example, by distinguishing between necessary and accompanying characteristics, or by following the classificatory rules of the 'insiders', the society we are studying. The fourth problem is that of internal variability, of trying to decide which class to put a case when the case has diverse characteristics which fit more than one class. Here the chapter suggested that the solution lies in placing a value on all the characteristics that belonged to each class and putting the case in the class with the characteristics having the highest aggregate value.

■ *Chapter 6* ■

To Count or Not to Count?

Up to this point our discussion of the methodological problems that confront social historians has been based on the key assumption that the solution to these problems is constrained by fragmentary evidence.

This chapter is something of a diversion but a necessary one, I think. Rather than broaching another problem, I intend to revisit what I have said in the previous chapters but within the framework of an entirely different assumption. Let us imagine that instead of being constrained by fragmentary evidence, we are fortunate enough to be working in an area where there are a lot of systematic data or to stumble across data that are not fragmentary but are susceptible to quantitative analysis. Should we employ mass quantification to solve the problems specified in Chapters 2 to 5? Or should we instead persist with the messy but more comprehensible non-quantitative methods which have been outlined so far? By mass quantification, I mean the use of advanced statistical techniques and/or numerical data as the sole or principal means of supporting a claim.

The reason these questions arise is related to a fundamental dilemma that currently faces social historians. Let me discuss this dilemma at some length.

One side of the dilemma comes from the fact that statistical method has proved itself to be an extremely useful tool of enquiry in many domains, notably the physical and the social sciences. Statisticians have created and refined all manner of powerful and sophisticated quantitative techniques that can solve problems, provided the right technique is applied to the appropriate data set. On the face of it, many such techniques are extremely useful for social historians as well. I will not attempt to describe these techniques since it would take up the rest of this book and would only duplicate the information contained in a large number of excellent textbooks on statistical techniques for historians and for those working in the social sciences. Moreover, if I did describe these techniques I suspect that most of my readers would bitterly complain that they did not have slightest idea what I was talking about, saying either that number crunching has nothing to do with history, or that like all historians they are hopelessly innumerate.

Nonetheless, I will try to illustrate my point by taking as examples the three problems we have examined so far. The first such problem, it will be remembered, was that of making reliable generalisations about a large aggregate from a few known cases. Now, if we are lucky enough to have access to a data set that documents every case, this problem simply disappears: all we need to do when we want to demonstrate that an aggregate had a certain trait is to count all the cases that did have this attribute and show that these cases made up the vast majority of the total number of cases. To be sure, our aggregates are often too large to be analysed in a 'cost-effective' manner: if the aggregate contains hundreds of thousands of cases and the information in the archives on each case is documented in a separate file, it would take far too long (unless we belonged to a research team or the data base was computerised) to go through the hundreds of thousands of files on the whole aggregate to collect the information we were looking for. But the advantage of statistical method is that it has devised a variety of sampling techniques, requiring some very simple mathematics, that enable us without much effort to select from the hundreds of thousands of cases a representative slice of all the cases. Since the slice will be comparatively small, it will reduce to manageable proportions the task of drawing the information from the files.

Statistical method also has considerable scope – or so one would think – for tackling the extremely troublesome problems discussed in Chapter 5, those related to establishing similarities and differences. Statisticians have devised a whole battery of techniques for these sorts of problems. To be sure, it is often difficult, even for those with first degrees in statistics, to know which is the most appropriate technique. But straightforward problems (for example, whether the proportion of items within a set is significantly different from that within another set) can be readily identified and tackled by someone with an elementary knowledge of the subject.

The third example seems to be even more pertinent: the problem of determining important causes. Chapter 4 noted that under the constraints of qualitative data, the method of systematic comparison has severe limitations: it can only handle a tiny number of cases, it cannot cope with the problem of exceptions, and it cannot determine the strength of a common cause. But when systematic comparison is harnessed to certain statistical tests of association (the best known of which are correlation and regression analysis) these limitations vanish. Firstly, with the assistance of a computer, correlation and regression techniques enable us to analyse large numbers of cases. Secondly, they allow us to measure the strength of a hypothesised cause. The most basic technique, simple correlation analysis, can be visualised as if it were a graph that is seeking to compare the movements of two lines of numerical data. Each line consists of a series of data points, the information for every matching pair of data points coming from the same case. One line (technically called a variable) represents a hypothesised cause, the other line, the hypothesised outcome. Essentially, correlations measure in a precise summary fashion (a 'co-efficient') the extent to which the peaks and valleys on one line move in tandem with those in the other variable. If there is a very large degree of correspondence, then the correlation co-efficient will be high, and, by implication, the hypothesised cause is strong. Correlations move along a range between +1 (where all the troughs and peaks on one line move in the same direction with as those on the other line) and −1 (where all the troughs and peaks for one variable are the inverse of all those for the other); a zero co-efficient means that there is absolutely no correlation. Thirdly, correlation analysis accommodates exceptions with ease. A correlation co-efficient of less than −1 or +1 but more than zero measures the extent to which a postulated cause (independent variable) fits a postulated outcome: the residual represents the exceptional cases, those with data points that move against the overall trend. A more complex technique, multiple correlation, can be used to reduce the residual. In effect, it takes several hypothesised causes (independent variables), combines them into a group, and plots the movements of the group against the movements of the variable expressing the postulated outcome. (Regression analysis is a prediction device which measures the best fit that can be made between a straight or curved line and a series of matching data points.)

So far what I have attempted to show are some of the advantages that seem to be linked to statistical method. These advantages constitute one side of the dilemma: on the face of it, statistical method offers a great deal to social historians. Since it can be such an effective means for supporting a claim, why not use it?

This brings me to the other side of the dilemma. With a few key exceptions (notably the economic, demographic and *Annales* historians) most practitioners in almost every field of history dislike mass quantification and currently there is very strong social pressure within the discipline against using it. To be sure, the hostility is by no means absolute. Although mass quantification (as I defined it at the start) is practically taboo, a little bit of simple enumeration is not. Some historians have been known to cite a few tables in a book; most will put a population in context by referring to its size; a small minority see nothing wrong with quoting a handful of percentages to measure changes over time and to compare the composition of several entities; and not a few will occasionally refer to averages in order to summarise a range of figures.

Social historians, of course, are more likely to engage in and tolerate number crunching than traditional historians. As the subject-matter of social historians generally consists of big aggregates, they have to be far more precise when using such phrases as 'few people', 'more people', 'many people' than traditional historians whose subject-matter generally consists of the history of elite ideas, elite biographies, tiny elite groups, and elite institutions.

Even so, it is true to say that most social historians are very wary of mass quantification – of supporting a claim with a lot of numbers and with statistical techniques which go beyond averaging and percentaging. As I said earlier in the book, mass quantification has become quite unfashionable in social history, partly because of a natural reaction against the excesses of the mass quantification craze of the 1970s, and partly because of the extraordinary upsurge during the last decade or so of the 'cultural turn' in social history. Spearheaded by post-modern and some hermeneutic theorists, the advocates of the cultural turn are sceptical of causal explanations, and give primacy instead to the role of symbols and interpretation, of culture and language, in ordering social life and in our understandings of it. As a consequence, for example, the history of crime which two decades ago was preoccupied with the 'scientific' counting and explanation of crimes, has moved into the study of the ways in which language and beliefs 'constitute' notions of dangerousness and deviance. It is now common for conference papers on almost any area of social history (apart from demography) which have a large statistical component to be disparaged for being 'mechanical' when once they might have been praised for their 'rigour' and technical inventiveness.

In the rest of this chapter, I will outline the arguments that have been levelled against mass quantification, assess the validity of these arguments, and then illustrate the points by examining two influential works. The underlying intention of the chapter is not to condemn mass quantification in principle or to worship at its feet. Rather the intention is to urge a purely pragmatic approach to statistical method. If the method is useful for solving a social historical problem we should use it; if it is not, we should overlook it. If non-statistical methods are more useful for solving a specific problem than mass quantification, we should use them; if they are not, then it would be irrational to reject statistical methods. Alternatively, if there is advantage in using both methods together as a means of solving a problem, then we should have no hesitation in doing so. The only qualifications I would make to this purely pragmatic position would be to say that if we decide to use statistical method, we should also ensure we employ the most appropriate technique *and* that we meet certain other conditions which I will specify later in the chapter.

The arguments against mass quantification

The arguments against mass quantification fall (very roughly) into two classes, those that are qualified (the conditional arguments), and those that are uncompromisingly dismissive and hostile (the fundamentalist arguments). I will take the conditional arguments first.

The conditional arguments are not arguments that are levelled against all works using mass quantification. Instead they consist of complaints which non-quantifiers – and even many quantifiers – frequently make when discussing specific works that use mass quantification. Although the critics might grumble that the problems they are talking about are far too common, they do not imply that the faults are inherent in mass quantification and are inevitable. The implication is that the works in question would have avoided the problems had they followed certain procedures or followed them more carefully. As I do not disagree with any of the conditional arguments, I will outline them without comment.

The first such complaint often levelled against cliometric works is their unscholarly and slipshod use of sources. More specifically, they are criticised for not checking and assessing ('auditing') their raw data; for placing too much reliance on raw data that are inaccurate, incomplete or shaky in some other respect; for failing to ascertain and (if necessary) correct the biases in the data which almost inevitably result from the ways the sources were originally generated; and for using 'proxy' variables that have only a remote relationship to what they are supposed to represent and hence are ambiguous in their meanings or are quite misleading. (A **proxy variable** is one that stands in place of something for which there are no direct measurable data. For example, the rate of suicide is sometimes used as a proxy for the concept of anomie.)

Another area where mass quantifiers are often said to go astray is in their categorisation decisions. Mass quantification necessarily involves comparing people by putting them into categories. This in turn requires the analyst to make decisions about what sorts of people should be included in which category or left out of the analysis altogether. In these respects, mass quantifiers are frequently criticised either for failing to make their categorisation decisions explicit, for not defending their decisions adequately, for making their categories too broad (i.e. for lumping together people with markedly diverging attributes), for uncritically accepting the categories of an original source, or for excluding from the whole analysis large numbers of people who if included would have made a substantial difference to its results. A case in point is Peter Burke's statistical analysis of the backgrounds of the artists and writers who comprised the 'creative elite' of the Italian Renaissance from the fifteenth to the sixteenth centuries: the analysis has been criticised for not selecting the cases according to a consistent set of criteria, and for the ways in which the conclusions are biased by the lack of data on the social origins of 57 per cent of all the cases.[1]

Then there are the criticisms which dwell on the presentational deficiencies of particular cliometric works. Singled out for criticism are works which make no concessions to the less numerate readers, bewildering them with algebraic equations and mathematical jargon, overwhelming them with mountains of indigestible numerical data, referring them to incomprehensible tables, and confusing them by failing to distinguish clearly between different sorts of data bases.

Lastly, there are the criticisms that are directed to the conclusions of many quantitative works. Typically, these dwell on the extravagance of the inferences which the works draw from the data; or the failure of the works to deal with change over time (this is a common criticism of works analysing **longitudinal** – otherwise known as time-series – data with correlation and regression techniques). A good example of criticism of a study's extravagance is that which was heaped on Fogel and Engerman's study of slavery in the USA in the first half of the nineteenth century, which found (amongst other things) that slavery did not undermine the black family, that slavery was more efficient than northern agriculture, that a substantial minority of slaves enjoyed upward mobility, that slaves enjoyed a higher standard of living than workers in the North.[2]

If the conditional arguments against mass quantification concede that the problems are preventable, the fundamentalist arguments do not. The fundamentalist arguments see mass quantification as intrinsically and irredeemably flawed irrespective of how competently it might be applied in particular instances. As the fundamentalist arguments are far more serious than the conditional arguments, I will critically assess them. There are seven fundamentalist objections.

The first is that the arcane nature of the more advanced works in cliometrics is unintelligible to the vast majority of historians who thus cannot assess their validity. They cannot tell whether these works employ the proper techniques in relation to the data, whether the works accurately translate the meaning of their numerical results when they describe them non-mathematically, and whether the works draw defensible conclusions from these numerical results. All this is bad for historical scholarship, so the critics conclude, because it reduces the exposure of such works to peer review, isolating them from the critical scrutiny of the general historical community.

To some extent this argument is overstated. It ignores the fact that not all ordinary historians are completely innumerate and that the majority of social historical works that employ advanced techniques limit themselves to the most standard techniques. As a consequence, at least some social historians have enough grounding in statistics to understand or potentially understand the bulk of advanced mass quantification.

In addition, the argument is unfair. It fails to take into account that most academic disciplines have become fragmented into numerous specialisms, and the historical discipline is no exception. It is now highly divided into a multitude of specialisms and most practitioners in each only talk to themselves. Much of the process of peer review and criticism has thus been taken out of the general historical community and placed in the hands of fellow specialists. The growth of mass quantification reflects this development; cliometricians talk in an arcane language because that is the language of their specialism, of their specialist journals and monographs. Their language may be opaque to outsiders and filled with ugly jargon but so is the language of those operating in the post-modern genre and, to a lesser degree, those working in specialised fields like legal history.

Where the argument does have substance, however, is when cliometricians write for a more general historical audience. In this situation we should expect them to make their processes of reasoning accessible by avoiding jargon and algebraic formulae, taking readers by the hand through the technically difficult patches, writing in clear and lively prose, explaining their techniques in simple terms, illustrating their points with interesting examples and so forth. Popularisers of scientific knowledge, such as Steven J. Gould and Richard Dawkins in evolutionary biology, do this very well; social historians employing mass quantification should be able to do it too.

The second fundamentalist argument against all cliometric studies is that the evidence they draw upon – their 'data bases' – cannot be independently verified, or at least can only be so verified with extreme difficulty. When conventional historians cite a primary document as evidence, they give a reference specifying where the document can be found, enabling other scholars to go to the source to check the evidence for themselves. But the scholarly underpinnings of a data base are not open to public inspection and assessment. Data bases consist of coded groups of umpteen individual items expressed as numerical values. Seldom is there enough space in a publication to describe the data bases in detail. Although summary tables of the information in the data bases are frequently presented in cliometric publications, the reader has no access to the data bases and thus cannot check the accuracy of the summary tables. Even if the data bases are accessible, the reader is in no position to determine how faithfully the individual items in the data bases were transcribed from the original sources since there are such huge numbers of individual items, often taken from many different – geographically scattered – sources. All this is very serious, so the fundamentalist opponents of mass quantification allege, since the generation of a data base goes through several stages each of which is highly susceptible to human error. There is a chance that the researcher will misconstrue the nature of a source, attributing the wrong meaning to it; when raw statistics are being transcribed from a manuscript, there is a chance the hand-writing will be indistinct and thus misread; when raw statistics are taken from tables in a printed document, there is a chance that the items will be taken from the wrong columns or lines; if the individual items are words that must be identified and counted, there is a good chance they will be misidentified and miscounted, when individual items are entered into the electronic data base, there is a chance that they will be misread, put in the wrong file or placed in the wrong column and line; when the researcher has to calculate estimates for missing values, there is a chance that the arithmetic will be wrong; and so on. Moreover, the chances of error are greatly magnified if, as often happens, inadequately trained and super-vised research assistants are employed to collect and enter the data, the decisions of research assistants are not guided by a good set of standard rules and so forth.

This objection, however, is unfair in that the problem it points to is not unique to cliometric history. The scholarly apparatus underpinning much traditional history is also closed to public inspection. Sometimes the footnotes in traditional works are very difficult to follow, or cite material produced by personal inter-views which no reader could replicate, or refer to material in for-eign languages which the reader cannot read, or refer to papers which can only be consulted with special permission of a private owner or some security-conscious branch of government.

Furthermore, the objection is overstated. Although it is usually impossible for mass quantifiers to publicise every item in their data bases, they can (and should be expected to) adopt a range of procedures that enable readers to make up their own minds whether the data bases were compiled with all due care and are trustworthy ('robust'). These procedures are the equivalent of audit trails. They include providing detailed descriptions of the original sources and how these were generated; discussing the biases in the sources, adducing the direction and probable magnitude of the biases and, if necessary, showing how these biases were corrected; providing scatter-plots (types of graphs) of the data and demonstrating that any extreme values ('outliers') were to be expected and were not the product of error; spelling out how the data were categorised and justifying the categories; indicating how many ambiguous cases there were and how they were dealt with; and so forth.

The third fundamentalist attack on mass quantification takes its cue from the sociology of knowledge and maintains that cliometricians use their scientific pretensions to disguise their political agendas. Cliometric studies, so the argument runs, have an air of objectivity, of scientific rigour. The function of this scientific mystique, the argument asserts, is to deter people from critically examining the assumptions of cliometrics and seeing that, as with all forms of knowledge, these assumptions promote the particular values and interests of the existing social order and/or of the particular occupational group to which the practitioners belong.[3]

In my view, this attack is the weakest of all the fundamentalist objections. Like all relativist arguments, it is self-refuting: if mass quantification had a scientific mystique, then how are the critics taking this position able to see through the mystique? Moreover, if mass quantification like all forms of knowledge has a political agenda and cannot make truth claims, then the statement that cliometrics has a political agenda must suffer from the same problem: as the statement purports to be a form of knowledge, it too must have a political agenda and cannot make truth-claims when it criticises cliometrics.

The fourth fundamentalist objection to mass quantification is that it dehumanises people because it treats them as objects, takes no account of their individual differences, and forces them into categories. This objection points to a problem which is not unique to quantohistory. It exists, at least potentially, in almost all areas of social history since the usual subject-matter of social history consists of collectivities and categories of people and not individuals. Most social historians who are not quantifiers avoid the problem (inadvertently, at least) by referring in detail to individuals to illustrate or demonstrate their points. Mass quantifiers can avoid the problem by employing the same device; indeed, for rhetorical reasons, it is to be recommended as a tool for communicating the results of analyses employing the more advanced statistical techniques.

The fifth objection made by the hardline critics of mass quantification is that the techniques most favoured by advanced cliometricians – correlation and regression, 'multivariate analysis' as it is often called – prove nothing. High correlation or regression co-efficients are necessary but not sufficient conditions for cause and effect relationships. In consequence, where there are strong associations between variables we have no warrant at all for claiming that certain variables were the causes and the other variables were the effects; nor for inferring from the strong association itself the presence of some sort of causal relationship. The association may be completely spurious. For example, a high correlation between the birth rate and the sightings of storks in nineteenth-century Belgium is hardly good evidence that the babies were brought by storks! (Such examples are often said to represent an **ecological fallacy** – the fallacy of believing that because two objects occur in the same environment they are therefore causally linked.)

This objection is technically correct. *If used by themselves*, correlations and other tests of association cannot demonstrate cause and effect relationships (which is the reason why at the beginning of the chapter I was careful to refer to 'postulated' causes and 'postulated' effects when introducing the technique of correlation).

But the problem highlighted by the objection can be overcome. If the correlation or regression co-efficients are strong, we can use them to demonstrate cause and effect relationships provided we satisfy two other conditions. First, we have to formulate a coherent theory that explains the cause and effect relationship in detail. Second, we must show that the explanation and the correlations are consistent with a variety of other forms of evidence.

Then there is the sixth fundamental objection: that mass quantification by its very nature deals with trivial issues. In the much quoted words of the famous American historian, Arthur Schlesinger, 'almost all important questions are important precisely because they are *not* susceptible to quantitative answers.'[4] What these important questions and answers are Schlesinger did not say, but often the opponents of quantification have asserted that they include anything to do with the life of the mind – ideology, ideas, sentiment – culture in the broadest sense of the word (or what the *Annaliste* historian, Pierre Chaunu, called history at the 'third level').

I agree that mass quantification is very often completely unsuitable for dealing with issues connected with ideology, ideas, sentiment; one only needs to think here of the notorious efforts of the French historian, Michel Vovelle, to measure the decline in piety in eighteenth-century Provence by taking as one of his indicators the weight of wax candles![5] But it is not always unsuitable: cultural historians themselves make quantitative judgments when they claim, for example, that certain books were bestsellers, certain sections of a population were literate, certain sentiments were typical and so on. Apart from this, there is no evidence whatever that cultural issues are *invariably* more important than the non-cultural.

There is, of course, another sense in which mass quantification is condemned as trivial, namely, that all too often its findings are negative or inconclusive. Yet negative or inconclusive findings are not necessarily valueless. Negative findings eliminate possibilities, tell us where not to look for answers and thus reduce the amount of 'search space', or provide counter-evidence against a widely-held theory, forcing us to rethink our views; an inconclusive finding indicates that we would be prudent not to commit ourselves to a theory until supporting evidence can be found. An example of a valuable set of negative findings is Dudley Baines' monumental study of overseas emigration from 51 counties in England and Wales between 1861 to 1900. Baines established that there were weak or negligible statistical relationships between the per capita rates of emigration from all of the 51 counties on the one hand and, on the other, their percentages of urban population, their rates of internal migration, their percentages of people engaged in agriculture, the earnings of their agricultural labourers, the proportion of young adults in their populations and their per capita rates of adult literacy. Although not flawless, the analysis nonetheless provided good counter-evidence against several widely held views, such as that a major cause of emigration was the poverty of English rural labourers.[6]

The seventh and last fundamentalist objection to cliometrics comes from historians of a hermeneutic persuasion. They maintain that mass quantification is premised on two fundamentally erroneous conceptions. First, it is wrong ontologically for it is deterministic and behaviouristic: it assumes that people are entirely driven by causal structures when they have a capacity for agency. Secondly, it is wrong methodologically. The conduct of a whole lot of people cannot be expressed within the meaning of a single variable since any given area of human conduct is subject to an indefinite range of *localised* meanings. To illustrate their point, hermeneuticians often cite the example of a person whose eyelid moves: this could be variously interpreted as meaning that the person has an involuntary twitch in the eyelid muscle, that the person was winking, that the person was parodying the wink of someone else, or that the person was rehearsing a parody of the winking of another person.[7] According to hermeneuticians, the meaning of every aspect of outward human behaviour such as eye movement is not universal; it varies from group to group. Thus group usage defines the meanings of each aspect of human behaviour. Only the 'insiders', the members of a group, know what the repertoire of meanings is and which meaning in a repertoire fits a particular context (the 'language rules'). In this respect, say hermeneuticians, the problem with mass quantification is the same as causal explanation: it is completely insensitive to local context. Since it is concerned to find regularities, mass quantification attributes a universal meaning to the same examples of human behaviour when there is none. Given all this, hermeneuticians believe that it is utterly pointless trying to study human conduct by counting how many people behave in a given way. Indeed, hermeneuticians insist that in attempting to lump together a lot of people exhibiting the same outward aspect of behaviour, mass quantifiers end up imposing on people motives, beliefs and values which they do not possess. It would hence be typical for mass quantifiers when classifying people prior to counting them to put people with rapid eye movements in the muscle spasm category when in fact some of them were winking and the others were parodying winkers! Or to count every cross as a crucifix when in some contexts it symbolised a kite frame and in others the

Ku Klux Klan. In short, hermeneuticians argue that the only proper
way to study human conduct is to take the local contexts in which
human interaction occurs and try to understand how the actors in
each context interpreted their own actions (I do not use the word
'behaviour' since this is a taboo word for hermeneuticians).

The hermeneutic objections to cliometrics are overstated.
There is no evidence that humans always have complete agency.
And there is no evidence that all signs vary in meaning from local
context to local context; in fact, the analogy of the eyelid is quite
misleading: in pre-modern societies the analogy might hold, but
not in industrialising societies from the nineteenth century
onwards where the growth of mass communications allowed certain signs to possess common national meanings and even to have
similar meanings in many different societies. Besides, I am not at
all sure that a characteristic of cliometric studies is that they
assume that human conduct is entirely determined by causal
structures and that they attribute a universal meaning to repeated
examples of the same behaviour. There is nothing in mass quantification that necessarily commits it or leads it to these positions.[8]
Finally, there are problems with the hermeneutic position which I
will deal with in Chapter 8.

Having said all that, let me also say that the cliometricians can
learn a lot from hermeneuticians. To understand this, let us go
back to square one. In essence what all mass quantifiers have in
common is that they investigate regularities in aspects of social
conduct expressed in terms of measurable information called variables or indicators or indices. Thus, for example, they might want
to find out whether the standard of living of agricultural labourers fell during the industrial revolution. To carry out the investigation, they might start by assuming that labourers' standard of
living can be measured in terms of an annual real wage index.
After collecting statistical information on the total wages paid to
all agricultural workers each year and on the prices labourers
paid for their food each year, they would then see if the index fell
or rose or was stable over the Industrial Revolution. If the index
fell, they would conclude that the living standards fell. Or they
might want to find out if falls in agricultural labourers' living
standards caused the labourers to engage in social protest; and to
do this they might correlate the annual real agricultural-wage
index or the food price index with the total number of rural riots

occurring each year. If they found a strong correlation, they would surmise that rural riots were caused by falling living standards.

On the face of it, there seems to be nothing wrong with these sorts of studies. But when looked at more closely, they can have glaring defects. The defects lie not in the lack of robustness in the data, their inaccuracy in a strict accounting sense, but in the assumptions that the studies make about the actors, in the ways they conceive the actors. As it happens, there has been a long-standing practice of economic historians to measure the living standards of late eighteenth- and early nineteenth-century English agricultural workers in terms of real wages, and as one historian has argued (plausibly I think), this measure is conceptually wrong. The trouble with it is that it is far too remote from the experiences – the values and beliefs – of the agricultural labourers themselves. A close examination of the statements made by labourers indicates that they seldom perceived their living stand-ards in terms of real wages. Instead they defined their living standards according to a range of other 'non-modern' criteria such as the availability of poor law relief, of access to common land, of pasture for grazing a few animals, of wage work for their wives, and so on.[9]

The point I am trying to make is that mass quantifiers are often unreflective about their assumptions and too casual about the ways they derive their concepts. They derive their concepts about the actors in times past not from a close study of the beliefs, values, perceptions of the actors themselves but through other means: either by deducing the concepts from a general theory or by generalising from their own common sense experiences or by fol-lowing a convention practised by modern historians. As a conse-quence, they can end up attributing to the actors a set of values, beliefs, desires and motives that have been drawn from modern culture and are alien to the actors, and thus represent one of the cardinal sins of the historian: anachronism. I do not deny that it is difficult for people to avoid interpreting another culture in terms of their own. Nonetheless, social historians with a mass quantitat-ive bent should strive to be 'culturally sensitive'. Fortunately, there are some procedures that can help them in their endeavour, and the procedures have been devised by microhistorians. In my view, microhistory is virtually indispensable for mass quantification

projects in social history. I will leave a discussion of microhistory
and its various procedures to a later chapter.

Illustrating the problems: the case of *The Rebellious Century, 1830–1930* by Charles, Louise and Richard Tilly[10]

During the mass quantification wave of the 1970s in the United
States, Charles Tilly pioneered the application of advanced statistical techniques to social history. After winning renown with *The
Vendée* (1964), a regional case study of counter-revolution during
the French Revolution, Tilly in the 1970s broadened his interests
by engaging in some bold quantitative studies, which often had a
strong comparative dimension, of the long-term incidence of collective protest in France and other countries in western Europe in
the nineteenth and twentieth centuries. Much of his enormous
output during this time was co-authored and drew upon the
efforts of teams of research assistants.

Published in 1975, the co-authored work which we shall examine, *The Rebellious Century,* exemplifes Tilly's interests and orientations in that decade. For its time the work was highly innovative
and sophisticated. Its key innovations lay in its self-conscious
attempts to integrate sociological theory with history, its novel
conclusions, its extensive use of the computer to analyse vast
amounts of data, and its attempts to test hypotheses with **epidemiological** (otherwise known as 'ecological' or probabilistic) techniques, partly with the help of correlation analysis. In social
history, the epidemiological technique is variously exemplified by
the graph, the chart, correlation, regression and so on. It is a
coarse-grained technique which seeks to explain some aspect of a
large aggregate by examining the relationship between multitudes of events of one type and large numbers of events concerning other types of things happening in the same broad
environment (the same country for example). The epidemiological technique differs from the other common technique of mass
quantification called **prosopography.** With prosopography, the

researcher also examines a large aggregate of people and tries to explain some aspect of them. But prosopography is much finer grained: the researcher *collects information on every known member of the aggregate under the same headings (occupation, age, religion, etc.)* and from the resulting pool of information ('collective biography') the researcher extrapolates explanations about the aggregate's conduct. Now before Tilly and his associates, there had been many prosopographical studies of rebellious crowds (the most notable in the Anglophone world being those by George Rudé).[11] Moreover, there had been not a few epidemiological studies of rebellious crowds as well. Where the Tillys in *The Rebellious Century* broke with these traditions was that they virtually abandoned the prosopographical technique and took the epidemiological technique far further than almost anyone else had ever taken it. For its time, the scale of their project was huge. They took a hundred year period in three countries and measured the relationship in each country between the trends in all known incidents of crowd violence each year and the trends in a large range of indicators (indices) representing different theoretical explanations of collective violence.

The aim of *The Rebellious Century*, in essence, is to test three competing theories about the mechanisms driving collective violence in France, Italy and Germany between the 1830s and the 1930s. (The term 'collective violence' is the authors'; by this they really mean 'group violence' since a crucial aspect of their preferred theory is that aggrieved people cannot mobilise unless they have prior links.) Two of the theories highly favoured by social theorists in the 1970s attributed to the participants in collective violence little capacity for agency. The first, 'hardship' theory, is the notion that collective violence 'necessarily sprang from a blind and impulsive response to hardship'.[12] The second theory is what the Tillys term call 'breakdown' theory. This also claims that collective violence is irrational and blind, but says it is a form of antisocial behaviour like crime and drug addiction that arises when rapid social change cuts people off from traditional moorings and social restraints. By the 1970s, social breakdown theorists had been in the habit of attributing the causes of this sort of social sickness – termed 'anomie' by the famous French sociologist, Émile Durkheim – to rapid industrialisation and urbanization.[13] Against these two theories, the authors put up their own theory. In their view,

most collective violence in this period was the by-product of politically motivated social protest. The protesters were well integrated into the organisation of society, and had well-defined goals:
the rectification of specific grievances and increased share of
political power. The collective action they took to secure these
goals – demonstrations, meetings, strikes, factory occupations and
so on – were not blind and unconscious behaviours but rational,
calculated and deliberate: politics by another name. The violence
associated with the protest, the Tillys maintain, was usually
unintended by the protesters. More often than not, the violence was
initiated by the state or by bully boys organised by the dominant
groups attempting to clear the protesters off the streets. In other
words, the theory favoured by the authors is largely an intentionalist explanation of social protest. As such, it gives the lie to the
assertions by hermeneuticians that cliometrics are inherently and
unavoidably deterministic and behaviouristic.

But if the explanation favoured by the authors is largely intentionalist, the methodology they employ to demonstrate it is the
very opposite we would expect from the advocates of an intentionalist explanation. Whereas the methodology of most intentionalist explanations depends on close interpretation of texts (in
the mode of E.P. Thompson's *The Making of the English Working
Class*), the Tillys rely on mass quantification in an epidemiological
form.

The book is divided into three case studies followed by two concluding chapters which generalise the themes of the case studies,
drawing the themes together and putting them into a broader
context. The first case study is devoted to France, the second to
Italy and the third to Germany. The formats of the case studies
follow very similar patterns. Each starts with a lengthy narrative
on the main outlines of the social, political and economic transformations of the country in question; proceeds to a summary statistical description of the long term trends in the country's collective
violence; then provides a statistical investigation discounting the
possible connection between the trends in collective violence and
statistical indicators of 'hardship' and 'breakdown' theories; and
ends with an attempt to demonstrate the plausibility of the favoured theory.

Despite having the same formats, the three case studies employ
quite different indicators and modes of analysis. The authors say

the lack of uniformity was forced upon them by the enormous differences in their respective source materials. The most sophisticated and systematic epidemiological approach is Charles Tilly's on France. The period it covers, 1830–1960, is longer than the other two. The raw statistics on collective violence were very largely derived by scanning two daily national newspapers. Collective violence was defined as episodes involving more than fifty protesters where there was either seizure or damage of property or at least one person injured (exclusive of external wars and prison riots). As indicators for 'hardship' theory, the study employs real wages, wholesale food prices and wholesale manufactured goods prices. The indicators for 'breakdown' theory are per capita rates of suicide, of vagrancy, of major property crimes, of major violent crimes, the annual rates of industrial production, and annual rates of urbanisation. To test the linkages between these indicators and collective violence, the techniques very largely consist of correlation analyses, graphs and charts, mainly of a time-series (longitudinal) nature. Lastly, heavy use is made of a highly schematic political narrative to show that the trends in collective violence were linked with the phases in French history when there were intense struggles over political power (1830, 1848, 1869–71, 1891–3, 1902–6, 1911–13, 1934–7, 1947–8, 1958).

As Italian society was so regionally divided, there were no national newspapers from which the Italian study by Louise Tilly could draw raw statistics on collective violence. Instead four secondary sources had to be used (including a chronicle of nineteenth century political events published in 1918) which were heavily supplemented by the data the central government collected and published on strikes. Presumably because the Italian state collected so few or such poor statistics on practically everything other than strikes, the study provides no systematic indicators for any of the theories. For all these reasons, the analysis for Italy is less sophisticated and far more impressionistic than that for France and Germany and does not do much to support the book's overall arguments.

The German case study by Richard Tilly embraces a somewhat dissimilar period (1816–1913). As with France, the bulk of the raw statistics on collective violence were derived by scanning every issue of two daily national newspapers; but unlike France, the definition of collective violence involved smaller crowds (twenty or more). As proxies for the 'breakdown' theory, rates of industrial and urban growth are used; and an index for agricultural crop prices is taken as the sole indicator for the 'hardship' theory. To test the linkages between the collective violence indicator and the 'hardship' and 'breakdown' indicators, the German study depends on graphs, tables and charts, some of a longitudinal nature, some **cross-sectional**. A lot of the quantitative evidence is presented in a highly summarised form.[14] Although compared with the French study less correlation analysis is evident in the text, it seems to inform many of the evidential summaries. Less attempt is made than in the French study to use schematic political narrative as evidence that the trends in collective violence corresponded with periods of major power struggles.

To what extent does *The Rebellious Century* exemplify the problems ascribed to mass quantification and to what extent does it avoid them? (Note that the following assessment excludes discussion of how far the work measures up to other kinds of criteria.)

The first thing that must be said is that unlike many works relying on mass quantification, this one goes out of its way to make itself accessible to the innumerate. The book is eminently readable. Correlations are cited judiciously (though the innumerate are not told what a correlation is), the text is completely free of mathematical formulae and jargon, narrative is extensively employed to render the discussion attractive to traditional historians, the writing is light and breezy, the text is not clogged with figures, and all the statistical evidence is liberally leavened and illuminated with maps and anecdotes.

There are two major respects, however, in which *The Rebellious Century* epitomises the faults which are often seen in cliometrics. The first is that the authors do very little to describe the nature of their data. An appendix describes how the collective violence data were generated for the three cases. But nowhere is there a description of the data employed for the myriad other indicators. The text certainly provides references for the sources from which the data were taken for these indicators. There is even a reference in the appendix to publications by the authors and their associates that tells us where we can find 'detailed discussions' of their sources and methods.[15] But if we are unfamiliar with the sources, and as the reference in the appendix refers us to eleven publications, the data are not readily open for inspection.

The authors could have overcome this problem had they provided us with audit trails or at least given some signal that they subjected their data to scholarly scrutiny and that they consider their data to be robust. But the text contains no audit trails and there are no signs in it at all that the data were subjected to scholarly scrutiny.

As a consequence, the reader has no idea whether there are biases in the data and how far any such biases might have influenced the results of the analyses. How much weight therefore can we put on the results? Are the results trustworthy or are they the product of biased data? Is the finding that there is no long-term correspondence between trends in collective violence and the 'hardship' and the 'breakdown' indicators a reflection of quirks in the data or of historical reality?

The problem is most acute with the 'hardship' indicators. With France and Germany, the Tillys find that all of their 'hardship' indicators have a weak long-term correspondence with trends in collective violence and infer from this that hardship was not a major cause of collective violence. Yet their 'hardship' indicators are few in number and cover a very limited range of phenomena: real wages, wholesale food prices, and wholesale manufacturing goods prices in the case of France, and agricultural crop prices in the case of Germany. Since the text does not tell us anything about these indicators, we have no idea whether their poor correspondence with collective violence is simply a reflection of their inappropriateness as indicators of the living standards of protesters. What heightens this suspicion is that the French and the German studies both find that their respective food price indices do have a strong correspondence with trends in collective violence in the first half of the century but not in the second.[16] By implication, then, the weak correspondence in the second half offsets a strong correspondence in the first half, producing an overall poor relationship for the long term. What the Tillys do not consider is the possibility that the weak correspondence in the second half of the century simply tells us that food prices are an inappropriate measure of the living standards of protesters for that half. The indices might have been an appropriate measure in the first half since food comprised a very large proportion of the budgets of protesters.

But as incomes rose in the second half of the century and as the proportion of income spent on food falls as incomes rise, then it follows that food prices are not a good long-term measure of living standards: as the period progressed, subordinate people spent a falling share of their budgets on food, therefore they were far less likely to protest when sharp rises in food prices occurred. In other words, the food price indices are bad indicators of living standards of the whole period because they do not reflect changes in the actual consumption patterns of protesters. The same problem applies to the other indicators used to measure 'hardship' – real wages and wholesale manufacturing goods prices in the case of France. It is quite possible that the reason these do not have strong long-term relationships with rates of collective protest is that they measure an unchanging mix of goods whereas the actual mix of goods consumed by potential protesters changed over time. It is also possible that these indicators include goods which never played a big part in the consumption of protesters. The Tillys needed to assure us that they checked on these possibilities – that the data were biased *against* finding a hardship/collective violence linkage – and eliminated them. Without these assurances, the Tillys make themselves open to the charge that they have not demonstrated that 'hardship' theory is a poor explanation of collective violence.

Even with the collective violence data the Tillys fail to provide a proper audit trail. A proper audit trail should assure us that the biases in the data are not responsible for the conclusions. In the appendix the authors tell us in detail how they generated their collective violence data; and they even tell us how the data are biased: they virtually admit that the bias works in favour of their preferred theory. That is, the data overstate the incidence of collective violence during periods of acute political crisis.[17] But having all but admitted the bias exists, they make no attempt to correct it or allow for it.

I hasten to add that the peaks in collective violence for Germany and France are so high that it is unlikely that they were solely the product of the bias in the collective violence data. I should also hasten to add that the methodology employs a device that minimises the suspicion that biases in the data for the 'breakdown' indicators were responsible for the very poor correspondence between these indicators and collective violence. The Tillys employ a large number and variety of indicators to measure 'breakdown' theory: the per capita rates of suicide, of major violent crimes, of major property crimes, of vagrancy, the rates of economic growth, industrial production and urbanisation in the case of France, and the rates of growth of urbanisation and industrialisation in the case of Germany. We might justifiably suspect that some, perhaps most, of these indicators are lacking in robustness; but can we justifiably suspect all were? I do not think we can. Surely at least one must be reasonably robust – yet not one has a good correspondence with collective violence.[18] It is thus very hard to resist the authors' claim that 'breakdown' does not cause collective violence. In the context of the 1970s this was a very important finding since it contradicted the conventional wisdom of the time.[19]

This brings us to the second respect in which *The Rebellious Century* epitomises the criticisms made of mass quantification: it fails to check that its variables are culturally appropriate. The criticism does not apply to the 'hardship' and 'breakdown' variables. The apparent aim of the book is to refute these theories *in their own terms:* both theories (at least in the form that the authors have summarised them) do not stipulate that hardship and social breakdown are culturally defined; therefore, the authors are not obliged to check that the indicators are compatible with the motives, beliefs and values of the actors.

The criticism, however, does apply to some of the components in the favoured theory. The theory states that collective violence will occur when (a) subordinate people develop a sense of injustice, (b) subordinate people are equipped with the social resources (common membership of networks and groups) that enable them to mobilise, (c) they seek political power to control their own circumstances; but (d) they cannot express their grievances through conventional channels, (e) the state lacks the power and the will to prevent the formation of protest groups, and (f) the state (or other elements in the dominant classes) subsequently employs force to crush protest action. With (a), (c) and perhaps (d), the theory claims to be explaining protest within the framework of the values and beliefs of the protesters themselves: the explanation is not causal but intentionalist.

The Tillys do not provide any microhistorical evidence to support (a), (c) and (d). They cheerfully admit 'We have made no effort to peer into the minds' of the protesters.[20] Instead they employ two procedures to support these claims. One is to draw on hermeneutic studies of protest in other countries in the early nineteenth century. More specifically, claims (a) and (d) are largely grounded on E.P. Thompson's *The Making of the English Working Class.*[21] In other words, the Tillys support (a) and (d) by assuming that what Thompson demonstrated in the particular case of England, is equally applicable to France and Germany: if popular protest in England was motivated by a sense of injustice and the inability of people to express grievances through conventional channels, then, by analogy, popular protest in France and Germany must have been driven by the same factors. Whether this analogy is plausible, we cannot tell, for the Tillys do nothing to persuade us that it is.[22]

The other procedure is a very bold one and is applied to (c). Here the Tillys support their claim that protesters had political ambitions by observing that the incidence of protest in France, Italy and Germany always shot up when these countries went through periods of acute political crisis. Putting this another way, the authors assume that as most riots, factory occupations, strikes, demonstrations and other mass gatherings took place in peak periods of political struggle, then these rioters, factory occupiers, strikers and so forth must have sought political power. Unfortunately, this assumption (like so many others in *The Rebellious Century*) is not defended but taken for granted, and I am not sure that the conclusion necessarily follows from the premise. A period of acute political strife in a country might well heighten the political consciousness of subordinate people and make them unusually politically ambitious. But it is also possible that the incidence of popular protest rises sharply in times of acute political crisis because subordinate people calculate that protest action to achieve *material goals* is more likely to succeed in crisis periods than in times of political stability because employers and the authorities are at their most vulnerable and hence most likely to make *material* concessions during periods of political crisis. Readers may well think of other logical possibilities. Had the Tillys included some microhistory in their research, it might have given weight to their favoured theory.

Illustrating the problems: the case of Stephan Thernstrom's *The Other Bostonians; Poverty and Progress in the American Metropolis 1880–1970*[23]

This work was also a major and highly influential product of the quantitative wave that hit the historical profession in the United States in the 1970s. Its author was one of the pioneers of what was known as the 'new urban history'. Whereas traditional histories of towns and cities had largely dwelt on the administrative and political activities of the elite, Thernstrom, along with the other innovators of the 'new urban history', focused on the anonymous mass of urban dwellers, specifically their long-term patterns of **social mobility**.[24] In helping to open up this area, Thernstrom asked new questions (for example, was the American city a place of opportunity? Did social mobility have a conservatising effect on politics?); exploited new sources (notably, city directories, census schedules and local tax records); used a research technique known as **record-linkage** that few American historians had attempted before; and applied the prosopographical approach to huge projects that had few parallels in the English-speaking world.

The structure of Thernstrom's enquiry was very simple. First, he generated a data base. As the population of Boston was so large (one third of a million in 1880 and two and three quarter million in 1970), he drew the bulk of his data from four random samples of the city's population. The four samples covered the years 1880, 1910, 1930, and 1958, and thus provided a series of roughly equidistant 'snapshots' of the city's social structure (such 'snapshots' are often called **bench-mark years**). The samples were taken from different sources: the 1880 one from census manuscripts, that for 1910 from city marriage records, the 1930 sample from local birth records, and the sample for 1958 from the city directory. Altogether there were 7965 males in the samples (females were excluded for reasons and with consequences we will discuss later). Information was collected on every sample member's occupation, age, religion, ethnic origin, marital status and on a variety of other topics. The subsequent careers of each male in each sample was traced mainly through city directories (none of those leaving the city was traced). Having generated the data base, Thernstrom then drew on it systematically to address a series of very precisely formulated questions. We will only deal with the principal results of his analysis.

One thing he asked was whether the inhabitants of Boston between 1880 and 1960 dwelt in the city for long periods, were residentially stable ('persisters'). He found instead that they were rootless, highly transient: over the whole period, about 40 to 60 per cent of the males living in the city at the beginning of any given decade disappeared within ten years. From this fact, he inferred that, contrary to a popular notion, the urban masses in this period in America did not form permanent ghettos.

Another issue Thernstrom investigated was the openness of Boston's class structure: was it rigid or very fluid or something in between? To determine the degree of **closure** (as it is technically called), he devised a model of the class structure that consisted of an occupational hierarchy divided into five broad strata. High white-collar occupations were in the highest stratum, low white-collar occupations in the second, skilled manual occupations in the third, semi-skilled manual in the fourth and unskilled manual occupations in the bottom. The two white-collar strata were assumed to equate with the middle class, the three manual strata with the working class. Thernstrom then used various procedures to work out how far the occupational and class composition of Boston changed. One set of procedures measured **intragenerational mobility** (the extent to which people move up or down the social ladder during their careers); another set measured **intergenerational mobility** (otherwise known as class or stratum 'inheritance', the extent to which people change their position on the social ladder in relation to the position held by their parents). What his indicators of intragenerational mobility revealed was that over the whole period the class structure was remarkably stable: for example, over the whole period the vast majority of men (roughly 60 per cent) ended their careers in the same occupational stratum where they had started, while an even larger proportion (80 per cent) ended their careers in the same class positions where they had started. In addition, his measures of both intragenerational and intergenerational mobility showed that most of the vertical movement was of a short distance not a long distance nature: only a tiny percentage of the unskilled men and their sons who were upwardly mobile vaulted up into the higher white-collar stratum, and an even smaller proportion of upper white-collar men and their sons plummeted down into the ranks of the unskilled. Lastly, Thernstrom discovered that the stability of the class structure expressed itself in terms of the very low rates of downward mobility of men born into the upper white-collar strata. They had an extraordinary capacity to retain their privileges from one generation to another.

But if the city's class order was strikingly stable, there were nonetheless, Thernstrom contended, substantial opportunities for its working class to be upwardly mobile. In terms of intragenerational mobility, the majority of unskilled men moved up the ladder (ending up, primarily, in the semi-skilled stratum). Moreover, in terms of intergenerational mobility, a very large proportion of working-class sons from all three strata managed to get on: over the whole period, almost 60 per cent of the sons of unskilled and semiskilled men ended their careers in a higher strata (principally in the lower white collar stratum) than their fathers; and about 40 per cent of the sons of skilled manual men ended up in the middle class (again primarily in the lower white-collar stratum). To be sure, there were also sons from skilled and semi-skilled manual backgrounds who ended up in worse positions than their fathers; but the unsuccessful sons were substantially outnumbered by the successful.

Perhaps, however, Thernstrom's most important finding was that the capacity for getting on varied markedly according to country of birth, religion, and ethnicity. Allowing for differences in class position, the foreign-born enjoyed far less upward mobility than native-born whites; and of the foreign-born, the British did best, followed by the Germans, Poles, and Swedes, while the Italians and Irish did worst; and the rankings did not disappear in the second generation of migrants. In terms of religious affiliation, the Jews enjoyed the highest rates of upward intragenerational and intergenerational mobility, followed by Protestants, with Catholics having the lowest. To explain these differentials, Thernstrom argued they were less the product of variations in social discrimination, marketable skills, residential segregation, and family size, than of cultural values, specifically of attitudes

towards education. He emphasises, however, that Blacks constitute an exception to the pattern: they had the worst rates of
upward mobility by far and, Thernstrom says, this was largely the
result of racial discrimination.

To what extent does *The Other Bostonians* exemplify the most
common complaints that are levelled at mass quantitification history? The first point to be noted is that the book is accessible to the
innumerate. Thernstrom goes out of his way to write in a lively
and lucid style, to simplify complex problems, and to take the
reader by the hand through the numbers. Moreover, he employs
only the most basic statistical techniques (which consist overwhelmingly of averages and percentages), and strenuously avoids
mathematical formulae and jargon. This is not say that the book
makes for good bedtime reading: the discussion refers to dozens
and dozens of tables, many of which are intricate and difficult to
take in at a glance. But though Thernstrom makes demands of
the reader, this is not a reflection on mass quantification or his
particular application of it. It is an expression of the richness of his
material which he generated through an extraordinary amount of
research, the sophistication of the questions which he addresses,
and the rigour and thoroughness of his attempts to answer them.
The demands the book places on the reader, in other words, are
an unavoidable product of original and exacting scholarship.

No-one, moreover, could complain that Thernstrom fails to inform the reader about his sources, his techniques for processing
them, his procedures for testing the biases in them, and his procedures for correcting any such biases. On the contrary. This part of
the book is exemplary in its explicitness and thoroughness. He
tells us of the procedures which he adopted to ensure that
research assistants handled with maximum accuracy the tricky
but mammoth task of record linkage.[25] More important still, he
uses two appendices at the end of the book to tell us how he tackled four crucial data problems. The first problem is one which
bedevils all record-linkage research – the problem of tracing common names. To deal with this, he tells us that he discarded each
common name from his samples and selected instead the next
name in the source which was distinct and therefore traceable.
The second problem arose from the manner in which he solved
the first. He says that by selecting only the uncommon names, he
left himself with samples that were not truly random and that, as a

consequence, may not have been representative of the total population. To test for this possibility, he compares the samples and the entire Boston population as regards the composition of their respective occupational, residential and ethnic patterns, and shows us that the differences between the samples and the entire population are insignificant. The third data problem which he explicitly discusses is the problem of whether his static model of the occupational hierarchy is reliable. To assure us that it is, he lists all the occupations that he grouped in each stratum, and then demonstrates that *over the whole period* his rank order of the various strata is perfectly aligned with their rankings according to other objective criteria: earnings, education, property holdings, and susceptibility to unemployment. This in itself is a striking result: it contradicts, as he says, a common view that over the late nineteenth and twentieth centuries lower white collar occupations diminished in earnings, prestige and so on in relation to skilled manual occupations, until, by the end of the period, the skilled manual were superior to the lower white-collar in the class structure.

Some of his data problems, it must be said, he does not (and cannot) adequately resolve. One such problem is the reliability of city directories, his main source for tracing the subsequent careers of sample members. Although he acknowledges that a large minority of the members of each sample were untraceable in the directories and had to be excluded from his analysis, he does not allow for the effect of their exclusion.[26] To be sure, it would have been almost impossible for him to make this allowance: most of the untraceables were working-class transients who disappeared from Boston and its suburban environs. But the exclusion does raise serious questions about the validity of the results of his analysis. There is no guarantee that the careers of the working-class untraceables were similar to the careers of the working-class traceables. Indeed, it is reasonable to believe that the untraceables would have been less likely to enjoy upward mobility than the traceables since they were abnormally transient and, as Thernstrom notes himself, rates of transience were inversely related to economic success.[27] This being so, his analysis may overstate the extent of working-class upward mobility.

Another unresolved data problem is that his samples exclude women. He defends their absence, saying that for much of his period most were not in the paid workforce, and that they are exceedingly difficult to trace, partly because they changed their surnames after marriage and partly because the directories often failed to list their occupations. Although these defences are reasonable, the absence of women nonetheless may bias his results. As women may have had fewer opportunities for upward occupational mobility than men, their exclusion from his samples may give an exaggerated impression of the openness of the whole occupational structure. In addition, it is almost certain that his samples grossly under-represent the floating poor, the 'residuum'. If so, he provides an excessively optimistic picture of the opportunities of Boston's poor to be upwardly mobile.[28]

The greatest weakness in *The Other Bostonians*, however, is its failure to relate its findings on upward mobility to their cultural context. Throughout the study, Thernstrom keeps on saying how 'impressive' are Boston's rates of working-class upward mobility. He states, for instance, that 'There was throughout the entire period a great deal of upward career mobility for men situated on the lower rungs of the class ladder'; that 'Really impressive, though, is the fact that youths born into working-class homes displayed substantial upward mobility.'[29] He also keeps on commenting on the 'striking fluidity' of the social order. In one passage he says that the 'main point' of the book is that 'the Boston social structure over the past century has been strikingly fluid'; in another passage, he writes that the 'lower levels of the community occupational structure were strikingly fluid'; in yet a further section, he says the same thing, the 'occupational structure of Boston ...was remarkably fluid...offering significant opportunities for self-advancement to a very substantial proportion of the men who started work in menial manual jobs'.[30]

The difficulty with all these judgments is that they lack appropriate yardsticks. They beg questions of meaning, questions about how much upward mobility is a good deal and how much fluidity is a lot. To be sure, Thernstrom recognises the difficulty. But his way of looking at it does nothing to help him solve it. Towards the beginning of the analysis he makes the extraordinary claim that there are 'no absolute standards' for determining whether upward mobility rates are high or low; we can only decide what constitutes a good deal of upward mobility by referring to our own individual expectations; what one analyst regards as a high level of upward mobility, another analyst will take as a low level.[31]

In effect, therefore, he is saying that he has little rational justification for any his judgments cited above, that the proportion of working class Bostonians who enjoyed upward movement is 'impressive' and that the fluidity of Boston's occupational structure is 'striking'. The logic of his relativistic position commits him to the general view that all such judgments must be purely personal and arbitrary, based on nothing other than the prejudices and feelings of the individual observer.[32]

Although Thernstrom may be right in saying there are no absolute standards for making these judgments, he is wrong to jump to the extreme opposite conclusion that there are no standards at all. In fact, there are two different kinds of non-absolute standards he could have adopted. First, he could have compared Boston's rates of working-class upward mobility with those of other societies, or with those achieved by Boston in other periods, or with those of other parts of North America. Putting this another way, *he could have adopted a notional average standard*. Second, and perhaps better still, he could have compared the actual rates of upward mobility with the rates that Bostonians expected and desired, *with their standards*. That is to say, he could have established whether the actual rates were high or low by putting them in their cultural context, by relating them to the values and beliefs of the actors, by taking a more hermeneutic approach. This would have required him to investigate all manner of issues his study ignores: how Bostonians perceived upward mobility; whether their perceptions differed from category to category; how strongly Bostonians valued upward *occupational* mobility in relation to the goals of security and other forms of vertical mobility, and so on. Answering these questions would no doubt have been very difficult, but microhistory would have helped.

■ Conclusion

There are many problems with mass quantification but the problems are avoidable or can be minimised as long as the practitioner meets or tries to meet the following seven conditions:

- ensures that the techniques are appropriate to the particular nature of the statistical data;

- conducts a scholarly audit of the raw data;
- leaves an 'audit trail' for the reader that pays special attention to describing the biases in the data, the influences of the biases on the conclusions, and (if necessary) the procedures which were employed to allow for and correct the biases;
- makes concessions to the innumerate when employing advanced statistical techniques and communicating to a more general audience;
- provides a detailed theory and other forms of evidence to support claims about causes and effects where high correlation and regression co-efficients are taken to denote these causes and effects;
- demonstrates that the indicators used as proxies of an explanatory theory are adequate representations of the theory; and
- checks that the meaning of the variables are reasonably compatible with the actual beliefs, values and motives of the actors and, if they are not not, demonstrates that it does not matter.

■ *Chapter 7* ■

The Problem of Socially Constructed Evidence

It is a truism that the ideology of the dominant groups shapes their observations of the subordinate elements in a society. It is also a truism that the dominant groups consciously or unconsciously act to shape the collective beliefs of the subordinate elements, so that the subordinate elements will observe the world as the dominant want them to observe it. In one form or another, both truisms appear in all kinds of claims by social historians that the sense of reality of past people – dominant and subordinate – was 'socially constructed' (or 'culturally constructed'). The truisms pose a serious problem for our attempts to recover the actual ways of life of subordinate people. It is the object of this chapter to spell out the problem and to assess some of the methods used by practitioners to solve it.

Before we start, I should make clear that when referring to the 'dominant groups' and the 'subordinates', I am using the terms in the broadest possible generic sense and not relating them to any particular kind of theoretical perspective. Thus, 'dominant groups' and 'subordinates' could be interpreted in the Marxist sense; or in the feminist; or in the sense employed by the historians of race and colonialism who equate the dominant with whites/colonial governments/slavery regimes and the subordinate elements with ethnic minorities/indigenous people/slaves; or in the sense used by historians of deviance who associate the 'dominant groups' with state institutions (prisons, the police, the judiciary, asylums and so forth), and the 'subordinate elements' with all the different kinds of people that these institutions label as deviant. Moreover, the terms could cover the concepts of domination and subordination used by the French theorist and

historian, Michel Foucault, who argued that the pattern of domination and subordination in society is not structured in any
particular overarching fashion – in terms either of class, race,
gender or whatever – but takes multiple forms and exists in every
social relationship.[1]

With these things in mind, let us now spell out the problem of
socially-constructed evidence. As is well known, our information
about the actual ways of life led by subordinate elements in the
past is, as a rule, extremely one-sided. Little of it was generated by
subordinate people themselves since either they were illiterate
and belonged to an oral/aural culture, lacked the self-confidence
and leisure to write about themselves, or had no resources to pre-
serve their written testimonies, and so on. Although people whom
Peter Burke calls cultural 'mediators' have left us with some information about subordinate people, most of our source material about the subordinate was generated by dominant groups.[2]
The material comes in all manner of *genres* such as comments by
employers about individual servants, impressionistic accounts by travellers about the inhabitants of a particular place, reports by parliamentary committees of enquiry, pamphlets on social problems,
published official statistics (rare before the nineteenth century),
parish records, the files of official institutions such as the courts
and almshouses, to mention but a few. The observations contained in these sources can be classified into the purely qualitative or
literary ('impressionistic'), the overtly statistical, and the potentially quantifiable.

The fact that these observations provide the bulk of the available evidence about the ways of life of subordinate people, creates
a dilemma which epitomises the problem of socially constructed
evidence. We cannot do without them, but they are obviously
unreliable since they may well have been socially constructed –
distorted by the preconceptions that the observers had of the
subordinate and by the conscious or unconscious desires of the
observers to shape the collective beliefs of the subordinate. If we
knew which observations were biased, the product of preconception and ideological contamination, we could of course take all the
others as our evidence after checking them for other kinds of
errors. But how do we distinguish the ones which were the product of preconception and ideological contamination, from those
which were not?

A good knowledge of the period and the material may, of course, allow the investigator to detect and sift out the descriptions that are patently biased, including the extremely bigoted, the self-contradictory, the physically impossible, blatant propaganda, and so forth. Moreover, where the topic is confined to one individual or a tiny group, traditional methods of textual scholarship will probably enable the biased reports to be separated from the unbiased reports if a variety of sources of detailed information are available and much is known about their authors. But while the patently biased descriptions may be easy to distinguish, this still leaves the problem of distinguishing all those that may be more subtly biased. The traditional methods of textual scholarship, furthermore, reach their limits where (as is frequently the case) the topic is concerned with a large aggregate of people and the available source material is of one kind and cannot be checked against other sources, or little or nothing is known about its author(s)/ compiler(s).

Some commentators, especially the followers of Michel Foucault, claim that as knowledge plays a crucial role in acts of domination, every observation by the dominant of the subordinate is socially constructed. Accordingly, they argue that the only proper approach to such documents is to 'analyse the discourse' – that is, decode its language so as to unmask its hidden political intentions. The object of discourse analysis is to expose the author's preconceived beliefs about the subordinate elements; show how the imagery of the text allows the dominant to believe that their unequal relationship with the subordinate is various just, natural, necessary, rational or inevitable; and, if the text is for public consumption, reveal how its language attempts to shape the beliefs of the subordinate, persuade them of the legitimacy of the established order. Discourse analysts also contend that their approach can reveal the hidden politics of the text by paying as much attention to the 'unsaid' as the 'said' since the 'silences' in a text are often as significant as its statements.[3]

Discourse analysts, then, assume that every historical document written by the dominant elements, irrespective of the conscious intentions of the author, imposes a tendentious meaning on 'reality'. Even in reports written by authors of seemingly impeccable impartiality, the facts will always be presented to serve dominant values and interests. For example, a prominent deconstructionist,

Joan Wallach Scott, states, without qualification, that published statistical sources,

> are neither totally neutral collections of facts nor simply ideological impositions. Rather they are ways of establishing the authority of certain visions of social order, of organizing perceptions of 'experience'. At least since the eighteenth century, numbers have been used to establish the authenticity of interpretive or organizational categories. Thus the collection of population statistics according to households (rather than, say, villages or places of work) reveals and constructs a certain vision of social organization based on a particular idea of the family that is 'naturalized' in the course of presenting the data.[4]

Discourse analysis has some interesting things to say. It has, furthermore, deepened the appreciation by historians of the role and power of language and the problematic meaning of documents. But its followers have never advanced any empirical evidence to show that *all* reports by the dominant about subordinates are socially constructed. Very often discourse analysts sustain their claim that all observations by the dominant about subordinates are constructed, with the *a priori* argument that it is in the interests of the dominant to do so since this prevents subordinates from seeing their oppression. But the argument does not necessarily follow. There must also be situations where it is in the interests of the dominant to make and collect *accurate* observations about subordinates; if the knowledge concerns of the dominant were limited to constructing the subordinate sense of reality, how would the dominant know what devices were most effective in controlling the sense of reality of subordinates? Given that the effective exercise of power requires access to accurate information about the *actual* beliefs, values, behaviour and actions of the adversary, then we would expect that at least some of the information-collecting activities by the dominant about subordinates would strive to see subordinates *as they are*. The problem of socially constructed evidence, thus, is not misconceived, fundamentally or otherwise; it is a real problem.

Let us now examine three works of social history each of which has attempted to solve the problem with a different method.

The method of comparing trends in observations with trends in the control response: V.A.C. Gatrell, 'The Decline of Theft and Violence in Victorian and Edwardian England'[5]

Published in 1980, Gatrell's long article sets itself several ambitious goals: to impose order upon a chaotic collection of published police and justice statistics on violence and theft in England between 1834 and 1914; to audit the data so as to pinpoint their errors and discontinuities; to demonstrate that the trends in the actual incidence of violence and theft fell over the long term, despite the upheavals brought by the industrial revolution; and to suggest several explanations for these long-term trends.

The article, a work of exemplary scholarship, achieves all these goals – and a lot more besides. Perhaps, however, what stands out most about the article is its rigorous application of an elegant and ingenious method invented by Gatrell to tackle a central problem in criminology and the history of crime, one closely akin to the problem of socially constructed evidence which for the last twenty years has been the object of a large and increasingly sophisticated body of writing by social control theorists. Let me outline the problem as simply and briefly as I can.

The problem, in essence, is that official crime statistics do not just record what criminals do. They also *to an indefinite extent* record what is called the 'control response' to crime. The control response is the reaction to acts perceived as crimes by all the social actors involved in the criminal justice system. The actors include the legislators who formulate the provisions of the criminal law; the general public (including victims) who report offences to the authorities; the police (if the society has a police force) who observe offences, arrest offenders and decide whether to proceed with prosecutions; the courts who decide if an offence has been committed; and the organs of public opinion (such as the media, social movements, moral entrepreneurs) who shape social attitudes about crime. In a sense, then, these social actors are the crime observers.

Given all this, then it follows that official crime statistics are completely unreliable sources of information about the number of crimes that *actually* occurred at any given point, and about the trends over time in the numbers of *actual* crimes. As the public (including victims) do not report all offences and the police do not observe or arrest all offenders, many actual offences fail to appear in the official statistics – they are the 'dark' figure of crime. Moreover, all kinds of things can cause fluctuations in the intensity of the control response over time such as changes in the definitions of crimes, changes in police resources, and changes in public opinion towards offending. As a result of these fluctuations, trends in official statistics may well bear no relationship to the trends in the 'dark' figure.

Before the appearance of Gatrell's article, historians of crime devised various strategies to circumvent or accommodate these problems. One strategy was to abandon the study of official statistics altogether and to make surmises about the trends in offending based on what contemporary 'experts' said about them. As we saw in Chapter 2, the strategy failed since, for example, it took no account of the biases of the experts. Another strategy was to restrict the study of offending to the crimes which probably had the smallest 'dark' figures. This strategy, however, could only be applied to the most serious crimes which, as in the case of murder, were exceptional by their very nature.

A completely different strategy was to turn the issue on its head. Under the influence of the radical social control theorists in the mid and late 1970s, some historians of crime claimed that the idea that crime statistics were unreliable was quite misconceived: crime statistics represented nothing but the control response. Anticipating many of the ideas of the later 'discourse analysts', the radical control theorists argued that crime statistics were completely socially constructed. Crime, they said, does not have an objective existence, it is not something 'out there'. It is an act which only has meaning as crime when labelled as such by the controlling institutions, namely, the police, the courts, the legislators, the media, and the penal establishment. Hence, they concluded, the only proper way of handling official crime statistics, was to treat them as source material for studies of the ideology and the vested interests of the controlling institutions and the powerful people who ran them – the dominant elements in society.[6] The theory, however, is overstated. It ignores the very strong possibility that the definition of at least some crimes is the product of consensus within a society, and that victims and offenders alike know when an offence has taken place in relation to those provisions of the criminal law which are precise.

The starting point of Gatrell's strategy is the assumption that crime does actually occur independently of the labelling process; but that the proportion of crimes which are represented in the official statistics is vitally dependent on the control response and this in turn may well be governed by the controlling institutions. The strategy cannot and does not try to determine what proportion of actual crime is represented in the official statistics at any given point. But it can exclude the possibility that a *trend* in the crime figures must have been engineered by changes in the control response, changes governed perhaps by the controlling institutions.

The strategy is a variant of a technique that traditional historians apply to reports in historical documents. The objective of the technique is to distinguish the observations in the document that *may have been* distorted by the bias – the preconceptions – of the reporter from the observations *that were not* distorted by the reporter's bias. The technique works by comparing the slant of the reporter's bias with the direction of the observations. If the bias *moves with* the observations, there is no way of telling if the reporter consciously or unconsciously only observed the things that fitted his or her preconceptions. But if the reporter's bias *moves against* the observations, it is legitimate to conclude that the observations were not shaped by observer bias – although these observations may be inaccurate for other reasons. (Note, too, that this technique has a certain similarity with the crucial case method discussed in Chapter 3.)

With Gatrell's strategy, the direction of reporter bias is analogous to the trend in the control response, and the direction of the observations is equivalent to the trend in a given series of crime statistics. *In broad principle, Gatrell's strategy requires us to compare the trend in the intensity of the control response to crime, with the trend in a given series of crime statistics.* If the two trends move in the same direction, we cannot tell if changes in the control response are causing the trend in the crime statistics: the changes in the structure and culture of the control response may or may not be causing the trends in the crime statistics. But if the two trends follow diverging paths, we know that changes in the control response are not causing the trend in the crime statistics: this being the case, the trend in the crime statistics must reflect the actual trend. In short, the key to Gatrell's strategy is to find whether the trend in the control response and the trend in the crime statistics converge or diverge. With a convergence it is impossible to tell whether the control response caused the movement in the crime statistics. A divergence, however, allows us to be certain that the movement in the crime statistics reflects not changes in the control response but the movement in the actual amount of crime. A finding of divergence is obviously far more valuable than a finding of convergence. Once we know the trend in the crime statistics represents the actual trend, we can explain the trend. Or we can use it to make all kinds of inferences about the changing social and material circumstances of the subordinate classes – *in the certain knowledge that the inferences are not based on data that are contaminated by the ideology of the dominant classes or their preconceived beliefs about the subordinate ways of life*.

To illustrate the method, let us say we have a period when the trend in crime statistics for theft is rising and we want to determine whether this trend reflects the actual trend in theft ('dark figure' plus 'known figure'). Applying Gatrell's strategy, we would examine the control response and determine whether it was growing in strength (an upward trend) or diminishing in strength (a downward trend). If we found that it was growing we would not be able to tell whether it had caused the rise in theft statistics or whether the actual incidence of theft had increased (or a bit of both). But if we found that the control response to theft had diminished over the period, we could safely conclude that the fall represented a real fall since it cannot possibly be explained by a strengthening control response.

So far we have outlined the principle behind Gatrell's strategy and how the strategy works in broad terms. Let us now see how he has converted the strategy into a set of four powerful procedures that permit the detection and verification of a trend in the control response to crime over a given period. I will list these procedures, then discuss them, drawing attention to the restricted conditions under which they apply. As I will explain later, one of these conditions is that the last three procedures cannot be applied to a composite index embracing all crimes but to a specific category of crime. The labels for the procedures are my own.

☐ *1. The preliminary procedure*

This procedure involves a search for the most obvious evidence of change in the *overall formal structure* of the control response. It entails examining the institutional components of the whole criminal justice system – policing, court procedures, definitions of offences, the punishment of offenders – and making an assessment about whether on balance the reaction of the criminal justice system was intensifying, softening or fairly stable. In some periods the signs of change will be plainer than in others. For example, in most industrialising societies during the nineteenth century the perceived or actual growth of widespread social unrest led the state to overhaul and modernise its whole criminal justice system and engage in an unparalleled crackdown on working-class crime. The characteristics of these transformatory periods were the establishment of professional police forces (along with perhaps rising police to population ratios, the adoption of new and more effective policing tactics, increasing police budgets), the increasing assumption by the state of the responsibility for criminal prosecutions, the extension of summary justice to facilitate prosecutions, the broadening of police powers under vagrancy legislation, the introduction of a wide range of moral or public nuisance offences, revision of penal codes, and so on.

☐ *2. The procedure for measuring changes in public attitudes to the police*

Gatrell claims that longer-term movements in the rates of assaults on police are a 'nice index of the public's tolerance of its servants', of public 'acquiesence' to the police, and hence of the public's willingness to co-operate with the police and, by implication, to report other offences to the police.[7] This procedure is a proxy of the control response which, being quantified, is more precise than 1.

☐ *3. The procedure for measuring attitudinal changes towards offences by magistrates and juries*

Gatrell contends that such changes are detectable within the crime statistics themselves. They are indicated by longer-term movements in: (a) the proportions of arrests that lead to convictions (or of trials that lead to convictions); and (b) the proportion of convictions to 'court orders' (cautions, probations, referrals to welfare institutions and so forth). Indirectly, these indicators also measure changes in attitudes towards crime of the wider society. As with 2, procedure 3 creates proxy measures of the control response which are more precise than 1. Thus the assumption behind (a) and (b) is that if the control response to an offence strengthened over time, it should manifest itself in a growing proportion of convictions (to arrests or trials) and a shrinking proportion of court orders (to convictions) over the same period; and vice versa.

☐ 4. The checking/corroborating procedures

These are employed when we have evidence (produced by the first three procedures) of a divergence between the trend in the observed amount of crime and the trend in the control response to crime. The checking procedures establish whether (a) the divergence is substantial; and (b) related crimes also exhibit the divergence. The purpose of these checking procedures is to anticipate residual doubts about the claims for a divergence. A divergence that is substantial is much harder to dispute than one that is slight. Demonstrating that the divergence is shared by every related offence eliminates the possibility that the divergence for one specific offence was the result of a subtle change in the categorisation of the offence over time. With (b) it is desirable that the related offences include some serious offences: petty offences are more prone to erratic swings in the control response than the serious. Thus a divergence for a mix of petty and serious offences is weightier evidence that the control response is not causing offence trends than a divergence for one petty offence or several.

The four procedures produce the most reliable results under certain conditions. To begin with, the last three conditions cannot be applied to a composite index embracing all crimes. The intensity of the control response tends to vary enormously from offence type to offence type; hence lumping all types of offences into a composite index hides these differences, ensuring that a divergence (if any) is dominated by the intensity of the control response to the most common offences such as drunkenness, traffic or administrative offences. In other words, procedures 2, 3 and 4 work best with a specific crime category, though 4a will be inapplicable if the category has no related offences. Moreover, all four procedures are not sufficiently sensitive to pick up short-term shifts in the control response, those lasting less than a decade or so. In addition, the application of many of the procedures will obviously be constrained by the particular nature of a criminal justice system and the surviving records; for example, very few studies of pre-nineteenth century societies will be able to apply procedure 3. Lastly, the ability of the procedures to demonstrate a divergence will greatly depend on how many are applied, the mutual consistency of their results, and our capacity to explain away any inconsistencies.

At first glance Gatrell's procedures may seem complex – and costly if their end result is to show a convergence or a highly ambiguous divergence. But the complexity is the price of their rigour – and could be rewarded with the delivery of a lot of information about the changes in the behaviour and circumstances of the subordinate classes which we would not otherwise have and that is free of ideological contamination.

To end this section, let us briefly illustrate how the four procedures operate by seeing how Gatrell himself applies them in his article on 'The Decline of Theft and Violence in Victorian and Edwardian England'. For the sake of brevity, our summary will confine itself to his analysis of assault.

The assault statistics studied by Gatrell are based on court convictions. To derive the data, Gatrell aggregated three categories of assaults: the annual totals of common assaults tried summarily, committed for trial, and aggravated assaults tried summarily. The annual aggregates (which he calls assaults) are expressed as rates per 100, 000 population. The series start in 1857 and end in 1914 (1857 was the year in which official sources began to publish assault trials and convictions).

Now Gatrell rightly emphasises that assault statistics are highly unreliable. The reason for this is partly that the common assault component (the largest in the aggregate) was regarded as a minor offence, and partly that the legal definition of common assault over his period was very vague and inherently subject to wide interpretation. As a consequence, not only was there bound to have been a very large 'dark figure' of assault over the 1856–1914 period, but also there is a very good chance that the intensity of the control response to the offence was unstable during most of the period. Hence the question he confronts is this. Given that there was an overall tendency for the rate of assaults to decline from 1857 to 1914, was this downward movement in the recorded incidence reflective of a real decline in minor acts of violence in the society or of a lessening in the intensity of the control response to minor violence? Is it possible, he asks, that a 'greater tolerance of petty violence' was responsible for the decline in the observed assault rate?[8]

To solve the problem, Gatrell first of all invokes procedure 1. What this tells him is that there were momentous changes in the English criminal justice system, especially in the first half of the nineteenth century. These changes saw the introduction of professional policing to many parts of England, the extension of summary justice, the increasing assumption by the state of responsibility for prosecutions, and many other institutional re-forms which would have tended to expand the state's overall capacity to reduce the dark figure of crime. Although the growth of this capacity slowed after mid century, it certainly did not stop; the ratio of police to population, for example, constantly increased. In short, the application of procedure 1 indicates general signs of a possible divergence from 1857 to 1914; the long term trend in assault rates was downwards, while the overall structural ability of the state to apprehend offenders was steadily increasing.

Gatrell then applies procedure 2. He finds that between the mid-1850s and the quinquennium of 1910–14, his proxy indicator of public co-operation with the police – the rate of assaults on the police per 100,000 population – dropped by 64 per cent. In a more precise way, this fall confirms what is indicated by procedure 1.

Following this, Gatrell applies procedure 3. That is, he finds out whether the attitudes of magistrates and juries (and by implica-tion social attitudes) towards assaults softened or hardened over the period. What he finds here, however, is *not consistent* with the results of procedures 1 and 2. He finds, firstly, that the proportion of all trials for assaults that resulted in convictions *tends to fall* from the mid-1880s to 1911 (from 65 to 55 per cent); and that, secondly, the proportion of trials resulting in court orders, after consistently registering zero until 1907, first emerges as 2 per cent in 1908 and gradually shifts upwards to 5.4 per cent in 1914. In other words, both indicators suggest that the attitudes of magistrates, juries and, by extension, the society at large, towards petty violence, is softening, becoming less punitive. As the results of procedure 3 are at odds with procedures 1 and 2, Gatrell turns to his checking/ corroborating procedure, procedure 4.

The application of procedure 4 satisfies Gatrell (rightly so, I think) that there must have been a divergence. For one thing, the extent of the drop in the rate of assaults (71 per cent from 1857–60 to 1911–14) is too steep to be explained by a late century softening in social attitudes towards violence which procedure 3 indicated. For another thing, the steep downward movement in recorded rates of petty violence was also followed by two other categories of crime related to assaults, namely, homicides and woundings. As both woundings and homicides are serious and highly visible offences (especially homicide), they are subject to minimal *long-term* fluctuation in observation error. Taking all these things into account, Gatrell concludes that the fall in observed rates of assaults was not caused by the changes in the control response or governed by the controlling institutions but reflects an actual and probably substantial reduction in the level of violence in English society.

The interpretive method: Elaine Showalter, *The Female Malady: Women, Madness, and English Culture, 1830–1980*[9]

Perhaps the hardest source of observer bias to detect and correct is the bias that enters the observations by dominant people about the madness of subordinate people. There are two reasons why this is so. The first is that within any given society the definitions of madness tend to be vague and highly unstable. The second is that different cultures tend to have very different ideas about what insanity means. For example, medieval Moslem society, which was highly sophisticated, believed in the existence of entities of mental disease which are quite unknown in modern psychiatry: these include 'lycanthropy' (where people have delusions that they are wolves), love-sickness, and phrenitis (a condition of delirium brought on by yellow bile). And on the other side of the coin, medieval Muslim society had no equivalent to the modern disease entities of manic depression, paranoia and schizophrenia.[10]

A very interesting book which attempts to tackle the problem of how to detect observer bias in observations by the dominant of madness in the subordinate is Elaine Showalter's *The Female Malady*. Published in 1985, Showalter's work is a pioneering, highly readable and superbly illustrated study of the part played by the male-dominated psychiatric profession in justifying and enforcing the subordination of women in England between 1830 and 1980.

The study was part and parcel of an outpouring of studies on the manner in which a large variety of patriarchal institutions operated to control women in the past. It has inspired many closer-grained studies of the ways in which individual asylums and psychiatric regimes in a variety of societies have defined madness in gender terms.

As Showalter sees it, the history of psychiatric medicine in England during the 1830–1980 period went through three stages. In each of these madness was characterised as an embodiment of the supposedly feminine traits of childish dependency, irrationality and emotional instability. In each stage, however, the psychiatric profession constructed a new entity (or new entities) of mental illness to designate supposed abnormalities in female behaviour. Showalter claims that these entities were theory-laden. Although in some cases the entities corresponded with actual diseases, they were projections of the prevailing beliefs held by men about proper gender differences in society. On this basis, Showalter advances what we will call her primary thesis, that these constructed disease entities had a dual function. One was to enable the patriarchy to marginalise and institutionalise women who transgressed the highly restrictive norms of proper female conduct. The other function was to give psychiatrists the licence to brainwash their female charges into accepting these highly restrictive norms. In Showalter's words, the various entities and the therapies which psychiatrists devised to treat them 'operated as ways of controlling and mastering feminine difference itself', of 'managing women's minds'.[11]

Showalter terms the first stage in the growth of psychiatric medicine as 'psychiatric Victorianism' (1830 to 1870). This stage is associated with the key figure, John Connolly. According to his ideas, insanity was not a loss of reason but moral deviance caused by loss of will power the symptoms of which, in the case of women patients, were displayed in a severe want of traditional feminine virtues, notably the home-making capacities. Curing mad women required placing them under the close supervision of a home-like institution where they could be morally re-educated: inculcated in Christian doctrine and immersed in household activities such as cleaning, washing, cooking and sewing. A new disease entity, puerperal madness, was invented to describe the behaviour of women whose disturbed reproductive systems led them to transgress gender roles by rejecting their household duties and the conventions of female propriety.

The next stage, 'psychiatric Darwinism' (1870–1920), is chiefly associated with the figure of Henry Maudsley who adopted a rigorously 'scientific' approach to madness. His notion was that madness was a form of racial degeneration that had inheritable organic causes, manifested in outward physical defects. Motherhood, so psychiatric Darwinism claimed, was natural to women; if women defied nature, they would develop mental disorders which might be passed on to future generations. A traditional female disease entity, hysteria, was redefined as an inheritable disposition towards intense emotionality by women whose maternal desires had been frustrated (anorexia, a disease entity invented in 1873, was sometimes classified as a form of hysteria); and another 'ailment', neurasthenia, was invented to designate a state of nervous exhaustion which both sexes were liable to, though in women it was associated with their movement out of the home into the higher echelons of the paid workforce.

The third stage, 'psychiatric modernism' (1920–1980), is chiefly associated with the influential work of W.H.R. Rivers at the beginning of the period and the 'anti-psychiatry' theories of R.D. Laing towards its end. (One of the ironies of Showalter's feminist history is that she implicitly embraces a 'great man theory of history' approach to explain change.) Rivers, she says, helped to transform English psychiatry by making the 'talking cure' (Freudian therapy) professionally acceptable, and by demonstrating that hysteria was not specific to women but also affected men, a conclusion which he was led to by his observations of the condition of shell-shocked veterans of the Great War. After Rivers, she goes on to say, the period saw the growing replacement of hysteria with the notion of schizophrenia. Although schizophrenia was not specifically associated with women, Showalter argues that its crueler 'cures' (lobotomy, ECT and insulin shock treatment) were mainly applied to women, notably those who transgressed the codes of feminine behaviour. Showalter then gives R.D. Laing credit for repudiating the dehumanising treatments of schizophrenia and for explaining it in social terms, but criticises him for not seeing that in the case of women it is a direct reflection of their plight. It should be noted that Showalter often indicates schizophrenia is a real disease entity,[12] but here the discussion, I think, confuses schizophrenia as a mental disease entity with erroneous or inappropriate diagnoses of schizophrenia (I shall return to this point later).

But if Showalter's primary argument is that the entities constituting female madness were invented by men so as to enforce and reinforce the subordination of women, this is not her only argument. She also pursues two secondary arguments. The first is that female insanity could also be real, *the pathological by-product of female subordination*. Thus when summarising *Cassandra*, Florence Nightingale's semi-autobiographical novel, Showalter concurs with the message of the novel that men's oppression of women drove them to insanity: '*Cassandra* is a scathing analysis of the stresses and conventions that drove Victorian middle-class women to silence, depression, illness, even lunatic asylums and death'. When recapitulating the chapters on psychiatric Victorianism, Showalter declares, 'the rise of the Victorian madwoman was one of history's self-fulfilling prophecies. In a society that not only perceived women as childlike, irrational, and sexually unstable but also rendered them legally and economically marginal, it is not surprising that they should have formed the greater part of the residual categories of deviance from which doctors drew a lucrative practice and the asylums much of their population'. And later when discussing schizophrenia she states, 'schizophrenic symptoms of passivity, depersonalization, disembodiment, and fragmentation have parallels in the social situation of women'; it is 'expressive of women's lack of confidence, dependency on external, often masculine, definitions of the self, split between the body as sexual object and the mind as subject, and vulnerability to conflicting social messages about femininity and maturity'.[13]

The other though less prominent secondary argument is that female insanity could also be *a more or less rational form of protest by women against their subordination*. For example, when discussing psychiatric Victorianism she says, 'Case histories of mental breakdown ... suggest both gender conflict and protest against sexual repression'. In another place, she contends that hysteria was often a passive or silent protest against patriarchy ('protofeminism'), a none too effective protest she adds, which on the protest spectrum was the polar opposite of active feminism ('the determination to speak and act for women in the public world'), a more effective form of protest, she seems to say.[14]

From the above it can be seen that Showalter's concept of female madness is far more complex than the concept of crime held by the radical social control theorists who argue that crime is not real and does not exist until labelled as such by crime enforcers. What makes her concept of female madness complex, is that it appears to be working on two levels, though she does not clearly distinguish the two in her discussion. On the first she is dealing with mental disease *entities* 'constructed' by men, some of which she says do not exist in reality (puerperal mania, for instance), while others she indicates do exist in reality and are caused by the powerlessness of women (schizophrenia, for example). On the second level she is dealing with *diagnoses* of women by men who believe (or want to believe) the women in question are mad and accordingly label as mad. Although she suggests that sometimes these diagnoses could be wrong (as in the case of women who successfully fooled doctors that they were suffering from hysteria), she also suggests that sometimes they could be right (as in the case of females who were so powerless, passive, lacking in choices and disembodied that, when they were diagnosed as suffering from schizophrenia, the diagnosis was necessarily correct).

The intriguing possibility raised by Showalter's complex concept of female madness is that it could lead to women being 'correctly' diagnosed for disease entities which were not real, or to women feigning the symptoms of a disease entity that was not real but being positively diagnosed as suffering from the disease!

Where, I think, Showalter is a constructionist is that she insists that a mental disease entity affecting women only exists when it has been labelled as such, and the labelling is usually a complete projection of male beliefs (a pseudo-disease entity). But at the same time she wants to maintain a weak realist position in that she says that at least some of these labels *could* refer to real disease entities.[15]

This brings us to the crucial questions: how does Showalter differentiate between the mental disease entities that were phantoms and those that were real? How would she tell, for example, if a women was acting out hysteria in order to make a protest and managed to fool the male clinician that she had hysteria, or was not acting out hysteria but was wrongly diagnosed as having hysteria by a male clinician, or had hysteria but was not diagnosed as having it by a clinician?

Unfortunately, there is no explicit discussion in the text about how Showalter thinks such questions can or should be tackled. Even so, it is obvious from her narrative that she does employ a method to deal with them to a limited extent. First, she makes a general assumption that female observers were far able than male clinicians to make accurate observations about female madness. Then, to determine the particular realities of female madness, she draws her supporting evidence from the accounts of madness written by women themselves. Some of these accounts are novels (like Florence Nightingale's *Cassandra*); others are autobiographies. Showalter treats such accounts as if they have a privileged access to the facts of the female condition. For example, while describing psychiatric Victorianism she asserts that 'The accounts of female insanity by Nightingale, Brontë, and Braddon are psychologically much richer than the descriptions by Victorian doctors'. When describing a short story about a woman's depression by the American socialist and feminist, Charlotte Perkins Gilman, Showalter says, 'Gilman's haunting and passionate protest against the rest cure has become a modern feminist classic. . . . it shows how solitary confinement within the bourgeois family could be maddening for intelligent women.' She approvingly quotes the feminist novelist, 'George Egerton', as saying, '"When we shall have larger and freer lives, we shall be better balanced than we are now"'. Discussing the advent of psychiatric modernism, she says, 'More than any other novelist of the period, [Virginia] Woolf perceived and exposed the sadism of nerve therapies that enforced conventional sex roles.'[16] And writing on the barbaric nature of the 'cures' applied to female schizophrenic patients, she comes very close to equating the perspective of these women with objective reporting,

These cultural and medical associations of schizophrenia and femininity were given a particular interpretation in the very extensive English women's literature dealing with madness, institutionalization, and shock. In scores of literary and journalistic works produced between 1920 and the 1960s, from inmate narratives protesting against the asylum to autobiographical novels and poems, schizophrenia became the bitter metaphor through which English women defined their cultural situation. Individually and collectively, these narratives provide the woman's witness so marginal or absent in the nineteenth-century discourse on madness; they give us a different perspective on the asylum, on the psychiatrist, and on madness itself; and they transform the experiences of shock, psychosurgery, and chemotherapy into symbolic episodes of punishment for intellectual ambition, domestic defiance, and sexual autonomy.[17]

Showalter's method is a version of a strategy we encountered in Chapter 1: 'the insider's view' or hermeneutics otherwise known as the *interpretive method*. The proponents of the interpretive method justify it on the premise that an observer from inside a culture (society, group) *necessarily* has a privileged access to knowledge about it and is an inherently reliable informant about it – or at least, will necessarily know more about it and will thus be a more reliable informant about it than an observer from outside the culture (society, group). Now, the interpretive method is a common one and, under certain circumstances, very useful. However, the validity of the premise it is based on is problematic and hotly debated. Showalter, unfortunately, does not anticipate any of the objections to the premise, many of which are powerful objections, as we will see in the next chapter.

Apart from this, there are several difficulties with her particular application of the interpretive method. To begin with, there are the obvious difficulties. Do the accounts she uses – nearly all of which were written by middle-class women – typify the experiences of *all* women who were labelled as mad and treated by male psychiatrists? Are novels reliable sources of evidence about the realities of a certain category of people? These questions are never addressed in the text.

Another difficulty relates to the limited scope of her particular method. Suppose we agree that female accounts of madness are good guides of when the observations by male psychiatrists about female madness – the disease entities they conceived and the diagnoses they made – were biased and thus highly error-prone. This being so, how can we, as historians, use this information to produce more knowledge about female madness? It would be pointless, I think, simply to keep on doing studies showing that male psychologists were biased; ultimately, this would only duplicate what we already know. Alternatively, we could use the information to explore the actualities of female madness. But if we wanted to take our research in this direction, how would the results generated by Showalter's method help us? The limitation of the method is that it has no capacity to measure the degree of bias – to estimate how often the observations by male psychiatrists were biased and the extent to which in aggregate they were biased. Hence, it has no capacity to shed light on the approximate extent of actual madness in a female population or on the trends in the incidence of actual female madness. Without this capacity, moreover, we have little or no means to establish the finer causes of actual madness in the female population, the variations over time in the strength of these causes or compare the differences between the causes of male madness and the female.

The last difficulty with Showalter's method relates to its robustness. Showalter presupposes, as we saw, that female accounts of madness tell us about the realities of female madness (or at least tell us more about the realities than the accounts by male clinicians). But it so happens that some of the female accounts she mentions share the biases of the male medical establishment. For example, when describing neurasthenia, a disease entity which she obviously thinks is a pseudo-entity, she summarises the views of a female doctor, Margaret Cleaves, who implicitly confirms the views of male psychiatrists about the causes of the disease in women: '[Cleaves] attributed female neurasthenia not simply to overwork but to women's ambitions for intellectual, social, and financial success. . . . she conceded, "that girls and women are unfit to bear the continued labor of mind because of the disqualifications existing in their physiological life."'[18] A little later, when describing the approved medical attitudes towards anorexia, Showalter admits that such attitudes were reflected in, not repudiated by, a best-selling novel by a female novelist, Sarah Grand.[19] Moreover, Showalter acknowledges that, although the feminist Charlotte Perkins Gilman in her short story (cited above) wrote a 'haunting and passionate protest against the rest cure', another feminist, Elizabeth Robins, wrote a novel where the rest cure 'is a rescue from an impoverished life, and the doctor–lover is a savior. . . . [the novel] shows that even for feminists, the rest cure might have had creative and sexual advantages.'[20]

Showalter does not say whether she thinks the female accounts that shared the biases of male psychiatrists were right or wrong. Her silence here stands in sharp contrast with her readiness to use the accounts which diverge from the biases of male psychiatrists as evidence for the psycho-pathology of women's subordination. To be sure, the accounts which shared male biases could well be untrustworthy or be more untrustworthy than the accounts which diverged from male biases. But if this is the case, we need to have some non-arbitrary criteria that justify the claims that the untrustworthy accounts are untrustworthy or more untrustworthy than the others – and it is unfortunate that in Showalter's text such criteria are never offered.

Oral history and the method of maximising the weight and variety of evidence: Eugene D. Genovese, *Roll, Jordan, Roll: The World the Slaves Made*[21]

Yet another attempt to solve the problem of socially constructed evidence is contained in Eugene Genovese's classic study of the ways of life of slaves in the American south in the first half of the nineteenth century. Before we examine his method for dealing with the problem, we will briefly outline the contents of the book and its main arguments.

In the Preface, Genovese says that his primary aim is 'to tell the story of slave life as carefully and accurately as possible. . . . of the black struggle to survive spiritually as well as physically – to make a livable world for themselves and their children within the narrowest living space and harshest adversity.'[22] On the face of it, the study strives to attain this vague goal by being encyclopaedic. The topics covered by Genovese include the paternalistic relationship which slave owners imposed on slaves, the living standards of slaves, the role of religion in the lives of slaves, the work habits of slaves, house-slaves, slave drivers, slave artisans, free slaves, miscegenation, slave language, the naming of slaves, the slave family, the sexual mores of slaves, slave wedding ceremonies, male slaves as husbands and fathers, female slaves as mothers and wives, slave children, elderly slaves, the housing conditions of slaves, the subsistence plots of slaves, slave eating habits, slave clothing, slave literacy, slave leisure pursuits, and slave forms of accommodation and resistance.

Yet the study is not in the mode of unfocused description. All the topics contribute towards the elucidation of a central problem, a problem of a 'how-possibly' kind: how were slaves able to endure their oppression, their abject status? Genovese denies that slaves responded to their plight with apathy and dull resignation, or by submitting entirely to their masters and internalising the racialist images which their masters had of them He also rejects the opposite view, that slaves preserved their sense of dignity by engaging in active resistance; although slaves did engage in some resistance, he claims that the regime was too oppressive to permit it to any significant degree. Instead, his explanation, which takes a sort of middle course, is that slaves managed to survive by *accommodating* themselves to their oppression, *mainly on the psychological and cultural plane*. Three arguments are involved.

The first argument is that slaves manipulated the meaning of the ideology of slave-owner paternalism in a way that gave them a measure of self-respect. Genovese's chain of reasoning here runs along the following lines: that slave owners attempted to justify their oppressive regime with the moral claim that slavery was beneficial to slaves (without it blacks would not survive); that to demonstrate the sincerity of this claim, slave owners were forced to treat their charges paternalistically ('kindness'); that paternalism implied a reciprocal relationship; that reciprocity implied that the master owed a duty to the slave; that the slaves were able to extract a concept of rights from this notion of duty; and that by possessing a concept of rights, the slaves were able to keep their self-respect.[23]

His second argument makes much of the positive effects of Christianity – more specifically, the slave version of Christianity – on slave morale. Christianity, he says, consoled slaves with the thought that they would receive their just desserts in the life hereafter. In addition, it provided them with a collection of values that stopped them from feeling degraded, that helped to furnish them with a common code of conduct of mutual love, and that gave them a set of standards by which they could judge their masters. On top of this, the prayer meetings that slaves organised for themselves contributed to the development of a black community.

The third argument (which overlaps the second) is that the collective practices and vibrant culture of slaves gave them the will to survive. Despite the small size of most plantations (one half of all units held four black families or less) and the high level of contact between slaves and slave owners, the plantations nonetheless provided many settings where resident and neighbouring slaves interacted free of white supervision, such as prayer meetings and on certain festive occasions. As a result of these interactions, Genovese maintains, slaves were able to forge an autonomous black community. Its importance, he says, was that it allowed them to practise and foster their own culture. Apart from being manifested in language, religion and music, the culture included a primitive system of mutual aid and solidarity which made their lives bearable. The system was manifested, for instance, in their readiness to assist runaways and to help each other in field labour, as well as in their relatively low levels of suicide, violence, and drunkenness.

In order to sustain these arguments, Genovese draws extensively on the written observations by slave owners about slaves. Yet he is well aware that such evidence is unreliable. He keeps on reminding us that slave-owner reports of slave conduct could be 'self-serving' and 'self-deceiving'. 'Slaveholders', he tells us in one place, 'usually interpreted every kind of behaviour among their slaves in such a way as to justify the status-quo', and that 'Southern whites had a genius for attributing their own faults to the slaves'. In yet another place, he insists that 'The whites' view of slaveholding as a duty and a burden was clearly self-serving and should hardly be taken at face value'. In a note on sources, he asserts that 'The slaveholders' papers and publications can hardly be accepted as "objective," especially when they purport to describe slave attributes.'[24]

But Genovese is not just mistrustful of slave-owner accounts of slave life. He also doubts the reliability of every other source. Thus, he doubts the reliability of the observations made by travellers to the South.[25] Similarly, he doubts the reliability of the published autobiographies by runaway slaves; these, he says, 'require enormous care, for when not distorted by northern abolitionist editing, they remained the accounts of highly exceptional men and women and can be as misleading in their honesty and accuracy of detail as in their fabrications.'[26]

Perhaps more striking still, he even doubts the reliability of a particular kind of 'insider' source, a source which many historians have taken as providing the most authentic and reputable accounts of slave life; that is, the oral histories narrated by ex-slaves to researchers engaged by the Federal Writers Project of the Works Project Administration during the 1930s. Although Genovese's discussion of the problems of these oral histories is sparse, it nonetheless refers to two problems which are general to oral history, problems which the practitioners of oral history all too often neglect. First, he says that the ex-slaves were asked questions about things that occurred a long time before, when they were children. He implies, quite rightly, that people cannot be relied upon to remember accurately the details of events which happened much earlier in their lives, partly because human memory is inherently faulty and partly because the concept that informants have of their lives at some point in the past can be influenced by their intervening experiences as well as by their present beliefs and values.[27] Second, he says that the ex-slaves were 'interviewed by whites under circumstances that may have imposed inhibitions'.[28] Here he is referring to a particular instance of a larger problem of oral history: that the expectations which interviewers have of the respondents and that the interviewers convey through their demeanour, voice inflexions, wording of their questions and so on, can affect the responses of the respondents (such a phenomenon is often known as the **Rosenthal effect**).[29]

How does Genovese solve the problem of socially constructed evidence given that, unlike Showalter, he is not prepared to privilege the accounts of slaves and former slaves, the 'insiders'? According to his own – and very brief – description, he says he tried to solve it partly by weighing different kinds of testimony against each other, and partly by becoming so familiar with the sources that he was able to make informed judgments about the veracity of the observations they contained. Although this may have been his conscious method, the text suggests that in fact he – perhaps unknowingly – made extensive use of another method: *an adaptation of the method of maximising the weight and variety of evidence*. One place where he uses it very effectively is in a section dealing with a very interesting question, the work ethic of slaves.[30]

Genovese starts the section by pointing out that the near universal opinion of slave owners was that slaves were naturally lazy. Genovese, however, says he greatly distrusts the veracity of these observations: it is highly probable that slave owners wanted to think this way since it helped them to justify their subordination of slaves. Having said this, Genovese goes on to argue that the 'insider's view', the testimony by ex-slaves themselves, on the matter can be just as unreliable. Although many ex-slaves stated that slaves were lazy, these statements must be taken with a grain of salt; given that slaves were so heavily exposed to the propaganda of their masters, it is very likely that at least on this subject slaves internalised the images that their masters had of them.

Following this, Genovese argues that slaves were not so much lazy as that they had little conception of regular or sustained effort. To support this claim, he cites many examples representing different types of (predominantly) circumstantial evidence that all converge on the same conclusion. First, he argues that slaves, by virtue of being slaves, generally did not have any material incentive to engage in sustained effort. Second, he argues that the aristocratic code of slave owners devalued the bourgeois virtue of steady application, that this attitude set the standard for the work habits of all other categories of white southerners, and that slaves necessarily followed suit since this was the only model of the work ethic they saw around them. Third, he argues from the objective situational logic of plantation work: that as plantation work was highly seasonal, with intensely busy periods interspersed with slack ones, it did not nurture an aptitude for steady application but a capacity to work in fits and starts. Lastly, he corroborates his case empirically, with a close reading of slave narratives. He notes that although the informants expressly describe their fellows as lazy, the informants also indirectly indicate that slaves toiled arduously and vigorously on certain key occasions during the year, and these occasions were the festivities associated with harvest time: corn-shuckings, log-rollings, hog killings, cotton picking and sugar grinding.

■ Conclusion

This chapter began by noting that when researching the actualities of subordinate elements in a past society, historians frequently have little choice but to take their evidence from sources generated by dominant people. We argued that the reliability of such sources can never be taken for granted since dominant people usually have preconceived beliefs about the subordinate and may describe the subordinate in a self-serving way. We did not, however, go along with the claim by many post-modern theorists that documents written or compiled by people in dominant positions should only be used to reveal the political strategies operating within the texts. We then looked at several solutions to the problem. These methods were V.A.C. Gatrell's method of comparing the slant of the observations with the bias of the observer; Elaine Showalter's method of appealing to the evidence of the 'insiders' themselves (a method which we think has to be treated with care); the resort to oral history (a variant of 'insider' history which also needs to be used with care); and Eugene Genovese's adaptation of the method of maximising the weight and variety of evidence.

■ *Chapter 8* ■

The Problem of Appropriate Concepts

Presentism – anachronism – is usually taken as a mark of bad history.[1] We engage in it when we think, talk and write about the past as if it were the same place as the present. Although most historians would concede that presentism is very difficult to avoid in practice, they nonetheless insist that it should be avoided as much as possible, and that we should strive to examine past people in their own terms, by their own lights, within their own context. Presentism is a form of ethnocentrism; the term 'historicism' was invented by nineteenth-century German scholars to denote the opposite of presentism.

There are many different types of presentism. The best known is material presentism, the presumption that past actors had access to the same material resources and capacities to solve problems as actors in the modern world. Perhaps the most serious types of presentism, however, are values-presentism, belief-presentism and their close relation, concept-presentism. Values-presentism occurs when historians examine a past people as if they have or ought to have modern values whether these be morals, desires, aims, ambitions, preferences, perceptions of rights, tastes, interests, goals or what have you. We engage in values-presentism when, for example, we make moral judgments about historical actors according to our standards which would have been foreign to the culture of the actors, or attribute modern desires to historical actors whose desires were quite different, or rank their desires in order of our preferences not theirs, and so on.

Belief-presentism arises when the historian projects onto past people modern views, which they would find alien, about the entities and structures that exist in the world (ontology) and about how the world should be studied (epistemology). By alien, I mean the views are not just unfamiliar to past people, but are incompatible with their whole belief system (world-views, para-digms, theories, modes of perception or whatever). An historian would perpetrate belief-presentism by, for example, stating that Polynesians practised science before Western contact, or that the sixteenth-century French writer, Rabelais, was an atheist, and so forth.

Closely linked to both values and belief-anachronism is con-cept-presentism, the false presumption that past people possessed our concepts and conceptual frameworks, attributed the same meanings to natural and social phenomena as we do. It occurs when we describe and explain the conduct of past people with present day concepts which the people in question did not know and would find alien. An example of concept-presentism would be to classify as 'democratic' the ideology of the Leveller move-ment of mid-seventeenth-century England, or to insinuate the language of genetics into the theorising of eighteenth-century biologists, or to discuss the ideas of sixteenth-century alchemists in terms of atoms and molecules. To avoid concept-presentism, the historian has to grasp the concepts and conceptual schemas of past people as they grasped them, and describe their values and beliefs with words that accurately convey the meanings that the values and beliefs had to the actors. To paraphrase the much quoted view by the historian and philosopher, R.G. Collingwood, the study of history should be based on 'the thought inside the event'.[2]

Gaining a proper understanding of the concepts of past people is perhaps more difficult for social historians than it is for histor-ians in other fields, especially the historians of diplomacy, politics and ideas. There are two main reasons why this is so. One is that social historians mostly study illiterate or poorly educated subor-dinate peoples whose modes of thinking tend to be more alien and less comprehensible than those of elite groups, the people usually studied by other kinds of historians. The second reason is that compared with the powerful and the famous, few subordin-ate people in past time wrote about their experiences. Hence social historians find it much harder than other historians to fol-low the convention of 'immersing themselves in the documents', the traditional procedure in historical scholarship for gaining familiarity with the ways of thinking of past actors. Not many social historians have the opportunity to emulate the example of

J.H. Hexter, the political historian of early modern England, who says that he soaks himself so deeply in the sources, that 'Instead of the passions, prejudices, assumptions and pre-possessions, the events, crises and tensions of the present dominating my view of the past, *it is the other way about*'.[3]

How, then, can social historians avoid the problem of concept-presentism? Are there any methods they can employ to understand properly the concepts possessed by subordinate elements in past time? A sub-discipline of social history has arisen partly to address these questions. The sub-discipline is microhistory.

Historians often refer to 'microhistory' as an all-purpose designation for any kind of study on a minute scale – say, a village or a family or a fragment of some event. But this designation should not be confused with the sub-discipline of microhistory. Sometimes called ethnographic history and ethno-history (though the latter term is also given to the study of indigenous peoples at the point of western contact), microhistory is of comparatively recent birth. Originating during the 1970s, its principal centres are Melbourne (where Greg Dening, the Pacific historian, and Rhys Isaac, the American historian, have been its seminal figures); the United States (where its leading lights are the historians of early modern France, Robert Darnton and Natalie Zemon Davis); and, most important of all, Italy (where it has its own journal, *Quaderni Historici*, and has been led by Carlo Ginzburg and Giovanni Levi).

The one variety of history that perhaps has the closest kinship to microhistory is the history of *mentalités*, established by the famous *Annales* 'school' in the late 1920s. Without doubt the two kinds of history have much in common. Both are almost exclusively concerned with the cultural and subjective dimensions of past human experience. Moreover, some historians of *mentalités* have written works that are virtually indistinguishable from microhistory; a key example being Emmanual LeRoy Ladurie's best-selling *Montaillou* (1978), a study of the village life of Cathar heretics in medieval France. Comparing microhistory to the history of *mentalités*, however, is misleading since the history of *mentalités* takes extraordinarily diverse forms. The studies which have been carried out in its name embrace, for example, the history of sensibility, of personality traits, of popular attitudes, of collective representations, of 'discourses' (common codes of knowledge), of ideology, of ways of thinking, of popular pastimes and so on.

Moreover, while many of these studies focus on subordinate people, others deal with other sectors: either the elite, the educated, or a complete cross-section of society. In addition, the historians of *mentalités* vary substantially in their theoretical perspectives (Marxist, Durkheimian, psycho-analytical, functionalist, structuralist, post-structuralist and so forth), and in their techniques (which range from the heavily quantitative to the highly impressionistic).

Microhistory, by contrast, is a more coherent sub-discipline. Amongst its distinguishing characteristics are its almost exclusive concern with ordinary people ('the voiceless'); its attempt, wherever possible, to use the self-testimonies written or generated by such people as source material; its limited attention to the unconscious causal mechanisms and structures that limit human agency and that produce change; its lack of interest in what happens over long periods of time; its rejection of quantitative techniques; its commitment to the narrative; and its suspicion of model-building and generalising theories.

What, however, is really distinctive about microhistory are three things. The first is that it has been more influenced by anthropology than any other type of history. Although microhistorians wear their theory lightly, they nonetheless have largely borrowed their approach from a strain in modern social anthropology called interpretive or symbolic anthropology, a strain which is closely identified with the writings of two scholars domiciled in America, Clifford Geertz (renown for his work on Bali, *Negra, The Theatre State in Nineteenth-Century Bali*, 1980) and Victor Turner (whose field-work in Zambia is the subject of such works as *The Forest of Symbols*, 1967).

The second thing which does most to set microhistory apart is its goal. The microhistorian is fundamentally concerned with grasping the concepts of subordinate people as they grasped them. The paradox of such concepts is that although they are quite unfamiliar to us, their users took them for granted, assumed that they were perfectly sensible ways for representing the entities and structures in their natural and social environment, especially social relationships. The goal has been nicely summarised by one microhistorian, Robert Darnton, as an attempt 'to get' the idioms of the people, to be able to speak and think like a native.[4] A fellow practitioner, Rhys Isaac, has defined the goal as 'The searching out of the meanings that...actions contained and conveyed for the participants'.[5] Another microhistorian David Sabean sees the goal as one where we examine the 'symbols and metaphors and the language of concrete experience, in order to understand ways in which villagers presented the flow of social processes and the nature of social relations to themselves and among themselves.'[6]

The third most distinctive feature of microhistory is, as the name suggests, its specificity and its close attention to detail. The name for this way of writing, 'thick description', has been popularised by the interpretive anthropologist, Clifford Geertz.[7] Hence a typical microhistorical study reads like an ethnographer's report on his or her field-notes: it consists of a fine-grained and highly nuanced description of the ways in which an ordinary person or tiny group of such people made sense of a very specific stimulus such as an unusual local event, a bit of social interaction typifying everyday life, a custom, a particular local ceremony, or certain texts.

In short, microhistory claims that it is specially equipped to deal with one of social history's more difficult methodological issues, namely, of how to understand the unfamiliar concepts of ordinary people as they understood them and thus avoid concept-presentism. In the chapter which follows we will critically examine this claim, focusing on a vexatious question which is at the core of the problem of concept appropriateness:

Should our descriptions and explanations of a past society *always* be framed within the concepts that the actors used; or can the descriptions and explanations draw upon different concepts and conceptual schemas (notably those of modern theories) which would not be understood by the actors? In other words, assuming we understand the concepts of historical actors, should our accounts of the actors be solely within their terms (**internalist accounts**), or are there justifiable conditions under which we can move beyond the understanding that the actors had of their situation and examine their situation employing our conceptual tools (**externalist accounts**)? To put this more bluntly, are there any circumstances in which we can legimately engage in concept-presentism?

The first section of this chapter discusses the question in broad terms. This section, it should be noted, hardly refers to what microhistorians say about the question since microhistorians, unfortunately, have written very little on it. Instead nearly all of the first section looks at the question from the perspective of a tradition in the social sciences called hermeneutics (or interpretationism). The reasons I have taken this line are that interpretive anthropology and, by extension, microhistory are directly derived from the hermeneutic tradition, and that hermeneutic theorists have put forward the best arguments for internalist accounts.

The second and third sections are a critical discussion of the value of a purely hermeneutic approach to social historians. Here I suggest that although a purely hermeneutic approach has much of value to offer social historians, it is nonetheless far too narrow for social historians. I argue, in other words, that social historians should not take an aversion to concept-presentism to extremes. The fourth and concluding section attempts to specify the contexts when a purely hermeneutic approach should be taken and those when it should not be.

■ The hermeneutic tradition

Although hermeneutics will be very well known to students of cultural studies, probably few students taking history will know anything about this mysterious-sounding subject. Hence, let me try to make it intelligible by putting it in a wider background.

In previous chapters of this book we discussed a range of procedures that in one way or another were concerned with two types of explanation, the causal and the statistical. In the chapter on the problem of important causes (Chapter 4) we saw that causal explanations are those that seek to establish an *invariable relationship* (or virtually invariable) between a particular class of causes and a particular class of outcomes. In Chapter 6 we indicated that statistical explanations (whether prosopographical or epidemiological) are those that demonstrate a close statistical relationship between the movements of two or more series of data.

Despite these technical differences, there is one thing both types of explanation have in common: they exemplify what is known as the 'naturalistic' tradition in social enquiry, which otherwise goes under the name of 'positivism'. Established in the nineteenth century by J.S. Mill, Auguste Comte and Émile Durkheim, the naturalist tradition assumes that human society is composed of the same basic stuff and subject to the same physical and mechanical forces as the inanimate and animate objects of the natural world such as plants, rocks, animals, earthquakes, insects and so forth. On the basis of this ontology (known as monism), the naturalist tradition maintains that the study of human society should be modelled as much as possible on the practices and aims of the natural sciences. Thus naturalists claim that when we practise our social investigations we should start by formulating theories about the causes of social behaviour, and then test these theories by systematically and objectively comparing cases to see how frequently the circumstances comprising the alleged causes are succeeded by the states comprising the alleged outcomes. As far as the aims of social investigation are concerned, naturalists argue that these should be to improve the stock of well-tested theories so that they increase in their predictive powers to the point where they become perfectly reliable and can be called laws. In short, naturalists are concerned with objectivity, systematic observations across cases, causes, predictions and laws.

In sociology and anthropology, accounts of a naturalistic kind arc usually designated as *externalist*. Other names are 'causal models', 'etic' accounts, 'objective' descriptions, 'behaviouristic' models, 'outsider' models, 'externalist' views, 'statistical' or 'unconscious models' (the phrases are those of Claude Lévi-Strauss, the French social anthropologist), amongst others. Exemplifying such accounts are those based on the generalising theories of anomie, relative deprivation, structuralism, Marxism and so on.

In the debates amongst historians and social historians about the relationship of history and social history to the social sciences, it is often presupposed that the naturalistic tradition is the only tradition in the social sciences. But this is far from the case. A competing tradition emerged in the eighteenth century with Giambattista Vico and took root in the nineteenth century, especially in Germany, where it was called the cultural sciences (*Geisteswissenschaften*), a name coined by the German philosopher, Wilhelm Dilthey. Although this competing tradition went out of favour and was overshadowed by the 'positivist' one from about the 1920s to the 1960s, its stocks subsequently rose and is now extraordinarily fashionable. Implacably anti-naturalistic, and sometimes labelled 'anti-naturalism', the competing tradition I am referring to is hermeneutics ('interpretation theory').[8] Within the social sciences, the anti-naturalist movement has affected sociology (where it often goes under the name of interpretive sociology and engendered the sub-discipline of 'ethnomethodology'), but perhaps has had the greatest impact on anthropology (where it gave rise to the sub-discipline of interpretive anthropology, which, as we saw, is the inspiration behind microhistory).[9] Although the social sciences these days generally define 'hermeneutics' as the art of interpreting 'forms of social life' or texts or culture, it was originally coined to describe a movement in biblical scholarship that sought to put back into the scriptures the meanings held by the people of the biblical period. Hermeneutic doctrine has changed considerably over time. Far from being a unitary theory, it currently has a multiplicity of different variants. As we cannot do justice to them all, the summary below is highly generalised and composite account that ignores important differences between the variants. It does, however, lean towards the influential 'rule-following' version chiefly associated with the philosopher Peter Winch, a version derived from the difficult theories of language use advanced in the later works of the famous philosopher, Ludwig Wittgenstein.[10] In consequence, it gives little weight to what is called the 'continental' approach to hermeneutic theory.

The advocates of hermeneutics make several key assumptions about the nature of human society and human beings (ontology). In summary form, these assumptions consist of the following points:

- The most important and distinctive feature about humans is their extraordinary capacity to create concepts in their minds and express them in a multitude of rich and powerful linguistic and non-linguistic symbolic systems. They invent multiple meanings – concepts – not only for words, phrases and gestures but for the natural entities they see around them as well as for their collective rituals, institutions, and all their other social practices such as marriage, eating, wearing clothes, fighting, working, recreation and so on. In the much-quoted phrase of the interpretive anthropologist, Clifford Geertz, 'man is an animal suspended in webs of significance he himself has spun'.

- There is a radical diversity of conceptual systems across human societies. Each society lives in a unique conceptual world of its own making. ('Meaning is local'.)

- Provided the society is small and close-knit, its linguistic and non-linguistic communication systems ensure that most of its concepts are shared by all its members, although individuals can and do have unique concepts about things. ('Meaning is shared', or in the jargon phrase, 'intersubjective'.)

- A society's conceptual world is holistic, a coherent language. The concepts which are associated with a particular symbol are only meaningful in relation to the concepts associated with all the other symbols. The concepts, in other words, are the components of highly integrated conceptual schemas.

- Each society has its own rules governing the usage of all its concepts and enforces these rules on its members. The rules ensure that all its members have the same or very similar understandings of social and natural objects and states of affairs. The rules, in short, bind the members together into a common conceptual community.[11]

Hermeneuticians reject the naturalistic view that social enquiry should be concerned with the scientific explanation and prediction of social behaviour in general. Instead they insist that it should be concerned with the elucidation of the unique systems of concepts and rules specific to each society.

Hermeneuticians justify their approach by claiming in essence that each society is largely *made* ('constituted' is the other favourite word) by the concepts of its members. On first acquaintance, this claim seems very mysterious if not absurd – how possibly can concepts, which originate in the mind, largely 'make' a society?

To understand this claim, we have to appreciate that hermeneuticians see society as being basically composed of four classes of phenomena. Although each is inextricably bound up with all the others, one – the society's language or body of concepts – is fundamental to the existence of the other three. The other three consist of the *actions* of the society's members, the *intentions* of actors, and the *rules* of the society. As I have already briefly described what hermeneuticians mean by the language of concepts,

I will now describe the other three classes, indicating why (according to hermeneuticians) the language of concepts is fundamental to them all ('makes' or 'constitutes' them).

Actions are forms of conduct which are under the control of people or could be.[12] They include writing and talking, establishing and performing institutional roles, forming and acknowledging customs and traditions, creating and performing rituals, initiating and engaging in all sorts of practices such as leisure, work, marriage, religious worship and so on and so forth. Actions exclude the involuntary behaviours that *happen* to and inside our bodies and minds such as birth, death, aging, the circulation of the blood and so forth. Hermeneuticians assert that actions matter much more to the society than the involuntary behaviours (otherwise called 'behaviour').

Hermeneutic theorists maintain that a society's language of concepts is the key to actions because it gives them meaning. A society's language of concepts *defines* the myriads of different sorts of actions which its members undertake. Without concepts, people would not be able to represent, express, identify and classify their actions in their minds. Consequently, they would not know what words, practices, roles, rituals, traditions and customs they were variously executing, expressing, observing, acknowledging, or performing. In short, a society's language of concepts 'makes' actions in the semantic sense. To be sure, the language of concepts does not 'make' actions in a physical sense. But hermeneutic theorists insist that the physical side of actions is far less important than their semantic side. When divorced from its specific conceptual context, an action (linguistic or non-linguistic) has no identity as an action. It will manifest itself as a blurry sort of undifferentiated physical movement. At best its significance would be highly ambiguous (it could any one of a vast number of 'things'). At worst, it would have no significance (an 'unobserved thing' or a 'vaguely observed thing').

To illustrate how crucial concepts are to actions, hermeneutic theorists are fond of citing examples such as that mentioned in Chapter 4: Clifford Geertz's example of the movement of the eye-lid. If we do not know with what intention the person moved his or her eye-lid, we cannot tell if it was a muscular twitch, a wink, a fake wink or a parody of a fake wink – and there is a vast difference between all of these things. Consider, too, the movement of a stroke of a pen: if we do not know what concept was expressed by this movement, we would not know if it betokened the breaking of a promise, the making of a promise, the renunciation of a birthright, an insult to a friend, the obedience to a command, the refusal to obey a command, or the committal of treason and so on. Similarly, unless we knew what idea to attribute to an arm wave, we would find it highly ambiguous: was it a farewell, a goodbye, a fascist salute, an attempt to improve the ventilation, an offensive gesture, a symbol of aggression, a signal for help, a warning, a traffic signal, a toast, a stretching exercise, or what? Finally, there is the example of the movement of someone's vocal chords. Without information about the semantic content of the sounds produced by the movement, there is no way of telling what the actor is doing: screaming, laughing, clearing her throat, coughing up phlegm, coughing with embarrassment, asking a question, disagreeing, speaking our language, speaking a foreign language, and so on.

This brings us to the next class of social phenomena, the *intentions* of actors. In the hermeneutic model of society, all actions are intended. Actions are not caused (involuntary) nor accidental. Instead, actions stem directly from the conscious reasoning of actors. In short, intentions are the considered thoughts – decisions – that lead people to act the way they do. Intentions come from a combination of desires, beliefs, and a capacity for rationality. Desires tell people what needs and wants they have; beliefs tell them how the world works; rationality gives them the capacity to make efficient links between their desires and their beliefs.

Social rules, according to the rule-following versions of hermeneutic theory, are vital to actions and the intentions of actors. Rules are a society's body of conventions, norms, maxims, principles, codes of conduct, its do's and don'ts. They are expressed in proverbs, folklore, myths, formal laws, ceremonies, rituals; most are embodied in 'common sense', unreflective principles about how people can and should find their way in the world. A large number of such rules are fixed to the social roles which individuals perform as parents, producers, consumers, players of games, office-holders, and so on. Hermeneuticians claim that what makes the rules of society so vital is that they *govern the semantic content of actions and intentions*. By specifying and defining the collective meanings of actions and intentions, rules ensure that all members of society have a common understanding of the outward significance of every sort of action, and (with some degree of play) can predict it as well as infer the subjective state, intention, behind it. There are rules stipulating the proper use (grammar) of verbal language; the proper performance of rituals and ceremonies; how gestures should be interpreted and used in which contexts; how every social practice should be performed (work, leisure, marriage, eating, wearing clothes and so forth); how social roles should be performed; how customs and traditions should be acknowledged; how true beliefs should and can be distinguished from the false; how 'good' explanations differ from the 'bad'; what constitutes morally acceptable desires and how these can and should be distinguished from the unacceptable; and so on and so forth. There are rules, for example, about spelling ('i' before 'e' except after 'c'); of good taste; about the use of colloquialisms (New Zealanders refer to one of the parts of their country as 'The South Island' and never as 'South Island'); about the interpretation of traffic lights; about playing games; about how to show respect to one's elders; about how pedestrians should cross the road ('look left, then right, then left, before crossing'); and so on and so forth.

One of the more important points hermeneutic theorists make about rules is that each society has its own rules: rules vary radically from society to society. The point tends to commit hermeneuticians to cultural relativism, a position which is now extraordinarily popular in the humanities and the social sciences. Those taking this position argue that if every society has its own rules governing actions and intentions, then the actions and intentions of every society are as valid as those in all the others, for there is no neutral or independent position (objective rules) from which actions and intentions can be evaluated: we can only evaluate these things according to the rules of the particular society where the actions and intentions are conceived and form its public discourse. Amongst other things, the implications of this position are that there are no universal human rights; that the meaning of 'common sense' is not pan-cultural but specific to each society; that we cannot say that the rules in pre-modern societies governing the study of the natural world are inferior to the rules of scientific method operating in modern societies; that there are no objective criteria for comparatively evaluating conflicting explanations by different conceptual communities about the same things; that there are no universal criteria of human rationality, only culturally-specific ones; and so on.

Hermeneuticians maintain that rules do not have causes. Whereas causes by their nature are unbreakable and unchangeable, rules can be broken and are changeable. Rules thus epitomise the human capacity for agency. Where then do rules come from? According to hermeneuticians, the members of a society themselves define the rules that govern the meanings of their actions. Rules evolve as a result of a continuous interplay between the capacity of each individual to think of new concepts for the observations they make about the world and the collective capacity of society to enforce rules about the usage of concepts. The great emphasis that hermeneuticians give to rules and how they govern the semantic content of actions and intentions, implies that, at least for radical hermeneuticians, the most important (or only) form of social control in a society is through the regulation of concepts.

How does hermeneutic theory explain why individuals follow rules, why most members of a society conform to most rules most of the time? How can they explain rule-conformity satisfactorily when they reject causal explanation? They do so in this manner. They start by referring to their claim that social rules regulate the semantic content of the bulk of each individual's desires and beliefs. They then elaborate the claim by pointing out that in regulating the semantic content of desires and beliefs, social rules in effect tell individuals what range of desires and beliefs it is possible to have, what feelings to attach to these desires and beliefs, and the relative value and importance of each desire and belief. Having made this point, they would ask us: 'do not human motives to act come from a combination of desires and beliefs?' Since we would have to agree with this truism, hermeneuticians would then say that it explains why rule-following is normal to a society: *social rules define the bulk of an individual's beliefs and desires, beliefs and desires motivate individuals to act, therefore when individuals act they generally conform to the social rules*.

Hermeneutic theorists claim that the ways in which a society works (its ontology) requires that it be studied with a particular methodology. The methodology, of course, has nothing to do with the practices and aims of the natural sciences – with objective and systematic observation, causes, predictions, laws. Instead it concerns something we mentioned earlier: the 'internalist' approach, examining a society within the framework of its own concepts.

The key to hermeneutic methodology is 'interpretation'. Conventional historians often think of 'interpretation' as a synonym for a line of argument (point of view) or a plausible conjecture which fills a gap in the empirical evidence. But for hermeneuticians 'interpretation' has a more specialised and special sense. For them, interpretation is the process by which we learn to understand how the people we are studying understand their own actions, desires, beliefs and rules. The goal of interpretation, then, is to achieve empathy with the minds – the conceptual world, the consciousness – of the people belonging to a different culture, to be able 'to read' their thoughts as they would 'read' them. Indeed, anthropologists and sociologists of a hermeneutic persuasion frequently talk about the task of interpreting the conceptual world of another culture as if it were a problematic text, a puzzling novel or poem, they were attempting to decode. Max Weber, the early twentieth-century German sociologist who made a major contribution to interpretative theory, labelled the process of interpretation as *Verstehen*.

In general, hermeneuticians admit that it is difficult for us to get on the same wavelength of the people belonging to another culture. Since the rules governing their concepts are quite different from our rules, we find their ways of thinking incomprehensible when we first encounter them. As a result we will be puzzled by their conduct, see it as irrational, and thus regard it as quaint or childish, and either laugh at it in a superior fashion, feel disturbed by it or become irritated by it. Hermeneuticians, however, insist that we can understand the concepts of another culture, at least to some extent, as long as we go about it in the right way. In their view, the tool that is absolutely crucial for achieving empathy is *thick description*, the term popularised by Clifford Geertz, the interpretive anthropologist.

In essence, thick description is a two-stage process. The first is the research stage. Here the investigator learns the concepts of a society and the rules governing their use by becoming thoroughly familiar with its various languages of symbols. The symbolic languages do not just take verbal form; they also consist of the non-verbal forms of communication such as demeanour, gesture, clothing, food, work, performances in rituals and ceremonies, the enactment of institutional roles and so forth. As one microhistorian, Rhys Isaac, has put it,

> A culture may be thought of as a related set of languages, or as a multi-channelled system of communication. Consisting of more than just words, it also comprises gesture, demeanour, dress, architecture, and all the codes by which those who share in the culture convey meanings and significance to each other.[13]

In other words, the symbolic languages expressing the society's language of concepts are its repertoire of actions. Just as concepts 'make' (constitute) actions; so actions symbolise concepts. To learn the rules of concept usage, the investigator must participate for long periods directly or indirectly in the culture being studied. The anthropological investigator, for example, will engage in extensive periods of field-work, living with the locals, closely observing at first hand the ways in which they use their symbols. The investigator will also handle these symbols so as to test predictions about their meaning and about the rules governing the meanings. The process is very similar to the manner in which conventional historians 'immerse' themselves in the documents so as to learn the meanings behind the idioms of the political and religious language of another era.

As a thick description requires a microscopic study of all the symbols of a society, it cannot readily be applied to a large population since the latter is likely to be culturally diverse, containing an exceedingly large repertoire of actions or even a multitude of different repertoires. Hence a thick description generally concentrates on a tiny, relatively isolated, group of people such as a village or a tribe. Not surprisingly, most of the research techniques of thick description have been developed by anthropologists since one of their traditional preoccupations has been to understand such groups from the inside.

With the second stage of thick description, the investigator writes up an account of the society. The object of the account is not to describe or explain the actions, desires, beliefs, rules and conceptual language of a society from an externalist perspective, that is, by referring to one or more of the generalising theories in the naturalist tradition of the social sciences (Marxism, relative deprivation, structuralism, functionalism and what have you).

Instead the aim of the account is to present the actions, desires, beliefs, rules and concepts both as the society understands them *and* in a form which would be intelligible to an audience from the investigator's own background who are unfamiliar with them ('making the strange familiar'). The second stage of a thick description, thus, is essentially a *translation exercise*: its goal is to translate the conceptual world of another society into terms which make sense to the members of the translator's audience but which accurately reflect their original meanings. To put this another way, the account has to be comprehensible to two cultures who otherwise find each other's ways of thinking mutually incomprehensible.

Producing good translations of conceptual worlds is a very tricky business because many concepts in one culture have no equivalents in another. Translators frequently have to strike a balance between intelligibility and accuracy; they have to be most careful not to veer too far towards one side in case they neglect the other. Many hermeneutic theorists say that accuracy is much more difficult to achieve than intelligibility; there is even a strong school of thought that denies that accuracy is possible. As a consequence, hermeneutic social theorists have tended to neglect the development of procedures to deal with the accuracy problem and have concentrated on developing intelligibility devices.

One intelligibility device is to tell a story about an action or a series of actions, organising and selecting the events according to a rule which is part of the culture of the audience. Another method for creating intelligibility is to break the story at suitable points and explicate the rules which the actors were complying with at those points. Alternatively, we can translate the concepts of the actors into terms which are the nearest in meaning to the concepts of the audience. A further option is to insinuate into the story revealing anecdotes about the actors' beliefs and desires, implying how these constrained and influenced their actions. Perhaps the most common translation technique, however, is to suggest to the audience how certain of their own experiences are analogous to those of the actors.

Thick descriptions of societies are frequently known as 'internalist accounts'. Other names include 'the insider's model', 'indigenous models', 'the insider's point of view', 'the native's model'; 'looking at things through the participant's eye', 'emic accounts' (after the term 'phonemic' used in linguistics), 'empathetic accounts', 'mechanical' or 'ideal' models (phrases coined by the famous structuralist French anthropologist, Claude Lévi-Strauss), 'conscious models', and 'contextual interpretation' (the name coined by Ernest Gellner, the philosopher and anthropologist). Such names capture nicely the objective of a thick description: to see the society as those belonging to it conceive it, *to describe and explain it (as far as possible) according to their rules of how it should be described and explained, or at least according to rules which are compatible with its rules.*[14]

Given that hermeneuticians claim that we should only examine a society in relation to its own rules, how would a hermeneutic social investigator account for social phenomena? Heremeneutic models of social phenomena can be divided into two different types, those which I will term 'governed by a society's cultural rules' and those which I will term 'governed by a society's principles of rationality'. Very often these two types of models are not separated, but I think it makes for clearer discussion if we do.

In the first type are accounts of specific actions by specific actors. The account would start with an intentional explanation of the action. Hence, it would attempt to demonstrate that the actor's decision to follow a certain course of action was reasonable *within the bounds of the actor's desired aims and the actor's beliefs about how the world works*. The account, in other words, would initially try to reconstruct what Popper calls the 'subjective logic of the actor's situation', or what W.H. Dray calls the 'rationale of action' (though note that Popper and Dray do not go past this stage).

In the next stage, the hermeneutician would elucidate the decision taken by the actor by putting it in its broader cultural context, or to be precise, by seeing what cultural rules informed the decision. Hermeneutic social theorists assume that these rules are implicit in the institutional roles and in the common-sense maxims of the culture to which the actor belongs. Social customs and conventions prescribe the performance of institutional roles, and roles govern the reasons for acting since roles carry rewards and sanctions as well as expectations – beliefs – about the outcomes of their performance. Hence, if the actor was in a situation where he or she was acting out a prescribed role (as parent, priest, employee, etc.), the investigator would explicate the action taken by describing the norms of conduct prescribed by custom and convention. In addition, the investigator might examine the society's body of common-sense maxims to see if any of these make the actions explicable. A society's broad common-sense maxims are variously expressed in its proverbs, myths, ideology, folk lore, practical wisdom, its rules of thumb. They consist of such generalisations as 'it is better to save for the future rather than spend now', 'it is more important for children to help their parents rather than help themselves', 'water will be found near the Adobe tree', 'better the devil you know rather than the devil you don't', 'a good Christian has faith, hope and charity', 'generosity confers more status than accumulating possessions'. A society's common-sense maxims, thus, are ground rules that give its members some general guidance about they should make their way in the world. They tell its members what emotions are pleasurable, what desires are appropriate, what values should be pursued, what causal properties to attribute to which natural and social entities. To understand the specific reasons that animated the actor to act in a particular situation, the investigator thus would see how they were conditioned by the corpus of ground rules, the framework of common-sense maxims, which the actor had been taught by the society.

The second type of rule-based account refers to a society's principles of rationality. Such an account deals with all phenomena that are unrelated to actions motivated by instrumental reasoning, namely, particular events in the natural world, particular outcomes of actions that were not intended and expected by actors (**unintended consequences**), and particular actions motivated by what is called **expressive rationality**. To grasp the society's interpretation of particular natural events and unintended outcomes, the investigator will relate them to its general belief structure (as expressed, say, in religious actions and the recounting of oral traditions), and show how this general belief structure, although irrational or incomprehensible in our terms, is entirely rational and comprehensible for the actors given their cognitive conventions, their prescriptions about the appropriate ways of observing the world, their criteria about what distinguishes false from true beliefs. The hermeneutic investigator will never presume, it should be added, that the actors' general belief structure, and the cognitive conventions underlying it, are inferior to ours; as far as hermeneutic social theorists are concerned, the actors' system of rationality is not inferior to ours, it is just different. As each society has its own rules governing the appropriateness of any given practice, including the epistemological practice of determining how the world should be known and what comprises proper beliefs, therefore there is no objective, pan-cultural, transhistorical, ground for contending that the evidential rules which govern modern science are superior to the epistemological rules of another culture

Some hermeneuticians go even further than this when explicating actions motivated by expressive reasoning. Such actions are not undertaken for some end, but for their own sake, for moral or spiritual or aesthetic purposes, or as a way by which the actors can communicate a shared view of life. Hermeneuticians claim that such actions occur in societies that are based on a principle of rationality that is quite alien to ours. An action such as a chant uttered when the seeds are sown or a rain-dance is not performed as a means toward an end (in the expectation that it will bestow control over some aspect of the world) but for its own intrinsic value. Expressive actions are usually associated with complex rituals and elaborate myths. To explain why a group is attached to them, the investigator will unpack the meaning of the symbols to the actors and try to discover what it is about the symbols that endows them with their resonance and emotional power.

Before we assess the hermeneutic claim that all accounts should be internalist, a few points need to be clarified and emphasised. The first is that although a thick description would concern itself with capturing the actors' conceptual world, it would not do this by postulating that the intentions were unconsciously either driven by certain causal mechanisms or constrained by certain causal structures. Hermeneutic theorists reject the validity of causal explanations and externalist models, as we have noted. Certainly, one strand in modern hermeneutics has attempted to reconstruct the unconscious psychological states of actors by using Freudian theory, but this is a minority strand which has tried to maintain that unconscious desires and beliefs in the Freudian sense are intended not caused.

Another point which needs to be clarified is that although hermeneutic theory and various post-modern doctrines have many things in common, the mainstream of hermeneutics diverges in key respects from hardcore post-modernism. Hermeneuticians assume that the societies they study exist independently of our thoughts and verbal language; hardcore post-modernists deny that anything is independent of our language-determined thoughts. Hermeneuticians contend that meaning is governed by the rules of a conceptual community; post-modernists (especially the followers of Derrida) go one step further. They say that there are no conceptual communities and no social rules governing concept usage, that in consequence every individual makes up his or her own rules, and that therefore meanings are neither shared nor stable.

The last point which should be emphasised is that this summary masks the key differences between the various strands of hermeneutics and is heavily slanted towards the rule-following strand. It has also deliberately excluded the views of a not insubstantial group of hermeneutic theorists who embrace a form of relativism called the **hermeneutic circle**. By this they mean that we are never able to step outside our own conceptual communities (at least, not completely) when we attempt to understand other societies: our understanding of 'them' inevitably contains projections of ourselves. Extreme forms of the 'hermeneutic circle' position, which I think are wrong, were discussed in the Introduction (pp. 5–7).

■ Externalist versus internalist models

So far we have seen that hermeneutic social theory makes the following claims:

1. The central, or only goal, of social enquiry is to understand the conceptual languages of another society by interpreting its languages of symbols as expressed in actions and practices;

2. To achieve this goal, it is essential to pursue a particular methodological strategy, one that examines another society within the framework of its own concepts and rules of concept usage, or at least one that employs concepts and rules of concept usage that are compatible with the society's;

3. Two procedures, one positive, the other negative, are required to carry out the strategy: (a) the positive procedure consists of cultural immersion, of learning how to think like

a native, of acquiring a knowledge of the society's 'internal model', by closely observing the society's activities at first hand and (where possible) participating in them; (b) the negative procedure consists of preventing the concepts in 'external models', the ideologies and theories which the investigator has picked up from his or her own society, from distorting and contaminating the investigator's understanding of the concepts in the internal model.

With this in mind, I will return to the question with which this chapter started. How far should social historians go in avoiding concept-presentism? Should the avoidance of concept-presentism be an absolute principle, or are there conditions under which its application is unnecessary and undesirable, or should it be abandoned altogether?

To initiate the discussion of these matters, let us make the assumption that the principle should be absolute – that concept-presentism must be avoided at all costs – and examine its main implications for how we would investigate the past. There are three such implications.

The first and most obvious implication is that our investigations, as a matter of logic and inclination, would be dominated by hermeneutic concerns. We would become hermeneuticians in spirit though not necessarily to the letter. Our objectives for studying the past would change, converge closely on the goal of the hermeneuticians, namely, to understand the conceptual languages of other societies (point 1 in the generalised summary above). Moreover, since our objectives would shift so strongly in the hermeneutic direction, so would our methodology. As hermeneuticians have developed by far the most effective, systematic and sophisticated methodology to understand the conceptual languages of other societies, we would have every reason to adopt it. Thus our methodology would become heavily dependent on the methodological strategy of the hermeneuticians and the two procedures (points 2 and 3 above). Perhaps the adoption would not be complete. History, after all, has its own conventions. Moreover, we cannot, in contrast to hermeneutically-oriented anthropologists, learn a society's conceptual language by directly participating in its activities. Even so, we would become so dependent on hermeneutic methodology that it would override all or most of

our other methodological orientations. In short, the first implication of our assumption that concept-presentism must be avoided
at all costs, is that social history would look very much like the
summary of hermeneutics itemised above: 1, 2 and 3.

The next implication, which flows from the first, is that our
accounts would be much freer of concept-presentism. We would
undoubtedly be far less inclined to misrepresent past actors, to
attribute false meanings to their actions and intentions, to impose
alien general theories on the past which wrenched things out of
their proper context, and to misconstrue the beliefs and values of
actors. There would be many other benefits, too. These I will spell
out towards the end of this section. In short, by adopting hermeneutic goals and methods, we would be more able to abide by the
long-standing convention of historical scholarship of 'examining
the past in its own terms'.

The third implication follows from the first and second. By
seeking at all costs to avoid concept-presentism, we would virtually become card-carrying hermeneuticians; but though the adoption of hermeneutics has many benefits to social historians, it
would also exact a heavy price. To put this in a more homely way,
by sleeping with the hermeneuticians rather than the presentists,
social historians would avoid being infected by concept-presentism, but in so doing they would become impregnated with serious
hermeneutic problems. What are these problems? There are
many such problems: we will confine ourselves to four groups of
them.

▌ Problematic aspects of hermeneutic ontology

1. *Hermeneutic ontology unwarrantably excludes a large range of
phenomena that is social or that affects social relations.* The excluded
phenomena consist of anything which is unrelated to the hermeneutic notions of symbols, actions, intentions, concepts and rules.
As a consequence, if we took the hermeneutic turn, we would not
be able to refer to impulsive behaviour, habitual behaviour, and
instrumental actions by otherwise rational people that were not
motivated by good reasons. Moreover, we would be prevented

from investigating entities and processes which were inconceivable to the society even though they affected it.

Key examples are microbes and long-term climatic changes. These phenomena had major influences on the demographic and ecological histories of pre-modern societies; the societies may even have vaguely noted their effects and presence; but as the phenomena were discovered by modern science, which has a radically different cognitive structure from that of pre-modern societies, we could not talk about them. Another example is that of 'latent functions', a term devised by the sociologist, R.K. Merton. These functions are a special kind of cause. They consist of social traits which, unbeknown to social actors, sustain other social traits. Explanations based on latent functions have been grossly misused and are now in disrepute; but recent work by analytic philosophers has demonstrated their validity under certain conditions. A more tricky and contentious example is the exploitation of the subordinate classes by the property-owning classes, a process of surplus extraction which Marxists claim is systemic to most societies. A hermeneutician would say (a point echoed by many historians) that we could not refer to exploitation in societies which, because they were dominated by ideologies such as paternalism, found the whole concept of exploitation an alien one. Presumably, too, a hermeneutically informed study of history would have to leave out any aspect of an actor's past if the actor was unaware of it even if it played a key role in the formation of the actor's personality, or any aspect of a society's past if the society had forgotten about it, or contextualise an event in any way that was beyond the 'local knowledge' of the people involved in the event. Hermeneutic ontology, in short, would impose severe (and unjustifiable) restrictions on the things we often want to study in social history if we adopted it in an all-out war against concept-presentism.

2. *The hermeneutic argument against the study of causal regularities is grossly overstated.* The key premise it is grounded on is that 'meaning is local', that actions cannot be compared across cultural boundaries because each conceptual community defines an action in a unique fashion. Certainly, hermeneuticians do have a point. As we noted in Chapter 6, cliometricians and the builders of general explanatory models have all too often lumped together pieces of social conduct that outwardly look the same but are radically different as far as the insiders are concerned. Even so, there is no

evidence that every action is culturally specific, certainly not radically so. This is a matter which can only be decided on a case by
case basis. The meanings of some actions may well be culturally
specific, perhaps fundamentally; but others may not be. Modern-
ising and modern societies are tightly integrated into international
and national systems of trade and communications which have
destroyed or corroded local concepts, and created new concepts
which have a national and international currency. The conceptual
language of a pre-modern society, furthermore, may overlap with
that of other pre-modern societies if they possessed comparable
ecologies or had common origins, or regularly exchanged goods
and peoples, or had been exposed to the same outside influences.
For example, most parts of Melanesia and Polynesia have the
same rules governing cross-cousin marriage. Many parts of early
modern western Europe seem to have attributed similar meanings to a considerable range of folk lore.[15] In short, the hermeneutic objection to causation is grossly overstated, and social
historians would deprive themselves completely of this crucial
tool if they embraced hermeneutics in a total war against concept-
presentism.

3. *The claim by hermeneuticians, that the symbolic side of an action is far
more important than the physical, is another exaggeration.* To support
this claim, hermeneuticians are fond of citing examples such as
eye-lid movements, arm-waves, and pen-strokes. With each of
these, they point out that the social impact of the action depends
not on its physical side but its symbolic side – the meanings that a
conceptual community attributes to it. The physical side is 'mere
behaviour'. Thus the physical movement of an eyelid does not by
itself have any impact on social life. It will only have an impact if
people attach significance to it and thus respond to it, and they
will only do that if they belong to a conceptual community that has
a rule that eye-lid movements are symbols and other rules that
indicate how the symbols are to be interpreted. In short, hermeneuticians assume that the power of an action, its social
consequences, depends on its symbolic-conceptual side, not its
physical nor its institutional.

Symbols and the concepts they represent are certainly a vital
and powerful aspect of an action. But the physical side of the
action can exercise a great deal of power as well, depending on
the strength and complexity of its causal links with the natural

world and institutions. With an action involving an eye-lid move-ment, the physical side has very weak and simple causal links to the natural world and institutions. Hence its physical side has a minimal impact on social life compared with the symbolic side. Many actions, however, have strong and complex causal links with the natural and institutional environment. In these instan-ces, the physical side makes all the difference to the outcome – the social impact – of the actions. Take the example of the issuing of orders. Would the impact of the actions of two generals be the same just because their orders to attack on all fronts were seen by their respective conceptual communities as having the same intentions? Surely that depends entirely on the physical and insti-tutional circumstances surrounding the actions in question: a command to attack given to a badly equipped rabble would have a very different impact than a command to attack given to a well equipped and highly disciplined unit. Another example is the action of spreading fertilizer over the land. According to some hermeneuticians, if two such actions occurred in different places within the jurisdiction of the same conceptual community, and that community regarded the two actions as the same, then they would have the same social impact. Again, surely, that depends on the institutional and physical circumstances of the actions in ques-tion. The effect of the two actions on crop yields and local eco-nomies would be quite different if the two areas of land had dissimilar weather patterns and soil types, or in one place the fer-tilizer was of the wrong sort, or in the other place it was applied at the wrong time and so forth. Of course, these are extreme exam-ples. It could be argued that a conceptual community would be highly unlikely to define two such actions of spreading fertilizer as the same; it would distinguish them, define them in different ways, taking into account the physical and institutional circum-stances. But that is precisely what hermeneuticians will not admit. Hermeneuticians refuse to believe that the world can influence concepts, that concepts are frequently modified when they fail to correspond to the world. As far as hermeneuticians are con-cerned, a society's conceptual language is 'self-constituting', gov-erned only by social rules which are themselves concepts. Hermeneuticians insist that conceptual language exists inde-pendently of the world and is uninfluenced by human encounters with the world.

4. *Given that hermeneuticians understate the importance of the physical side of actions, they are unable to allow for the effect that physical and institutional circumstances may have in determining the range of actions available to actors.* In some instances, of course, the physical and institutional context has little or no effect on the range of available actions. The physical side of the action can be performed virtually anywhere across time and space. Eye-lid motions can be done as readily in 30,000 BC as in modern Manhattan. But the performance of other sorts of actions is much more constrained. The actor's capacity to perform them is highly sensitive to structural conditions, including the society's overall level of technological development, the ecological setting of the action, the economic resources of the actor, the political power of the actor, demographic circumstances and so on. For instance, the range of actions open to a person who wanted a meal in 30,000 BC would have been radically different from that of a Wall Street stock broker in 1990. The range of actions available to an early nineteenth-century white male American who wanted to engage in such practices as litigation, performing a financial transaction, setting up a household, and engaging in recreation would have been far different from that available to a plantation slave. Similarly, the range of actions available to an unmarried mother in an English workhouse in 1900 who wanted to educate her child would have been more restricted than those available to a married woman belonging to the middle classes.

Let me now come to the point: how does all this affect social historians? The point is this. If social historians embraced hermeneutics in an all-out drive to rid their discipline of concept-presentism, they would end up with the same problem as hermeneuticians: they would not be able to talk about the structural factors that constrain the range of actions available to actors. Social history would be all the poorer as a consequence. It would not be able to discuss the institutional and environmental circumstances that to a large extent explain why the range of choices open to certain types of actors changes over time, varies between social categories, and differs between societies. Actors certainly have agency but their range of choices is seldom completely open. As Marx said in his famous *The Eighteenth Brumaire of Louis Napoleon*, 'Men make their own history, but they do not make it just as they please.'

5. *The exaggerated importance that hermeneuticians give to symbols and concepts creates a problem with the hermeneutic theory of social control.* According to hermeneuticians, social control is achieved by the regulation of concepts and symbols. The rules of concept-usage maintain and generate order and stability by 'constituting' (delimiting and organising) the beliefs and desires of the members of a society. In the radical version of this, the dominant elements in society exercise power over the subordinate by manipulating the semantic content of words, ceremonies, rituals and so forth. Research work on this sort of thing has become very fashionable, and the results have often been interesting. The hermeneutic view of social control, however, is far too restricted. It excludes all the other sources of social control – economic influence, legal sanctions, force of arms, informal sanctions such as social ostracism and so on. Hence, if social history took a major hermeneutic turn, in order to eradicate the problem of concept-presentism, it would acquire a useful tool for analysing power in a society but it would lose many others.[16]

6. *The hermeneutic emphasis on understanding societies exclusively in relation to their own rules, obliges its investigators to accept the validity of the collective beliefs of those societies.* The position that hermeneuticians hold here is a variant of cultural relativism called cognitive relativism (otherwise known as epistemological or belief relativism). According to this position, one culture's beliefs about the world are equal to another's, for there are no independent, universally valid, criteria by which its belief system can be evaluated from the outside. Every attempt to claim that there are such criteria, is based on local beliefs about what comprises valid criteria. If I insist that my society's standards (rules) for evaluating another society's beliefs are valid, I am arbitrarily taking my society's standards and imposing them on another culture which does not share them.

Cognitive relativism gives rise to serious problems, and social history would, I think, be seriously undermined if it completely adopted the hermeneutic methodology that gives rise to cognitive relativism. To demonstrate the point, let us start with a very interesting phenomenon we briefly discussed earlier, the 'unintended consequences of actions'.

As the name suggests, the unintended consequences of an action are those which the actor did not expect and intend. Certainly, many actions of actors completely succeed in achieving their expected and intended goals, nothing more and nothing less. Where this occurs, we can infer that the actors' beliefs about their respective situations were correct, at least in crucial respects, and thus we can readily explain the actions in question by reconstructing the beliefs of the actors. But many actions do have unintended consequences and these cannot be explained by reconstructing the beliefs of the actors since these beliefs must have been false.

Now, according to the argument from cultural relativism, there is only one permissible method for explaining why unintended consequences occur, and that is to do in Rome as the Romans do: to account for unintended consequences as the locals would. Thus, to determine why certain actions had unintended consequences, we have to see how the society (or the actors) retrospectively explained why they happened. The procedure commits us to draw our explanations from the society's stock of beliefs. To be sure, it is possible that an actor was an eccentric and had beliefs about the original situation, or about the unintended consequences of the action, that deviated from the prevailing beliefs that the society had about the situation (or the class of situations it belonged to). However, though this is possible, hermeneuticians are bound to say that it would be unusual given that rule-following by individuals, including their adherence to the dominant beliefs, is crucial to social control and therefore is the norm.

One problem with this procedure is that a society's stock of beliefs will not always contain a story which accounts for the unintended consequences we are trying to explain. Nor will a society's beliefs always be clear and unambiguous – even to its members. In addition, people frequently behave in a manner which diverges from or contradicts their society's ideology. Moreover, what do we do if we want to explain unintended consequences flowing from situations in multicultural societies or complex societies which have many sub-cultures? The society might have several competing stories about what produced the unintended consequences, say, one story told by Catholics and one by Protestants or one by the government and one told by the revolutionary movement – whose version do we chose and why and according to whose rules? To make matters even more hideously complicated, the story may change over time as the cognitive structure or ideology of the society changes. For example, which of the official versions

– 'the internalist accounts' – that have occurred since 1917 do we take to explain the Bolshevik revolution? Of course, the presence in a society of competing stories – myths, traditions – could stimulate subordinate categories to action and therefore could explain a whole series of other historical events. Treating history in this fashion is now widely practised by radical historians, particularly cultural Marxists. Indeed E.P. Thompson and Eugene Genovese pioneered the approach with great skill. But this brings us full circle. Though the approach might successfully explain the rebellious actions by minority and dissident groups, it cannot of itself account for the unintended and unexpected outcomes of such actions.

Perhaps the worst problem with the cognitive relativism that underpins hermeneutics, is that it commits investigators to accept a society's explanations uncritically even when they are patently false or consist of blatant propaganda. Furthermore, since hermeneutics rejects the naturalist tradition in the social sciences we would not be able to provide better explanations. Thus when studying ill-fortune in seventeenth-century Massachusetts we would have to accept the contemporary belief that it was caused by witchcraft; or if studying gender relations in nineteenth century Victorian England we would have to accept the idea in the dominant ideology that women were biologically inferior to men; or if examining slavery in the American south we could not reject the dominant view that it was essential for the welfare of racially inferior blacks; or if studying the purges in Russia in the 1930s we would uncritically accept the official view that they were needed because of internal subversion against the State; or if examining Hitler's Germany, we would follow the official line that Germany's defeat in 1918 was caused by an International Jewish conspiracy; and so forth.

To this point, we have looked at the implications that flow from taking the avoidance of concept-presentism as an absolute principle. We have seen that an absolute avoidance policy would lead us to embrace hermeneutics, and that hermeneutics would be of immeasurable assistance in solving the problem. We also saw, however, that our embrace of hermeneutics would create other sorts of major problems (unintended consequences!).

How, then, do we avoid concept-presentism without inflicting the problems of hermeneutics upon ourselves? In the next and concluding section, I will sketch out a strategy for solving the dilemma. The strategy involves a modified hermeneutics and it implies that we accept concept-presentism under certain strict conditions.

■ Conclusion: a suggested strategy

A hermeneutic approach to our examination of past social life is an essential preliminary to all studies of the social past, irrespective of the questions we are asking or the mode we are operating in. By preliminary, I mean the stage where we are engaging in primary research on a topic, collecting information. At this stage we should make every effort to understand the concepts of a society (or a subsection of it) in the same way as it understood them itself. In effect, our goals at this stage should be those of 'thick description': to learn the intended meanings that lie behind the categories employed in our sources and to learn how to translate these meanings as accurately as possible into our concepts.

There are several reasons why hermeneutics is vital at this stage. In the first place, it has humanistic value – it allows us to converse, at least to some extent, with the people of the past. In the second place, it is inherently interesting. In addition, the data generated by the hermeneutic stage may provide a good test of the veracity of a general theory. Moreover, practitioners like Carlo Ginzburg have maintained that the tiny details discovered by microhistorians may suggest fertile hypotheses that general theories may not provide.[17] Perhaps, however, the most important reason for adopting hermeneutics at this stage is the methodological one – it is fundamental to the generation of reliable data for historical arguments and explanations. *Unless we have an accurate knowledge of the meanings of the categories in the sources, our accounts are based on unreliable data. Thus if we crucially misinterpret the categories in the sources, and then treat the observations embodying the categories either as evidence for our claims, or as phenomena we want to explain, we end up respectively with bad evidence for our claims and explaining the wrong phenomena.*

A hermeneutic approach is also vital to accounts based on the intentional explanatory mode of enquiry or to those parts of them that employ intentional explanations. As these accounts attempt to understand the conscious reasons that led an actor to act in a particular situation, they need to explicate these reasons by putting them in the context of cultural rules, the rules inherent in the cultural norms prescribed for the institutional role the actor was playing, and in the cultural code of common sense maxims. The relevant cultural rules could, of course, either be those of the actor's wider society or those of a certain sub-culture to which the actor belonged. There is nothing novel about this approach. Political historians have long had a practice of attempting to understand the decisions of political actors by 'putting these in their own context' – which essentially has come down to seeing how these were shaped by the norms of political life, by the roles that were prescribed for the actor and the other decision-makers involved in the actions, and by the actor's interpretations of past political events.

However, there are limits to a hermeneutic approach in social history. An 'insider's view' cannot easily, if at all, account for the unconscious structures that constrain the range of options available to the actor in any given situation. It is also a highly unreliable way for explaining actions that were motivated by bad reasons; the unintended outcomes of actions; the forces in the natural world that affected the society and that it was aware of; those which the society may have vaguely felt but had no concepts for (such as microbes and long-term climatic change in pre-modern societies); human events and states of affairs which impinged on the society and of which it had no knowledge; spontaneous behaviour; and 'latent functions'. Under all these circumstances – but only under these conditions – it is perfectly legitimate to use our concepts embodied in our theories to describe and explain the society. For one thing, we usually have more information about these things than the insiders did since we have had more opportunity than they to observe more cases and to use these to test causal claims about similar kinds of events, states of affairs and unintended consequences. For another, our principles of rationality, being based on modern science, are usually more advanced than the insiders'. They generally stood on the other side of the 'great ditch' – Ernest Gellner's term for the scientific revolution – whereas we more often stand on this side.

In short, the strategy I am suggesting for dealing with the problem of concept-presentism rests on the recognition that neither the hermeneutic tradition nor the naturalist one is by itself adequate for social history. The hermeneutic preoccupation with recovering the original meanings of the society is a powerful antidote to the ethnocentric tendencies of historians. But it is not designed to deal with entities, events, states of affairs and structures that affect societies and that they cannot either conceive or adequately explain. The naturalist tradition is more able to deal with these things. But it is not equipped to put a society's concepts in their own context. The strategy is able to make the best of both traditions by subjecting all our sources of evidence to a preliminary hermeneutic treatment, and then examining phenomena according to the tradition they properly belong to.

■ *Chapter 9* ■

The Problem of Determining the Best Explanation

The problem of how to determine the best explanation is the final standard problem with which we will deal. The problem is obviously not general to all modes of social history, but specific to the explanatory modes, whether they be the causal, the intentional, the statistical or some combination of the three. The problem occurs when several competing explanatory theories are advanced for the *same* phenomena and we want to know which theory is the 'best'; that is, which one provides the best *explanans* for the *explananda* in question.

It is almost inevitable that any given set of phenomena will attract competing explanations. Social history indeed is filled with an extraordinary variety of debates over *why* things happen, large and small things, particular events as well as classes of events – revolutions, social movements, class formation, the rise of certain occupations, the growth of towns, the adherence to certain beliefs, changes in vertical social mobility patterns, changes in family size, deviance, the everyday actions of tiny groups, immigration, wars, shifts in sensibility and attitudes, to mention but a few phenomena. Amongst the causes of competing explanations are the theoretical pluralism of the historical discipline and the social sciences; the establishment of new research programmes (such as the *Annales* school); the chance entry into the profession of really talented individuals who develop radically new approaches; the strong tradition of debate in history; the largely pre-paradigmatic character of social history itself; the sharp differences in the backgrounds and experiences of individual researchers; the conflicting reports in the primary sources about the phenomena; the vagaries of intellectual fashion; and the competition within the profession for status and research grants.

A question which might be raised about the objective of determining the best explanation is whether it is necessary or desirable.
Why should we sort out which of several competing explanations
is the 'best' one? Are there not other, perhaps less tiresome or
more fruitful, ways of treating rival explanations? Let us consider
five possible alternatives.

The first alternative to determining the 'best' explanation is to
aim higher – to find the *right* ('true') explanation. Determining
the best explanation, it might be contended, is too limited; it
settles for too little: we compromise the search for truth by wanting
only the best explanation since the best explanation in any given
case might be the best of a very bad bunch and could be quite
remote from the truth, indeed it could be patently false. The
answer to this point is to say that it asks for far too much. It is nearly
always impossible in history to produce a 'true' explanation in the
sense that it comprehensively corresponds to the facts (a notion of
truth called the correspondence theory of truth). What makes it
impossible, amongst other things, is that in history our sources of
evidence are generally scanty and unreliable; unlike many of the
natural sciences we cannot replicate the experiences of our subjects under laboratory conditions; and unlike the social sciences
we cannot generate systematic data by organizing surveys. A
much more realistic objective is to determine the best explanation. If we sought only true explanations and treated all that were
untrue as equally unacceptable we would not make any advances
in our knowledge. The advantage of seeking the best explanation
is that it allows us to advance our knowledge; as slight as these
advances generally are, surely they are preferable to making no
advances at all. This does not mean that we should accept each
best explanation as true or ignore its problems. On the contrary.
We should take serious note of its problems, and strive to produce
a better explanation, a process of knowledge growth which Karl
Popper calls verisimilitude.[1] I shall have somewhat more to say
about this process in the next section.

The second possible alternative to determining the best explanation – and one which some people might think is a more positive approach – is to take all the rival explanations and synthesise
them. For example, if we had three competing explanations of the
phenomena, we could take certain parts from this one, take other
parts from that, and some parts from the third, and integrate all

these different parts into a new explanation. Now, it would be perfectly possible to synthesise the different parts of rival explanatory theories, provided of course that the theories were not radically incompatible and provided that the end-result was coherent (we do not want to end up grafting the head of an elephant onto the body of a mouse). In fact, social historians often attempt to create syntheses from opposing views when they discuss the historiography of a debate about the 'causes' of given phenomena. However, the synthesising option does not avoid the problem of making choices. If we want to synthesise competing explanations, how do we select which parts we should take from each? Presumably, we would match the theories part for part and take the *best* part from each matching set. There would be no point in taking a part from one if it was inferior to the corresponding parts of the competing theories. Synthesising rival theories, hence, merely shifts the problem of choosing the best theory to another level: from the theories considered as wholes to their respective component parts. Regardless, furthermore, of how we produce a synthesis from all the competitors, it would be very odd if we did not hope or expect it to be 'better' in some sense or another than all the theories we were synthesising. In other words, the synthesis alternative does not spare us from determining the best theory.

A third possible alternative is to take a historiographical approach. Instead, that is, of looking at each set of candidate theories and determining the best one, we could investigate the contexts of their historical production – the institutional pressures, the political experiences, the economic interests, and the ideologies that determined the content of each. There is a kindred approach in the philosophy of science, known as the sociology of knowledge, which is used to explain the content of scientific theories and their history. It is usually defended on the ground that cognitive changes do not come about through rational decision-making but through all manner of irrational factors. The objections to it are many, and we do not need to go into them here except to say that it conflates two things: the 'context of discovery' and the 'context of justification'. Investigating the context of discovery tells how new theories arise; but it cannot tell us how good each theory is – that is the domain of the context of justification. To illustrate the point let us suppose that Smith produces a sociological explanation about what caused James Cook to chart the New Zealand coast accurately but finds that Brown has already produced a different and incompatible explanation. Examining the context of discovery of both theories will not help Smith one jot to decide whether his theory has more going for it than Brown's; he can only solve the problem by examining both theories in the context of justification. In other words, the appropriate place for the sociology of knowledge is in the context of discovery; it has no place in the context of justification. And the same applies to a historiographical approach. The historiographical approach allows us to work out the lineage of rival explanations and the influences upon their history. But it will not enable us, at least directly, to work out if one explanatory account is variously more convincing, supported with better evidence, contains more internal contradictions, is argued more rigorously, is more scholarly, or has more truth than competing explanatory accounts. These are the sorts of questions that only a comparative evaluation can answer.

A fourth possible alternative to choosing the best theory and attempting to justify the choice, is to glorify in the pluralism; that is, celebrate the fact that there are different explanations and let them proliferate, indeed encourage their proliferation: *vive la différence!* However, this advice will be of no help to us where we find ourselves in research situations that *do* require us to determine the best explanation. What do we do, for example, when we are researching the causes of a certain event, and find that the documents suggest a hypothesis which differs substantially from the explanation offered by a standard work in the field? Or what do we do if we do not know how to explain a pattern in the data, we go to the works in related fields to see if they can solve our problem, and we find although some look promising they are mutually incompatible? Or what do we do if we are attempting to find the causes of a certain mass phenomenon and we discover that contemporary observers and commentators provide sharply contrasting explanations of it?

The fifth alternative to choosing the best theory, is to adopt what I shall label 'the agnostic position'. Characteristically, those who adopt the agnostic position acknowledge the existence of rival explanations, describe them, and may criticise them; but then state that there is no way of making a preference. Now, *in many specific instances*, agnosticism can be a perfectly reasonable position to take. Thus, we would be quite entitled not to make a choice between a particular set of rival theories if we could demonstrate convincingly that all the theories in question were equally poor (or equally good) in relation to an explicit and defensible set of criteria. Similarly, it would be eminently reasonable not to make a choice if we found that we needed vital information to make an informed choice and we did not have access to the sources of such information. But there is another form of agnosticism which is quite different in type. Its adherents object as a matter of principle to determining the best theory; they say that in every instance a choice should or can never be made. According to their view, all ideas are equal since there are no objective – universally accepted – standards by which ideas can be comparatively evaluated. The view is grounded on cognitive relativism, which as I suggested in earlier chapters, is untenable. It is self-refuting. Its logical endpoint is an indiscriminate scepticism or credulousness; it implies that patently absurd beliefs are as valid or as invalid as those which are not absurd. Moreover, I cannot see how it can be held with any consistency. In everyday life, especially when making decisions, we do not usually act as if all beliefs and sources of information are equally valid (or invalid); and I do not see why we should do so when we encounter rival historical explanations.

So far I have disposed of questions about the necessity and desirability of determining the best explanation. In so doing, I have kept on begging another, more fundamental question, if not *the* key question, namely, what does 'best' mean? The term is, of course, extremely vague and open to widely varying interpretation. Do we mean best according to moral criteria, political, aesthetic, the epistemological, the pragmatic or what we may think of as purely historical criteria? As a group, most social historians do not, of course, draw upon an unlimited range of criteria when they make comparative evaluations. Their discipline may be largely pre-paradigmatic but each practitioner does not invent criteria as he or she pleases. Most practitioners select their criteria from a pool of criteria, the limits to which are governed by conventions, the discipline's informal code of practice. Even so, the total number of possible criteria which practitioners can select from the pool is very large indeed. Moreover, the criteria are quite diverse, if not ill-sorted. According to my impressionistic observations, the criteria that are most commonly selected from the pool include such considerations as the quantity of supporting evidence; the weight of the counter-evidence; mastery of the primary source material; deviations away from the basic standards of historical scholarship (accuracy of quotation, referencing and so on); use of novel primary source material; imaginative handling of apparently unpromising source material; the degree of analytical rigour; the amount of ingenuity applied to the tackling of inherently difficult evidential problems; the logicality of the arguments; the forcefulness of these arguments; the crudity or sophistication of the concepts; readability and the quality of prose style; the tightness (or looseness) in the construction of the accounts; originality of theory; the inclusion of people 'hidden from history' (women and ethnic minorities); breadth of subject-matter; the failure or otherwise to discuss key works in the historiography; the capacity to open up new fields of enquiry; the use of a novel and interesting approach; avoidance of anachronism and sensitivity to the specifities of context; the capacity to give a good feel for the period; the capacity to empathise with the actors; and the presence or absence of illustrations in the accounts.

There are several problems with this pool of criteria, the conventions that regulate it, and the way practitioners make their selections from it. The first is that the conventions do not give enough prominence to explanatory power criteria – and these surely are essential criteria given that the purpose of an explanation is to account for the phenomena. The second problem is that since the pool of criteria is so large, practitioners cannot possibly use all the criteria in the pool when they engage in comparative evaluations of rival theories. As a consequence, they are forced to chose some criteria to the exclusion of the rest. The third and related problem is that the conventions do not, for the most part, specify the relative importance of the different criteria. As a consequence, the manner in which practitioners chose criteria from the pool is subject to a great deal of latitude and personal discretion. Certainly, there are some conventions about the relative importance of the criteria but these mainly cover extreme situations; most practitioners, for example, would give precedence to prose style criteria or scholarly criteria if one particular explanation in a set of rival explanations was expressed in incomprehensible English or flagrantly violated the canons of historical scholarship. In short, as the conventions governing criteria choices are very loose, it is perfectly possible to arrive at a series of quite different conclusions about which of several rival theories is the best one simply by selecting each time a different criterion or combination of criteria from the large pool which the discipline has accumulated. The fourth problem is that there is not much chance that conventions governing criteria selections will arise. Practitioners are not in the habit of defending and debating their criteria choices explicitly, let alone of stating why they give more weight to some criteria than to others when their comparative judgments are implicitly based on such distinctions. The *rationale* behind most criteria selections tends to be unspoken except where standards of traditional scholarship are obviously at stake or when debate rages over the merits and demerits of a particularly controversial set of rival accounts, impelling the protagonists to justify their respective positions by appealing to bedrock principles.

In short, the discipline has ground rules governing the range of criteria that can be selected for the comparative evaluations of rival explanatory theories. But it does not provide adequate ground rules – let alone guidelines – about how we should select and organize the criteria. The object of this chapter is to suggest a way in which a little more methodological order can be injected into the conventions.

The chapter is in four sections. The first section outlines the way I think we can rationalise the conventions that bind the ranking of rival explanations. Here I have attempted to organise the conventions into a coherent evaluative strategy. The aim of the three central sections is to test the *usefulness* of the strategy. Here we will see if it works well by applying it to two opposing explanatory accounts that deal with exactly the same phenomena – of a most disturbing and infamous nature, as it happens. In these sections we will outline the claims made by each account, discuss the procedures each employs to support its claims, assess the strengths and weaknesses of each theory, then try to determine which theory is on balance the best.

The reason why I have chosen these particular rival explanatory accounts to test the usefulness of the proposed evaluative strategy is that they are well-matched and hence provide an exacting test of the strategy's usefulness, of its inherent capacity to *distinguish* the best theory. As we shall see, there is considerable overlap in their confirmation methods and in their use of source materials. Moreover, both have to grapple with vexing evidential problems and do so with varying degrees of ingenuity and success; and both explicitly discuss methodological issues in an unusually reflective and sophisticated manner (more so than is normal in social history).

In the final section, I will draw on the lessons of the middle sections and suggest where the evaluative strategy is unsatisfactory and could be improved.

Working out an appropriate strategy for the comparative evaluation of competing explanatory theories

As we noted earlier, the criteria in the pool are many and very heterogeneous in character. To rationalise them, I have operated on the key assumption that an explanatory theory has three fundamental objectives – to have maximum explanatory power, to have maximum reliability, and to have maximum originality. On the basis of these assumptions, the evaluative strategy is designed around the three guiding principles of explanatory power, reliability and originality. I have then categorised each criterion according to its capacity to serve the purposes of one of the principles; distributed each criterion to the most appropriate principle; and attempted to weight the criteria subsumed under each principle. In effect, then, the proposed evaluative strategy ranks rival explanatory theories by determining how well each performs in relation to three guiding principles, each (with one exception) consisting of a rough hierarchy of criteria.

Now, the key assumptions which underlie the strategy, the identity of the criteria which have been subsumed under each principle, and the weightings which have been given to the criteria, are all matters requiring elaboration and justification. But let us leave these until we have described the strategy in detail and clarified a number of points. Although the strategy endeavours as far as possible to work within the loose social historical conventions for ranking rival explanations, it nonetheless diverges from these in many respects. For one thing, it gives far more prominence to explanatory power. For another, it refines and modifies some of the criteria so that they serve the purposes of the guiding principles more effectively. In addition, it incorporates certain criteria which are not normally used by social historians (including explanatory power criteria). Lastly, it relegates all criteria if these are valued for their own sake and do not serve the purposes of any of the three principles. In my view, these are second-order criteria and should only come into play after we find that on balance rival explanations in a set are equal in relation to the first-order criteria, those that serve the purposes of the governing principles. The divergences, however, do not depart radically from the conventions and I cannot see how they can be avoided if we want to reduce the problems generated by the conventions. Let us now describe each governing principle in detail.

☐ *The originality principle*

It seems self-evident that our appraisals of rival explanations should give a high value to their relative degree of conceptual and theoretical originality. The growth of knowledge about what produced social phenomena in the past depends on our ability to keep on thinking up new explanatory theories. Without them, we would be stuck with our existing explanations which we know are imperfect, if not seriously flawed, and may well have no relevance to a vast range of social phenomena which have yet to be discovered. Popper made a similar point with his famous argument that the growth of knowledge is an unending process requiring both severe criticism and the invention of bold hypotheses, whereby investigators invent bold conjectures about the world, severe criticism discovers their errors and, learning from experience, investigators advance new bold hypotheses that do not commit the same errors.[2]

Our appraisals of rival explanations, however, should also refer to other kinds of originality criteria. The growth of knowledge about what produced past social phenomena may not just depend on the capacity to think of new concepts and theories; for obviously it can also come from innovative methods, new ways of handling evidence, and the capacity to make imaginative guesses about the location of unexploited and unknown but rich primary source materials. Moreover, we would not be in the position to

explain the phenomena in the first place unless they had been discovered and identified by someone with the imagination to think
of the possibility of their existence and either to recognise them
when they stumbled upon them or take the initiative to find them
(as problematic as the ontology of these phenomena often is). In
sum, then, many different kinds of originality criteria need to be
considered when rival explanatory theories are evaluated. They
include (and this is not an exhaustive list):

(a) novel concepts and theories;
(b) innovative or unusual use of methods to solve difficult evid-
    ential problems;
(c) the devising of new approaches to the evidence (demon-
    strating, for example, the connections between different
    areas of evidence that had previously been thought to have
    little or no connection);
(d) the ingenuity to extract significant pieces of information
    from apparently unpromising sources;
(e) the discovery of hitherto unknown rich primary sources;
(f) the finding and identification of the phenomena and the
    pioneering of the field.

In the abstract, it is very difficult to weight these different kinds of
originality, apart from suggesting that perhaps (f) is the most
important since without it we would not know there were phenomena to explain. Moreover, it is very difficult in the abstract to
be definite about what values to attach to the sorts of factors making up each criterion – except to make the obvious point that
there are degrees of originality in each case. Hence, although I
have attempted to weight the criteria subsumed under the other
two guiding principles, I have not attempted to do so in this
instance. Thus, when appraising rival explanations in relation to
the originality principle, it seems that we must treat each set of
explanations very largely on its own merits.

☐ *The explanatory power principle*

By definition, the aim of an explanation is to explain the facts
embodying the phenomena. Broadly speaking, when we talk
about the explanatory power of a theory, we are referring to the

range of facts which the theory claims it can explain. (I have deliberately added the word 'claim' here since explanations do not necessarily entail the facts they refer to – as we shall see later when we come to the reliability principle.) The notion of explanatory power is thus essential to the business of ranking rival explanatory theories. An explanation which (on the face of it) can account for a large variety of facts associated with the phenomena is obviously far superior to a rival which (on the face of it) can only explain a very limited range. There are three criteria of explanatory power.

The first criterion – and the most basic – counts cases. It looks at each explanation to see how many comparable cases each has *actually* attempted to explain, and says that the explanation that (on the face it) accounts for the most cases has the greatest explanatory power. The criterion is restricted to studies that have investigated cases to find out whether in each one the same phenomena occurs in conjunction with the same preconditions ('factors', 'causes'). The comparable cases could be either individuals belonging to the same social category, or comparable groups of people, or comparable localities, or comparable regions, or comparable countries and so on.

The second criterion is an extension of the first but is more sophisticated. Although it will incorporate information derived from the use of the first criterion, it goes further. It pays more attention to the *logic* of the 'causal mechanism' implied or specified by each explanation, and says that the explanation with the greatest explanatory power, is the one with the causal mechanism that is applicable to the largest number of *conceivable* comparable cases – or even to other classes of cases. The criterion thus assesses explanations in terms of their *inherent* capacity to generalise. The criterion, in other words, values boldness in explanations; their preparedness to claim they will cover unknown cases and that their application is not restricted to the few known cases.

The third criterion of explanatory power is quite different. It works by determining which explanation accounts for more of the finer details – the variations, the nuances, the intricacies – manifested by the phenomena within a case. The third method, hence, comparatively evaluates rival theories according to their degree of coverage of the finer details at the micro-level; the theory that explains a greater range of finer details associated with the phenomena *within* the case, has the strongest explanatory power. This method for comparatively evaluating the power of rival theories is indispensable when, for some reason or another, it is not possible to generalise across cases. For example, we may only have information about a tiny number of the phenomena in one case, even though the phenomena were once common in a multitude of cases. Alternatively, the phenomena could have been of a non-recurring kind and intrinsically unique, or could have been rare. Such phenomena are the stuff of many intentional explanations and of what are called **sensitive dependent** circumstances (those where little differences in the preconditions produce disproportionately large differences in outcomes).

Sometimes comparative evaluations that use the first and second criteria yield indecisive results. Where this occurs, we can attach additional tests of explanatory power to the criteria. One test is to ask if any of the rival accounts attempts to account for the finer details associated with the phenomena within a case or cases, and if several do, establish which one covers the greatest variety of finer details. Another test is to see which of the rival explanations is most able to deal with and accommodate exceptional cases – those where the preconditions occur but not the expected outcomes, or vice versa. Human society is so complex, that exceptions are almost inevitable, especially if the explanations refer to a large number of cases. To apply the test, a series of increasingly finer sieves such as these can be employed: (i) an attempt to account for exceptions through *ad hoc* adjustment of the theory; (ii) the provision of a separate theory for the exceptions; (iii) the demonstration that a minor causal factor in the explanation, when inverted, accounts for some of the exceptions (or better still, most of them); (iv) the demonstration that the exceptions are minor exceptions (of degree), not major (of kind); (v) the provision of a good argument that the exceptions are **special cases**, or that they can be accounted for by inverting a major causal factor in the explanation.[3] Obviously, however, if the number of cases is finite and tiny, exceptional cases are not exceptions but serious – even fundamental – anomalies.

Perhaps the most stringent test, however, is to examine the logic of the causal mechanism implied by each explanation and to compare it to the others in relation to the following hierarchy: (i) neither necessary nor sufficient to bring about the outcome; (ii) necessary for the outcome; (iii) sufficient for the outcome; and (iv) necessary and sufficient for the outcome. To illustrate how this test might work, let us imagine we have two rival explanations. One postulates a causal mechanism that is neither sufficient nor necessary to produce the outcome (type i). Now this explanation will be greatly outranked by the rival explanation that postulates a causal mechanism which is sufficient to bring about the outcome (type iii). Why? Well, the first explanation admits its postulated causal mechanism is very weak: as the mechanism is neither sufficient nor necessary to bring about the outcome, the explanation accepts that the mechanism *by itself* will not bring about the outcome in any case *and* that there will be an indefinite number of cases where the outcome occurs without the mechanism. The rival explanation, however, postulates that a far stronger causal mechanism is at work; for, by claiming that the mechanism is a sufficient condition for the outcome, the explanation is committing itself to the prediction that in every single case where the postulated causal mechanism exists, the same outcome will occur.

Social historians, of course, do not often explicitly describe their explanations in the language of necessary and sufficient conditions. They are more inclined to use non-standard and vaguer terms, such as 'vital', 'central', 'key', 'decisive', 'major', 'of fundamental importance' and so forth. Even so, a close examination of the surrounding context of each of the several rival explanations will often suggest where each stands in the hierarchy of sufficient and necessary conditions.

☐ *The reliability principle*

We can talk about an explanation as an attempt to describe the 'causal mechanism' that generated the phenomena. I am using the term 'causal mechanism', in this instance, only as a metaphor covering all types of explanations and not those which are strictly 'casual'. To carry the metaphor further, we can imagine the mechanism as consisting of a system of cogs, wheels, wires, tubes and bells and whistles. When we thus explain the phenomena, we are attempting to describe the particular system of cogs, wheels, wires, and so forth that generated the phenomena in question. If our description is completely accurate, it would look like a comprehensive model which in every detail corresponded to the plans drawn up by some all-knowing designer ('a god's eye view'). Our problem, however, is that we are not all-knowing designers; we do not know what the causal mechanism is; from our position of ignorance, it looks like a black box. Hence, our attempts at description are basically educated guesses – claims that are filled with errors, large and small – about the actual contents of the black box.

I have used the reliability principle in a very broad sense to denote the various means by which we can determine *the relative degree of accuracy* of rival descriptions of the same causal mechanism. Note here the emphasis on the words 'relative degree of accuracy'; as indicated at the beginning of the chapter, it is unrealistic to evaluate any given set of competing explanations by social historians according to whether or not each completely corresponds to the truth (to all the facts). This requirement is far too demanding and no social historical explanation (except the extremely trite) would satisfy it given, amongst other things, the deficiencies of our primary sources. The notion of the reliability principle has some resemblance to Popper's idea of verisimilitude – the idea that there are degrees of truth, and that rival theories can be evaluated according to how far each approximates to the truth (to all the facts). But the reliability principle differs in major respects. The verisimilitude principle was designed for the natural sciences and consists of a hierarchy of 'critical tests' which are too stringent for most social historical explanations. For example, Popper rejects the view that the best theory will be that which is supported by the largest number of positive examples; he argues that as we can find any number of supporting examples we like to confirm our theories, we should instead concentrate on looking for the counter examples that refute our theories. But social historians have to look for both supporting and counter examples since the fragmentary nature of our sources make both kinds very hard to come by, and since nearly all social historical explanations take the form not of exceptionless universal laws (as is the case of the natural sciences) but of generalisations that admit to exceptions. Moreover, the idea of verisimilitude presupposes that rival theories yield precise – quantifiable – results (and most of ours do not), and can be tested under laboratory conditions (which we, of course, generally cannot do). Accordingly, although the reliability principle follows Popper in devising a hierarchy of tests, most of these expect much less and are far more modest than Popper's, and are strongly orientated to the peculiarities of social historical evidential problems.

The reliability principle has three tiers. In the lowest tier are what are called plausibility criteria; in the middle tier are what have been designated credibility criteria; and in the third and highest tier are the probability criteria. Thus when evaluating rival explanations, we start by seeing how well they compete against each other in relation to the plausibility criteria. Those that seem to satisfy the criteria of plausibility (or least do not deviate from them in any serious way), are then matched against the more demanding credibility criteria; and if two or more survive, they are evaluated in relation to the probability criteria. The principle assumes that we do not need to go outside the texts to apply the plausibility and credibility criteria; what they require is a very close and critical reading of the respective texts, though a good general knowledge of the subject-matter is necessary too. All the criteria in the third, however, demand a detailed knowledge of the primary source material and of the relevant historiography. Another assumption is that it is too easy to apply the criteria to petty matters; we should strive instead to apply them to the large.

The plausibility criteria

1. An account needs to give us at least some grounds for believing that the explanation is not impossible. To this end, an explanation should cohere with our common-sense beliefs.[4] Better still, it will do this as well as make some attempt to detail the process by which the postulated causal mechanism generated the phenomena. The process may be expressed as an explicit theory or through concrete illustrative examples. The latter are perhaps preferable since they also give us *prima facie* evidence that the process existed.

2. The major claims of the explanation must be logical. By logical, we mean that there should be no contradictions between the various major claims; and that major inferences necessarily follow from the given evidence. There are two things in particular we need to watch for here. First, if the account breaks the explanation down into several ancillary hypotheses, we need to check if the main ancillaries are mutually

compatible; if they are radically incompatible, then the explanation does not make sense and is quite implausible in its own terms. An analogy would be someone who asserted that *x* was true at one moment and then insisted that *x* was false in the next. (When we talk about ancillary hypotheses we are referring in effect to the more specific claims which an account might make about how its postulated causal mechanism produces the phenomena.) The second thing we pay particular attention to, is whether the explanation *logically entails* the facts embodying the phenomena. What we are looking for, in other words, is: (a) whether the postulated causal mechanism has the kinds of physical properties which would enable it to produce the outcome in question; and (b) whether a quite different causal mechanism could have generated the phenomena just as readily. By way of analogy, let us think of the dinner that has just appeared on the table. It would be implausible to conclude that mum *must* have put it there if (a) mum had died three years ago; or (b) dad (especially a new age dad) could also have put it there.

3. The last criterion of plausibility and perhaps the most decisive is testability, otherwise known as falsifiability. It embraces a variety of things. An explanation would not be testable if it was formulated in many different and inconsistent ways; inherently vague and ambiguous; or immunised from criticism by some in-built device. One such immunising device is to attribute the causal mechanism to a mystical or occult force; another is to assert that only people equipped with special innate powers are equipped to detect the causal mechanism; a third such device is to employ circular reasoning (the reasoning would be circular, for example, were we to argue that aliens are intelligent beings and exist on earth but are too intelligent to make their existence known to earthlings).

The credibility criteria

These focus on the empirical adequacy of the rival explanations. The object here is determine how successfully they compete against each other in relation to the following evidential questions:

1. To what extent can each assure us that it has not mistranslated the concepts in the source materials that it uses as evidence for the phenomena and the causal mechanism? Of course, only an expert knowledge of the documents and the society that generated them can allow us to arrive at definite answers to this question; but we can come to a preliminary decision by seeing how conscious the account is of the obvious problems of understanding an alien culture in its own terms.

2. How effectively has the account grappled with the problems of socially constructed – 'theory-laden' – evidence (discussed in Chapter 7)?

3. If the explanation depends on fragmentary evidence, how effectively does it deal with the problems of typicality inherent in such evidence? (Statistical explanations – those based on the analysis of systematic quantitative data – can be appraised according to the standards laid down for statistical explanations in Chapter 6.)

The probability criteria

These are composed of three sieves. First, all the published studies related to the field are exhaustively combed to search for counter-evidence to each explanation, the object being to identify the explanation that contains the fewest serious anomalies. If this fails to yield a decisive result, the rivals are put through the second sieve. Here the relevant primary sources are checked against the evidence advanced by each rival to see if the ways in which the evidence has been selected and interpreted by one account stand out as being markedly less problematic than the ways the evidence has been selected and interpreted by the rival account(s). If this fails to separate out the rivals, then they are put through the third and finest sieve. This involves carrying out independent research on the same explanatory problem, taking a new set of cases that are as similar as possible to those of the rival accounts, and seeing if the resulting data have a better fit with one explanation than with its rival(s).

As this brings to an end the discussion of the proposed evaluative strategy, we now need to assess its usefulness by applying it to two works that advance competing social historical explanations of the same phenomenon. The next two sections will outline the theory advanced by each work and evaluate it in relation to the explanatory power and the reliability principles (but not the probability criteria). The final section will then take the results of the analyses, discuss the relative merits of each explanation in relation to the originality principle, and come to a verdict about which one on balance is the best theory.

The first candidate theory: Christopher Browning, *Ordinary Men*[6]

The central topic in the study of genocide is the Holocaust. Although the Holocaust has produced an enormous literature since the early 1960s, most of it has been concerned with examining the experiences of the victims and debating whether it was the direct outcome of a long-held Nazi plan or the end result of a series of *ad hoc* bureaucratic expedients. Very few of the major works, however, have attempted to engage in detailed empirical investigations of a fundamental problem: why did a multitude of ordinary Germans – people who were neither rabid Nazis nor members of the SS nor trained killers – become 'Hitler's willing executioners', perpetrators of extraordinarily horrendous acts of murder and cruelty against myriads of defenceless victims? This question is the central concern of the two accounts we shall take as our case study, though, as we shall see, they come to quite different conclusions despite employing similar methods and sources. I will now deal with each account in considerable detail since the detail, at least in this particular instance, is crucial to our capacity to determine which account provides the best theory. We shall examine Browning's much acclaimed account first since it pioneered the field, was published four years before the other work – Daniel Goldhagen's *Hitler's Willing Executioners* – and unwittingly established the terms of what has become an extremely heated debate.

Browning attempts to answer the question with a highly focused study of a single group of mass killers, the 500 or so men belonging to Reserve Police Battalion 101, responsible for shooting at least 38,000 Polish Jews and the death camp deportation of 45,000 others during the peak of the Holocaust in Poland, between mid-1942 and early 1943.[7] Police battalions were lightly armed, regionally based, paramilitary units, composed partly of career policemen, partly of volunteers (who enlisted to avoid military service) but primarily of conscripted reservists belonging to the older age-groups. The battalions were organized at the beginning of the war out of various militarised police formations. Along with Germany's traditional municipal, small town and rural police forces, police battalions were centrally controlled by an agency set up by Himmler in 1936 called the Order Police, Orpo. (Another centrally controlled agency, the Security Police, set up at the same time as the Order Police, exercised jurisdiction over the Security Service, criminal detection units, and that infamous Nazi institution, the Gestapo.) By mid-1940, over one hundred battalions had been formed, all being deployed in German-occupied territories, 13 in eastern Poland (an area officially known as the General Government), and seven in the areas of northern and western Poland annexed by the Reich.

Nearly all the source material Browning took for his study is of one kind, namely, the official testimonies of Battalion 101's former members when they were interrogated about its suspected war crimes by the Hamburg Office of the State Prosecutor representing the German Federal Government between 1962 and 1972. There were 210 such testimonies, and Browning deployed these in three ways.

In the first place, he built a statistical profile of the Battalion from all 210 testimonies, analysing them according to age, party membership, SS membership and 'social background'. One of his most important findings was that in June 1942, *just before the Battalion became involved in its murderous activities,* most of its men were raw conscripts, reservists who had no experience of German occupation methods in eastern Europe nor, except for the most elderly who had served in the First War, of active combat. He also found that the Battalion's Commander, Major Trapp, a career policemen aged 53, was not a member of the SS and 'was clearly not considered SS material', though he had joined the Nazi Party in 1932. Of the ten other officers, seven belonged to the Nazi Party, two to the SS, and nearly all were aged between 33 and 48.

With the NCOs there was a similar pattern. As for the rank and file, they were overwhelmingly from working-class backgrounds; but as we shall note later, Browning sees some significance in the fact that very few had economically independent occupations and an education beyond the age of fourteen or fifteen. Their average age was 39; a quarter were Nazi Party members.

Although Browning thinks that the proportion of Nazi Party members in all ranks was 'surprisingly high', he concludes his statistical analysis by arguing that the men 'would not seem to have been a very promising group from which to recruit mass murderers on behalf of the Nazi vision of a racial utopia free of Jews.' Most 'came from Hamburg, by reputation one of the least nazified cities in Germany, and the majority from a social class that had been anti-Nazi in its political culture'. Moreover, as the men were largely middle-aged and not impressionable youngsters, they 'had known political standards and moral norms other than those of the Nazis.'[8]

In the second place, Browning created a narrative of the Battalion's deeds based on 125 of the most detailed of the 210 testimonies. The story begins by telling us how the Battalion (like many other police battalions) was initially deployed in the invasion of Poland in 1939 to protect installations, round up Polish soldiers, collect weapons and so on; and goes on to relate how the Battalion from late 1940 to early 1941 was involved in the wholescale expulsion of the peasantry living in the annexed areas of Poland, and guarding the Łódź Ghetto in Poland's General Government, operations which were not without excesses. In May 1941, however, the Battalion was practically dissolved, with the transfer of most of its rank and file to other units and their replacement by conscripted reservists. After a period of training, it returned to Poland in June 1942, where, unbeknown to its personnel, it was about to play its part in the Final Solution which, after beginning in the occupied areas of Russia in mid-1941, had been extended later in that year to Poland, from then on its major site.

The crucial deed that initiated Police Battalion 101 into mass shootings occurred on 13 July at Józefów village in the Lublin district of the Central Government. Trapp had received orders from his superiors on 11 July to round up all 1800 of the Jewish inhabitants, transport the able-bodied males to work-camps, and shoot all the rest. It is noteworthy that when the officers were

informed of the pending action on 12 July, one of them, a con-
script, Lieutenant Buchmann, who said he would refuse to kill
defenceless women and children, was not punished or repri-
manded but given a transport assignment instead. Even more
noteworthy is another series of events. When Trapp addressed his
Battalion about the operation early in the morning of the fateful
day, he was not only visibly upset but made an 'extraordinary
offer': he proclaimed that he would excuse any of the older men
from the task who objected to it. After a pause, one private
stepped forward, was berated by his Company commander for
breaking ranks, but Trapp cut the officer short, overtly taking the
private under his protection, thereby implicitly encouraging ten
or twelve other men – but only that number – to step forward as
well; all were assigned alternative duties. During the massacre,
Trapp was conspicuously absent and made his distress well
known, though in the preceding roundup he did nothing to stop
the shooting of Jews who could not walk.

Much attention is given by Browning to reconstructing the
events surrounding the massacre itself, a badly organised affair
requiring much extemporisation. After being separated from
their menfolk, the women, children and the infirm were shot after
each executioner had some personal contact with the victim. The
victims were taken in small groups to a nearby forest, formed into
a line, each victim was paired off with an executioner, and the column then marched to a section of the forest where each executioner shot his victim in the back of the neck – with horrific
physical consequences: '"The shooters were gruesomely besmir-
ched with blood, brains, and bone splinters. It hung on their
clothing"'. [9] The psychological burden was too great for some of
the men. After a few rounds of killing, some executioners asked
their officers and NCOs to be relieved, their requests being granted
in many instances. Others evaded covertly. They took advantage
of poor supervision and the relative privacy of the forest, either by
dawdling, or by shooting past their victims, or wounding, or dis-
appearing after several killings. Browning estimates, however,
that the vast majority of the members of the killing detachments –
80 to 90 per cent – stuck to their horrific task all day. Browning
goes on to maintain that after the Battalion returned to barracks,
it was 'pervaded' with a 'sense of shame and horror', with 'resent-
ment and bitterness' over what it was asked to do, feelings shared

even by the most obedient executioners. Probably as a consequence of the Battalion's demoralisation, Major Trapp abandoned plans to massacre the Jews of a nearby village several days later. Even so, only a handful of the whole Battalion (including Lieutenant Buchmann) asked for transfers back to Germany.

After the slaughter at Józefów, the Battalion's contributions to the Final Solution in Poland were somewhat different. Although units of the Battalion were involved in about ten mass shootings of Jews from August 1942 to late 1943, most of its actions were concerned with clearing and guarding ghettos, deporting their inhabitants to the Treblinka death camp, and so-called *Judenjagd*, hunting down Jews hiding in forests – actions usually undertaken with unbelievable brutality and attended by small-scale shootings. Even with the worst deeds, however, Browning found that in each case for which there was evidence only a few men either formally requested to be excused or took various covert evasive measures when the opportunity arose. With the *Judenjagd*, indeed, there was no shortage of volunteers.[10]

The third use to which Browning puts the testimonies is to address the fundamental question: 'Why did most men in Reserve Police Battalion 101 become killers, while only a minority of perhaps 10 per cent – and certainly no more than 20 per cent – did not?'[11] Browning's explanatory theory is a multi-factor one, the factors being a mix of the intentional and the causal. The primary reason for compliance, he argues, was peer group pressure. Although – 'at least initially' – almost all men 'were horrified and disgusted by what they were doing', breaking ranks 'was simply beyond most of the men'. He states: 'refusing to shoot constituted refusing one's share of an unpleasant collective obligation' – it violated the informal code of comradeship. 'Those who did not shoot risked isolation, rejection, and ostracism', and these were powerful sanctions given that 'stationed abroad among a hostile population', the non-conformists 'had virtually nowhere else to turn for support and social contact'.[12] As evidence for this claim, Browning cites several testimonies of two types: from non-shooters who told the interrogators that they justified their actions to their comrades at the time by pleading that they were 'too weak' to kill; and from shooters who told the interrogators that the reason they chose to kill was that they did not want to 'lose face' or admit they were 'cowards', 'weak'.[13]

What gave further weight to the decision of most men to kill when they had the choice not to, he clearly implies, were two interrelated secondary factors. One was racism. Browning concedes that there are few references to antisemitism in the testimonies. When interrogated, the former killers had every incentive to avoid admitting that they were motivated by antisemitism; otherwise they would have been liable to charges of war crimes. Moreover, killing for 'base motives' – which included race hatred – was a definition of homicide under German law.[14] Yet Browning asserts that the pervasive antisemitism of Nazi political culture 'made it all the easier for the majority of the policemen to conform to the norms of their immediate community'. It inclined, he says, the ordinary men of Police Battalion 101 to the belief that 'The Jews stood outside their circle of human obligation and responsibility'; that the Jewish victims had no 'common ground with the perpetrators'.[15] The other secondary factor was the polarising effect of war. Creating a 'siege mentality', it led the men to perceive Jews as 'part of a foreign enemy', to assimilate Jews into 'the image of the enemy'.[16] As evidence, Browning cites a portion of Major Trapp's address to the Battalion before the Józefów massacre where Trapp, justifying the unpleasant task the men were about to undertake, told them they had to remember that the enemy was bombing their own civilians, that the Jews had instigated the American boycott that had injured Germany, and that some Jews in the village were involved in partisan activity.[17]

In addition, Browning argues there were many minor factors of compliance. One was that most of the Battalion had previously held lowly civilian jobs and calculated that compliance would enable them to be upwardly mobile within the police force after the war.[18] Another was that, after Józefów, all the Battalion's mass murders were undertaken by small units led by officers who were less tolerant of non-compliance than Trapp.[19] In addition, after Józefów, the deeds were easier to perform since they incurred lower psychological costs: the men became hardened to the grotesque inhumanity of their tasks;[20] these primarily consisted of Ghetto clearings and deportations which were intrinsically less gruesome than outright killing; the most brutal parts of Ghetto clearances and deportations were performed by units of Security Police and 'Hiwis' (SS trained auxiliaries consisting of former Soviet POWs);[21] most of the mass shootings had a depersonalised character since the victims were grouped in large formations or the killers had no prior contact with them; and units of Security Police and 'Hiwis' also took part in the mass shootings, sometimes doing the lion's share of them.[22]

Having outlined Browning's multi-factor theory, let us now briefly assess its main strengths and weaknesses in relation to our basic criteria of explanatory power and reliability.

☐ *Explanatory power*

The key strength of the theory here is that it is potentially able to explain like cases: it is generalisable. Right at the end of the book, Browning contends that most members of groups of ordinary men would act as the men of Battalion 101 did under the same boundary and initial conditions.[23] His thesis, in short, is reducible to the following formula:

> peer group pressure + racisim + the siege mentality of war + the desire for upward mobility and other minor factors → a sufficient condition for majority participation in mass killing of the defenceless

Browning also makes strenuous efforts to account for the exceptional cases – the non-compliant. In respect of the men who formally requested to opt out prior to massacres, he takes one of the minor factors in the theory, the upward mobility argument, and inverts it, showing that some of these men had less incentive to curry favour because they came from superior occupations and did not need to pursue a post-war police career.[24] In respect of all the other sorts of non-compliance, he invokes two explanations, both extraneous to his theory. One is that these men were engaging in 'tortured attempts' to reconcile 'the demands of conscience' with the 'norms of the battalion';[25] the other is that the men were attempting to cope with the conflict between the Battalion's norms and a sense of personal revulsion aroused by the physical effects of shooting.[26]

☐ *Reliability*

Browning's theory passes almost without exception our tests of *plausibility*. For a start, the theory coheres with our common-sense views: it is not unreasonable to believe that a group of human beings will do monstrous things to defenceless people if they are under acute pressures to conform and they have racist ideas about their victims and they identify their victims with an external enemy with whom they are at war. Moreover, Browning gives the theory plausibility by illustrating nearly all of the explanations with concrete examples, and by providing a fairly detailed description of how the primary factor generated the phenomena – although the same cannot said for the secondary factors: his descriptions of how they generated the phenomena are unacceptably vague and underdeveloped.

In addition, the theory is falsifiable. The primary explanation is neither mystical nor vague and meaningless nor immunised from criticism with circular reasoning or assertions by the author that he belongs to an elect group of believers with privileged access to the truth.[27] Moreover, although he stipulates that a large number of factors motivated the men to become willing killers, he enhances the testability of the theory by ranking each factor, identifying the primary factor, distinguishing it from the implied secondary factors and the minor. Lastly, what makes the theory plausible is that there are no contradictions between any of its major claims.

But does the theory pass the stronger test of reliability, that of *credibility*? It does on one criterion: Browning gives us some grounds for being confident that he has not mistranslated the concepts underlying the testimonies partly because he consciously set out to understand the actions of the men of Battalion 101 from their point of view by immersing himself in their testimonies; and partly because prior to the study he spent over twenty years examining court records and archival documents generated by the perpetrators of the Holocaust.

But in four other major respects we can say that his theory is empirically inadequate. First, although he attempts to rank the factors that drove most of the men to become willing killers, he provides no evidence to justify his order of rankings.

Second, although Browning theorises to some extent about the finer componentry of his primary explanation, he offers us little empirical evidence for it. Since his key claim is that fear of informal peer sanctions deterred men from requesting permission to opt out of killing, we would have expected him to provide ample empirical detail showing how powerful the process of informal peer pressure actually was in those few instances where men made requests to opt out. Criteria of 'powerful' might include conduct where the whole of a Company or platoon turned against a violator, and where the violator was severely penalised and disadvantaged. Browning, however, documents only one instance where social pressure operated at platoon level and it is a poor example: his own evidence shows the platoon was obviously divided over the matter.[28] Although he cites several instances where a peer sanction was brought to bear against a violator, in every case the sanction consisted not of beatings or death threats or ostracism – the strongest sanctions – but variously of criticism, disparaging remarks, contemptuous comments or abuse – the weakest sanctions.[29]

The third area where the theory lacks credibility is its dependence on examples of unknown typicality. To confirm each of his explanations for compliance, Browning's procedure is to cite a few positive examples from the testimonies. As he does little to assure us of their typicality, we end up with the indeterminacy problem: he gives us no grounds for believing that the few known positive cases are representative of all the many unknown cases. Since his peer group argument must bear the greatest weight of explanation we would expect Browning to provide supplementary evidence for it in the most obvious way, by applying the method of maximising the variety and number of observations. But he makes scant use of this procedure. He does not refer to other cases of genocide where peer pressure might have been the key to compliance. He does very little to demonstrate the overall power of peer group pressure within the Battalion by documenting how it governed all sorts of other aspects of the Battalion's life.[30] His only substantial attempt to use it comes at the end of the book where he argues that his thesis is corroborated by one of the results of the famous laboratory experiments conducted in the 1960s by Stanley Milgram on obedience – and the argument is tenuous, given that, as Browning himself concedes, the willingness to inflict pain under laboratory conditions is not analogous to real-life events where men willingly kill myriads of defenceless people.[31]

The last area where Browning's theory fails to satisfy us about its credibility relates to his handling of his source materials – the testimonies. Their factual accuracy is highly suspect on five grounds. For one thing, they were obviously subject to all the usual psychological mechanisms that corrupt recollections of distant events such as memory loss, wishful thinking, suppression of the unpleasant and so on. For another, since they were generated after twenty-five years of radical changes in Germany's whole system of values, beliefs and climate of opinion, they were unusually subject to *post hoc* ideological contamination. Moreover, they could easily have been distorted by the particular nature of the questions asked by the interrogators and their general demeanour. In addition, since all the testifiers seem to have settled in Hamburg after the war, it is certainly possible that at least some of them kept up personal contact and 'remade history', evolved common myths about the Battalion's exploits. On top of all this, the testifiers had good reason to lie and suppress information if they thought that frankness and telling the truth would increase the risk that this would incriminate them or their former comrades in war crimes or homicide.[32]

Browning makes valiant efforts to limit the unreliability of the sources. He does this by *carefully and assiduously checking the observations in the testimonies against each other*, rejecting uncorroborated observations or treating them with great caution but treating the well corroborated as reliable. The procedure succeeds in the case of collective actions – deeds involving groups of men where one participant witnessed the behaviour of his fellows. Here Browning assumes, quite correctly, that if the same events are recounted in a lot of witness reports, we can be fairly sure (all things being equal) that the events actually occurred. It is possible, of course, that a lot of converging reports were the product of organised lying or mythologising, but this is unlikely: if organised lying or mythologising took place, we have to explain why it failed to conceal the Battalion's most monstrous deeds. However, the corroborative procedure is far less effective when applied to two other kinds of statements: (a) those where the testifier recounted the intentions that led him to act as he did in an action, and (b) those where the testifier claims he took certain courses of action and these actions were not observed by others. Statements in both categories include those of the non-compliant and compliant upon which Browning's primary explanation stands or falls. Such statements cannot be corroborated by witnesses since there are no witnesses to individual intentions and unobserved individual actions. To corroborate such statements Browning in effect alters the procedure. To establish the likelihood that one individual had a certain (unwitnessed) intention or took a certain (unwitnessed) course of action, he cites other examples of individuals whose alleged intentions or actions were similar in the same situation. The procedure might allay our doubts about the unreliability of each statement if a multitude of parallel examples could be cited for each situation. But Browning never cites more than about three examples – a sample size which is far too small. A case in point is his argument that it was mainly peer pressure that prevented all but a handful of men from taking advantage of Trapp's 'extraordinary offer' before the Józefów massacre: to confirm the claim he cites just three testimonies where the men state they did not step forward in case they were labelled as 'cowardly' or 'weak'.[33] Surely it would have taken very little to produce the same errors in three statements about an intention recollected two decades after the event. Three recollections on this particular point could easily have been corrupted in the same direction through organised lying or mythologising, or by some quirk in the interrogation process. Moreover, out of a total pool of 125 individuals who testified, it is quite possible that by chance there were three who happened, quite independently, to be subject to the same psychological mechanisms that led them to misreport their thoughts in the same way.

But in weighing up the credibility of Browning's theory one other thing has to be considered: towards the end of the book, he systematically applies, with considerable effect, the hypothetico-deductive (argument to the best explanation) method, *demonstrating that all alternative theories for compliance do not work – they either have no relevance to the particular circumstances of the Battalion or contain serious anomalies.*[34] Thus he refutes the possibilities that compliance arose from the brutalising effect of war on the men; from military discipline and the compulsion to follow orders; from the way in which the highly bureaucratic nature of the Holocaust diminished personal responsibility; from the presence in the Battalion of an abnormal number of sadists and psychopaths; from a policy of the Order Police high command to induct Nazi fanatics and hardened killers into the Battalion; and from a deliberate campaign to brainwash the men to kill.

So, the four problems of evidential typicality and reliability, when considered in isolation, cast grave doubt on the credibility of the theory. But when put in the context of his demonstration that all alternative theories are either inappropriate or false, the doubt diminishes. The demonstration does not make the problems go away. But it reduces the overall weight we would otherwise give them, making us more prepared to consider that the theory has a measure of credibility.

The second candidate theory: Daniel Goldhagen, *Hitler's Willing Executioners*[35]

The product of a Harvard doctoral thesis, Goldhagen's monumental book (it runs to some 600 pages) has been highly controversial. It is an ambitious attempt to come up with an entirely different answer to the same question that Browning addresses; indeed to a considerable extent it is directly concerned with criticising and overturning the Browning thesis. The book starts with an unusually extensive discussion of methodological issues, moves to a series of detailed empirical case studies, and concludes with a summary discussion which matches his theory against others in the field.

Goldhagen's central claim – his core theory – is very simple. He says that hundreds of thousands of 'ordinary Germans' were willing executioners of Jews and in order to explain their actions we do not need to look any further than the *exceptionally* pernicious antisemitism that lay at the heart of German culture:

> The conclusion of this book is that antisemitism moved many thousands of 'ordinary' Germans – and would have moved millions more, had they been appropriately positioned – to slaughter Jews. Not economic hardship, not the coercive means of a totalitarian state, not social psychological pressure, not invariable psychological propensities, but ideas about Jews that were pervasive in Germany, and had been for decades, induced ordinary Germans to kill unarmed, defenseless Jewish men, women, and children by the thousands, systematically and without pity.[36]

According to Goldhagen, all but a tiny minority of Germans possessed a peculiarly vicious 'eliminationist ideology' – an obsessive hatred of the Jews, a belief that their so-called malevolent characteristics were immutable, and a consequent desire to eliminate them completely from German life. It was this factor and this factor alone that motivated the vast majority of Germans when opportunity arose to choose to kill Jews with the utmost zeal and passion. In Goldhagen's formulation, Germany's uniquely vicious eliminationist ideology was the necessary *and* sufficient motivating cause of compliance by ordinary Germans.[37]

To demonstrate this ambitious claim, Goldhagen employs a sophisticated methodological strategy which can be divided into four parts. The first – and least sophisticated – part attempts to account for the historical origins of the eliminationist ideology and establish its centrality to German culture. Goldhagen strenuously denies that the ideology was created and imposed by the Nazi regime. He also insists that it did not stem from the disturbed conditions associated with the Weimar Republic during the 1920s and early 1930s. Instead, he says, the ideology arose much earlier in German history and was fixed by the late mid-nineteenth century, as a consequence of a fusion between two powerful antisemitic intellectual traditions, one religious, the other racist. The religious tradition sprang from the doctrines and practices of the medieval Catholic Church and the antisemitic preachings of Martin Luther during the Reformation. This tradition injected into German culture the demonic view of the Jews, the belief that they were agents of the devil, alien and hateful figures, although redeemable if converted to Christianity.[38] The racist tradition arose in reaction to the piecemeal steps taken from 1807 to 1871 to extend civil rights to the Jews and was strongly shaped by social Darwinism. Although it had many strands, it took over and built on the notion in the religious tradition that the Jews possessed alien and malevolent characteristics. But rather than projecting the characteristics as a threat to Christianity, it claimed that they imperiled the German people and nation. Moreover, instead of seeing the Jews as redeemable, it advanced a harder and broader claim: that Jewish characteristics were immutable, biologically fixed, and that the Jews were a powerfully organised and parasitic force.[39]

Formulated in these terms, the cognitive content of German antisemitism had a logic, Browning contends, that entailed eliminationist prescriptions. If Jews had characteristics that were hateful, threatening *and* immutable, then the only way of dealing with this intractable 'problem' was to remove it. As evidence, Goldhagen cites an unpublished study that engaged in a content analysis of 51 'prominent' antisemitic writings and authors appearing in Germany between 1861 and 1895. Most saw the Jews as unchangeable, and 28 proposed 'solutions' to the 'Jewish problem', 19 of which involved physical extermination.[40]

Goldhagen's narrative goes on to indicate that what popularised eliminationist doctrine and embedded it into the 'cognitive structure' of ordinary Germans, were Germany's institutions. These instilled and reproduced the ideology at every level. By the late nineteenth century as a consequence, the ideology was integral to the 'common sense', the 'general conversation', the sense of normality, of the vast majority of Germans:

> no non-antisemitic alternative image of the Jews found *institutional* support (the Social Democratic Party partially excepted), certainly not widespread institutional support.... This was true not only of political institutions but also of the Tocquevillian substructure of society, the associations that provided the staging ground for people's political education and activity.[41]

The second part of Goldhagen's methodological strategy is an attempt to put the core theory into verifiable form. This is a difficult task partly because the core theory is about the inner thoughts – intentions and motives – of the perpetrators, and inner thoughts are not observable; and partly because he completely distrusts the capacity of perpetrators in their war trial testimonies to be honest about what actually motivated them to kill during the Holocaust. To overcome the problem, Goldhagen employs an ingenious and elegant procedure: he sets up empirical tests of the core theory consisting of four auxiliary hypotheses about perpetrator actions that he deduces from the core theory. The procedure is based on the assumption that the existence of unobservable forces (intentions, motives) can be deduced from their observable consequences (actions). Hence, he says, if perpetrators were motivated by eliminationist ideology, we should be able to detect the effects of the ideology in certain kinds of actions they took towards Jews. To be more precise, he says that we will be able to tell if perpetrators were motivated by eliminationist antisemitism, if we find evidence that they engaged in four types of actions. All four types of actions presuppose that eliminationist ideology was a very powerful motivator, generating as it did feelings of profound hatred, obsessiveness and paranoia towards Jews. The four types of actions are (i) gratuitous killings, that is, actions where perpetrators slaughtered their victims without being ordered to do so; (ii) gratuitous cruelties and humiliations, that is, actions where they degraded Jews and tormented them without being ordered to do so; (iii) actions where they implemented orders zealously, eagerly and thoroughly; and (iv) actions where they rejected or ignored opportunities to spare the lives of victims and lessen their suffering.[42]

The third and most sophisticated part of Goldhagen's methodological strategy is his attempt to confirm the auxiliary hypotheses. The task he set himself here – which takes up the bulk of his book – is enormously daunting. For one thing, his theory is explicitly 'monocausal' in nature and monocausal explanatory theories in the social sciences and history are regarded as highly suspect.[43] For another, there is the problem of sources and evidential typicality. Goldhagen claims that his theory explains the motivation behind all killer actions conforming to his four types. Yet he acknowledges that hundreds of thousands of killers were engaged in the Holocaust; that they operated within a multitude of different killing institutions and situations; and that the bulk of their actions were either undocumented or poorly documented. Hence, there was no scope for him to confirm the auxiliary hypotheses by applying the techniques of mass quantification or by selecting cases of known typicality. Lastly, since he insists that German antisemitism was exceptionally vicious, *sui generis*, he cannot confirm his theory with cross-cultural comparisons, that is, by showing that in other societies the same precondition had the same outcomes.

To cut through these problems, Goldhagen employs another ingenious procedure – he draws his confirmatory data from **crucial cases**. Browning employs three such crucial cases which he describes with a wealth of illustrative detail.

With the first crucial case, Goldhagen revisits the trial testimonies of the former members of Police Battalion 101. For Goldhagen, what makes the Battalion a crucial case is that, according to various criteria he advances, its members were very ordinary Germans.[44] For this reason, he argues, it is all the more significant that in every deed the men's actions conformed to his four auxiliary hypotheses. We do not have space here to describe the evidence he uses to substantiate each hypothesis except to say that it consists of illustrative examples, most of which are mentioned by Browning, though Goldhagen relates them in more detail and with greater emphasis.

Goldhagen's second crucial case consists of a more generalised account of the German treatment of Jews in work camps. What makes this a crucial case, he says, is that 'Institutions devoted to economic production, whose calling card is rationality, should have been the least susceptible to the influence of a pre-existing ideology – in this case, to antisemitism.'[45] Thus it is significant, he claims, especially when we consider that Germany had an acute manpower shortage, that the camps severely undermined the productive capacity of their Jewish inmates *then* wantonly destroyed it. As evidence that the camps severely undermined Jewish productive capacity, he dwells on the examples of three camps in the General Government that inflicted certain kinds of 'routine cruelties' on Jews which grossly impaired their ability to work. As evidence for the wanton destruction of Jewish productive capacity, he quotes statistical data on another camp showing that the Jewish monthly death rate (mainly as a result of disease, work exhaustion and malnutrition) was 100 per cent, a figure radically higher than that for all other categories of prisoners.[46] Given this huge wastage of valuable manpower, so Goldhagen argues, the purpose of the work camps was surely not economic. It makes far more sense, he says, to explain the purpose of the camps in terms of eliminationist ideology. The real underlying motive behind the workcamps was to make the Jews suffer and die.

Goldhagen's third crucial case consists of a study of a death march in early 1945. This particular death march was one of many that occurred towards the end of the war, when concentration camps in the East were evacuated, their inmates being forcibly marched by their guards away from the advancing Soviet armies, experiencing huge death rates in the process. Using both survivor evidence and war trial records, Goldhagen's graphic study focuses on the horrendous treatment meted out by some 47 guards (half of whom were female) to over 500 Jewish women, former inmates of the Helmbrechts camp in eastern Germany, who were forced to march, aimlessly, for 195 miles over a period of three weeks. About 40 per cent of the Jews perished, many from random shootings and beatings, others from starvation, exhaustion and hypothermia induced by deliberate acts of cruelty. What makes this a crucial case, Goldhagen says, is that the guards were virtually unsupervised and thus had an abnormally large amount of discretion in the way they treated their defenceless charges. Moreover, early in the march, the guards received orders from Himmler not to kill. It is significant, therefore, that they exercised this large amount of discretion and disobeyed orders by killing and brutalising. Indeed, the guards preferred to take this option rather than to desert from the column and escape from the encroaching Allied forces. The only explanation which is compatible with these actions, Goldhagen concludes, is eliminationist ideology. The guards consciously chose to brutalise and kill their Jewish prisoners because that was their strongest desire.

The fourth and last part of Goldhagen's methodological strategy is an attempt to supplement the evidence of his crucial cases by applying the hypothetico-deductive procedure – by arguing that eliminationist ideology is a better explanation for the actions of ordinary perpetrators of the Holocaust than four alternative theories. Thus he systematically canvasses and rejects the theories that ordinary Germans killed because they were compelled to follow orders; because of peer-group pressure (a thesis which he attributes to Browning); because of the desire for personal advancement; and because the highly bureaucratic nature of the killing diminished the sense of individual responsibility.

Having outlined Browning's theory, let us evaluate it according to the same criteria which we applied to Browning's: *explanatory power* and *reliability*.

☐ *Explanatory power*

Since Goldhagen insists that eliminationist ideology was *sui generis* to Germany, his theory is not generalisable to other instances of genocide. Although this might be considered a limitation, Goldhagen claims that its compensatory strength is its robustness within the unique German case: it can explain why, within this unique case, the same outcomes occurred under such varied circumstances. To be more precise, it can explain why so many ordinary Germans acted in the same ways even though their personalities were highly diverse, they occupied such a wide variety of institutional roles, and operated in so many different local settings. Goldhagen, however, does not attempt to explain exceptional cases – the ordinary perpetrators who chose not to kill and brutalise Jews – even though he often mentions them.

☐ *Reliability*

The theory meets some of our plausibility criteria. For one thing, it is well illustrated with positive examples and goes to considerable lengths to specify the linkages between the postulated causal mechanism and the phenomena. For another, although monocausal explanations do not cohere with our background assumptions about appropriate explanations, Goldhagen's particular monocausal explanation is compatible (at least in very broad terms) with our background beliefs about the motives behind the Holocaust. But what about the criteria of logicality and falsifiablity? Does the theory pass these plausibility tests? There seem to be five major problems here.

1. It is impossible to falsify Goldhagen's thesis, within the terms it is stated, that eliminationist ideology had become embedded in German culture by the late nineteenth century – the origins argument. At the root of the problem is his concept of eliminationism. Goldhagen consistently defines late nineteenth-century eliminationism in relation to the prescriptions advanced by antisemitic ideologues and writers to solve the 'Jewish problem'. But his argument about what eliminationism meant to these antisemitic writers – and by extension antisemites in general – is inconsistent. Towards the beginning of his discussion of late nineteenth-century antisemitism, he says that 'all who spoke out on the "Jewish problem"' were unclear about how to eliminate Jewish influence, and that no one prescription was more favoured than the others. In Goldhagen's words, 'What "elimination" – in the sense of successfully ridding Germany of Jewishness – meant, and the manner in which this was to be done, was unclear and hazy to many, and found no consensus during the period of modern German antisemitism. But the necessity of elimination of Jewishisness was clear to all.'[47] He even states a little later that 'What is astonishing…is that a large percentage of the antisemites proposed no action at all, despite their belief that the Jews were dreaded and powerful enemies.'[48] As the discussion progresses, however, Goldhagen increasingly shifts his ground. His first step in this direction is to say that although many different prescriptions were proposed and

these were 'rough functional equivalents', 'the most prominent antisemitic writers increasingly accepted the logic of
their beliefs, calling for nothing less than the Jews' extermination.'[49] His second step is to make the emphatic statement
that '*The eliminationist mind-set tended towards an exterminationist
one*'.[50] By the end of the discussion he is stating, 'It is incontestable that racial antisemitism was the salient form of antisemitism in Germany....It is incontestable that this racial
antisemitism which held the Jews to pose a mortal threat to
Germany was pregnant with murder.' [51] In other words,
Goldhagen starts with the cautious claim that there was no
consensus amongst late nineteenth-century antisemitic writers about how to eliminate Jewish influence ('Jewishness'),
and ends up with the 'incontestable' claim that the 'salient'
view of late nineteenth-century antisemitic writers (and of
antisemites in general) logically entailed the extermination
of Jews. We begin with a claim that the writers had no consensus about how to solve the 'Jewish problem'; we end with
the claim that writers had a 'salient solution' 'pregnant with
murder'. We begin with the statement that the writers
sought the elimination of 'Jewishness' (Jewish influence); we
end with him virtually saying that the goal of antisemites was
the extermination of the Jewish people. In short, since Goldhagen fails to define late nineteenth-century eliminationist
ideology consistently, it is impossible to refute his origins
argument.

2. A similar confusion exists in Goldhagen's continuity thesis –
that the mind-set behind the exterminationist programme of
the Nazi regime was directly descended from nineteenth-
century eliminationist ideology. In some contexts, Goldhagen
seems to hold the position that the Nazi regime 'unshackled'
the ideology, 'mobilized' it, '*activated*' it, implying that they
simply adopted it and put it into practice without changing its
semantic content.[52] In other passages, he puts more onus on
the Nazis, stating that they 'accentuated', 'intensified', 'elaborated' the ideology, implying that they changed its semantic
content, making it more pernicious (appreciably more?) than
it would have been had they not come power.[53] In still another
passage, he takes both positions, contending that Hitler
'essentially unleashed, even if he also continually inflamed'

eliminationist ideology.[54] Then there are contexts where he says something different again, that the genocidal programme of the Nazis 'was a more extreme "solution" to a problem, the diagnosis of which had long been agreed upon in Germany', implying that the Nazis adopted and put into action the most pernicious version of an existing ideology which had many variants.[55] Given the differences between these formulations and the consequent lack of clarity in the argument, it is impossible to test Goldhagen's continuity thesis.

3. Earlier we noted that Goldhagen insists that perpetrators had every incentive to lie in their post-war trial testimonies about the fact that they were motivated by antisemitism to kill Jews. As a consequence, he says, the only proper way of ascertaining that they were motivated by antisemitism is to look at the evidence of their actions. To be precise, he claims that there are four types of perpetrator actions that tell us that eliminationist ideology motivated the perpetrators. Is he right? It is vital to remember here that his procedure is a deductive one. He deduces antisemitic motives from actions. He assumes, that is, that certain kinds of motives are unambiguously revealed in certain types of actions. If we know the actions, we know the motives. Now, as a general principle the deductive procedure is a quite legitimate form of enquiry. But its application can fail under two circumstances. One failure occurs where the investigator deduces auxiliary hypotheses from a core assumption and the auxiliaries are mutually incompatible – one or more of them contradict(s) one or more of the others. The second failure arises where the auxiliary hypotheses do not necessarily follow from the core theory – a problem known as the **fallacy of affirming the consequent**. In Goldhagen's case, the auxiliary hypotheses are free of the first problem but they are afflicted by the second. Goldhagen contends that perpetrators must have been motivated by eliminationist ideology since they killed gratuitously, engaged in gratuitous cruelties and humiliations, followed orders eagerly and diligently, and spurned opportunities to save victims and lessen their suffering. But the conclusion does not necessarily follow from the premise. There are other logical possibilities which Goldhagen's

explanation does not preclude. We could, for example, deduce from the same actions that what motivated perpetrators were various other factors such as sadistic or psychopathic person-ality drives, peer group pressure, special ideological and mil-itary training, a past career in a Nazi killing institution where they had learned that brutalising Jews was necessary and normal, the example of and standards set by brutal and pow-erful leaders of camps and killing squads, and so on. To be sure, Goldhagen implicitly attempts to anticipate this objection by saying that his explanation is better than alter-native explanations. Whether this argument is successful, is an issue that will be examined later.

4. Another of Goldhagen's key claims is the 'ordinary Germans' thesis – that perpetrators, irrespective of the perpetrator institutions they belonged to, were 'ordinary Germans'. Is this proposition coherent? Goldhagen goes to considerable pains in one particular part of the book to explicate his con-cept of perpetrators as ordinary Germans – the part describing the backgrounds of the men belonging to Police Battalion 101. Here he employs a range of criteria to deter-mine whether the men were 'representative Germans', 'ordinary Germans', and after examining a variety of statist-ical data comes to the definite conclusion that they meet these criteria. As Goldhagen puts it: 'Overwhelmingly, they consisted of ordinary Germans – of both kinds – those who were in the [Nazi] Party and, especially, those who were not.'[56] What makes him so certain? In his words, 'The most important characteristic' for 'assessing...the degree to which they were, as a group, representative of German society – that is, ordinary Germans – is their degree of Nazification.... It is those who had no Nazi or SS affiliation who are analytic-ally the most significant people, because they (and the thou-sands like them in other police battalions) provide insight into the likely conduct of other ordinary Germans, had they too been asked to become genocidal killers.'[57] True, he says, the data indicate that the proportion of the men who were Nazi Party members was rather higher than the German average; but, he says, we should not give too much weight to this since 'Being a member of the Party was a rather ordinary distinction in Germany'. What is far more telling is that so

few of the men belonged to the SS: 'the most remarkable and significant fact is that 96 per cent of these men were not in the SS, the association of the true believers'.[58] Given all this, how can Goldhagen designate all categories of perpetrators as 'ordinary Germans' when SS men constituted such a large segment of the perpetrator population? He says himself that the SS ran the vast camp system and that the operatives of SS mobile killing units considerably outnumbered the men belonging to police battalions involved in genocidal activities.[59] If a low level of SS membership is the key criterion that signifies that the men of Police Battalion 101 were 'ordinary Germans', then by the same criterion the myriads of SS men who bulked large in the perpetrator population were not 'ordinary Germans'. Either Goldhagen's key criterion of 'ordinary Germans' is wrong or masses of perpetrators were not 'ordinary Germans'. He cannot apply the concept 'ordinary Germans' both to Police Battalion 101 and to the perpetrator population as a whole.[60]

5. Lastly, there are the problems of logic in two of Goldhagen's crucial cases. (Remember here that a 'crucial case' is one which has properties that would lead us to expect it to confound a preferred hypothesis.) Now, Goldhagen says that we would expect work camps *not* to kill Jews since Jews were a valuable source of labour. The problem here, however, is that Goldhagen himself indicates that the SS higher authorities in their own highly ambivalent fashion wanted the camps both to make Jews suffer as well as to extract labour services from them. Consequently, we do not know how far the monstrous brutalities inflicted on Jews by the guards were the product of the expectations of the SS higher authorities and the implementation of camp rules, and how far they were the product of the free choices exercised by the guards. Certainly, Goldhagen's descriptions suggest that the guards did nothing to spare the suffering of Jews and carried out their orders enthusiastically. But given that a large portion of the guards were SS men – an 'association of true believers' in Goldhagen's own words – it is scarcely surprising that they failed when opportunity offered to act humanely towards Jewish inmates!

The death march is a bad crucial case but for a different reason. Goldhagen says we would expect the death march guards *not* to kill Jews since Himmler ordered them not to and since they could have been caught in the act by Allied forces, known to be closing in on the column. Now, with this case we certainly do find ordinary perpetrators – the guards – who killed, disobeying the orders of the Nazi leadership (Himmler). But it is not a crucial case because there is a key factor that would lead us to suspect that their motives for killing had little or nothing to do with eliminationist ideology. This key factor is the personality of Alois Dörr, the command-ant of the Helmbrechts' camp and leader of the march. Goldhagen says 'Camp commanders had it within their pow-er to ameliorate conditions, as some did. Dörr was not among them…. Dörr was an exacting superior and cruel to the prisoners…a passionate Jew hater'.[61] By Goldhagen's own definition, Dörr was not an 'ordinary German' but a member of the killer elite, having joined the SS in 1933. Goldhagen even says that Dörr could well have been selected by the higher authorities to be the Helmbrechts' comman-dant since he had all the requisite aptitudes 'to torture and slaughter Jews'.[62] According to Goldhagen's own evidence, Dörr was directly responsible for many of the deliberate cru-elties that helped to produce the high death rates during the march: it was his orders that may have initiated the march in the first place, that prevented the Jews from receiving addi-tional issues of clothing before the march, that prevented the column from taking adequate food supplies, that forced the Jews on 'several occasions' to sleep outdoors in the freezing weather, and that produced 'some' of the executions.[63] With-out doubt, many brutalities were committed by the guards (ordinary Germans) without orders from Dörr; but these are ambiguous examples of gratuitous actions by 'ordinary Germans': the guards were a tight-knit community whose norms appear to have been defined by their fanatical com-mandent.[64]

In relation to the criteria of *credibility*, Goldhagen's account has several strengths. One is his determination to comprehend the actions of perpetrators from their own perspective. Another is his acute sensitivity to the specificities of context. The last is his skilful use of photographic evidence. As against that, the theory has three major empirical problems.

The first concerns his claim that eliminationist ideology was entrenched by the late nineteenth century. We noted previously that to demonstrate the claim, he attempts to show (a) that eliminationist ideology originated from German antisemitic literature, and (b) that Wilhelmine Germany's institutions were responsible for fixing the ideology into German popular culture. To support (a), Goldhagen depends on, and generalises from, the unpublished secondary study of 51 'prominent antisemitic writers and publications' appearing between 1861 and 1895. Goldhagen's summary of the study begs vital evidential questions. Were the writings sampled by the study typical of the totality of antisemitic writings of the era? How did the study select these particular cases and how far does the manner in which it selected them determine the results of the analysis? In what terms were they 'prominent' – their popularity, their reputability, their notoriety and contentiousness, or the extremity of their views? And how numerous and influential were the writings of an eliminationist bent in relation to all the writings that were either not antisemitic or antiantisemitic? To support (b), Goldhagen cites a handful of positive examples of voluntary organizations that expressed or condoned antisemitic sentiments. Goldhagen does nothing to assure us of the typicality of these cases even though it is obvious that late nineteenth century Germany must have had myriads of voluntary organisations. Moreover, with one exception, he fails to demonstrate that these organisations echoed – and by implication popularised – the eliminationist prescriptions of the antisemitic writers. Lastly, he admits that this exception – the antisemitic political parties founded in the 1880s which favoured the exterminationist prescription – experienced a decline in their electoral fortunes during the early twentieth century.[65]

The second problem relates to his bold contention that Germany's long standing eliminationist antisemitism was the necessary *and* sufficient motivating cause of perpetrator actions. To demonstrate this bold claim, Goldhagen must (at the very least) show us that little or none of the eliminationist content of German antisemitism can be found in other strongly antisemitic cultures. But Goldhagen advances no such empirical evidence.[66] Indeed, he never discusses the content of antisemitism in other societies at all, some of which had a much worse record of antisemitism than pre-Nazi Germany.[67]

The third empirical problem resides in Goldhagen's claim that perpetrators were ordinary Germans. This is quite misleading since Goldhagen's own data show that many mobile killing squads and contingents of camp guards were partly or almost wholly made up of east Europeans (notably, Ukrainians and Lithuanians) and so-called 'ethnic Germans' (people claiming German ethnicity who had settled in eastern Europe).[68] Indeed, he narrates deeds involving both German units and 'Hiwis' (eastern European SS auxillary units led by German officers) where the 'Hiwis' behaved far more brutally than the German units.

■ Browning or Goldhagen?

Having analysed the respective strengths and weaknesses of the two rival theories, let us now decide which one is best. In terms of explanatory power, little separates them. As Goldhagen says that he has found the sufficient and necessary motivating cause of perpetrator actions, he claims to be able to account for all perpetrator actions during the Holocaust; but as Browning implies that he has found a sufficient motivating cause, he cannot account for all perpetrator actions during the Holocaust – only some of them. So as an explanation of perpetrator actions in the Holocaust, Goldhagen's theory is more useful. However, Browning says his theory has cross-cultural applications – it is generalisable to instances of genocide in every modern society at war – whereas Goldhagen says that his model is specific to the Holocaust and is not generalisable to other cultures. Hence, as a theory about genocide in general, Browning's theory is more useful. To be sure, Browning makes more attempts to explain the nuances of perpetrator conduct – the exceptions and the variations – than Goldhagen does. As against that, he does not attempt to deal with a variety of perpetrator institutions – and this Goldhagen certainly does.

How should we rank the two rival theories in relation to our reliability criteria? We saw that Browning's explanation of Police Battalion 101 has some serious empirical problems. We found that that his evidence for the motives of the men was thin; begged vital questions about its typicality; and, despite his scholarly methods, failed to overcome our doubts about its veracity.

But as unsatisfactory as Browning's direct evidence was, his theory did – with some minor exceptions – pass the tests of plausibility. Moreover, he is able to compensate for its empirical weaknesses by refuting alternative theories. The same, however, cannot be said for Goldhagen's theory.

As we saw, Goldhagen's theory failed critical tests of plausibility. His key claims – that eliminationist ideology was entrenched by the late nineteenth century, that the Nazi regime inherited the ideology and did not create it, and that perpetrators were ordinary Germans – are not coherently formulated and thus cannot be falsified. His method for confirming the theory is designed around the three crucial cases, and of these, one does not necessarily tell us anything about the volitional conduct of perpetrators as 'ordinary Germans', and the second does not fit the prescription of a crucial case. Most important of all, is the implausibility of his central claim – that the central motivating cause of perpetrator actions was eliminationist ideology. He rests the claim on the argument that we can deduce eliminationist ideology from four types of perpetrator action; but the claim is implausible since the supporting argument commits the fallacy of affirming the consequent – it is possible to deduce other sources of perpetrator motivation from the same types of actions.

To be sure, Goldhagen implicitly anticipates this objection to his central claim by subjecting many of these other theories to severe criticism. His main criticism is that they are generalising theories which cannot account for the peculiarities of the German case. To be more precise, they cannot explain why Germans killed Jews whereas other peoples such as Italians or Danes did not. One of these generalising theories – that perpetrators were motivated by peer group pressure – he attributes to Browning. But this misrepresents Browning's case. First, although peer group pressure is the primary factor in Browning's theory, it is not, as Goldhagen implies, the only factor. We noted earlier that Browning's theory contends that what led ordinary men to be willing killers was primarily peer group pressure *and* two secondary factors – racism and the polarising effects of war – *as well as* several minor factors. Second, the two secondary factors in Browning's thesis can, in combination, account for the peculiarities of the German case. Browning could account for the failure of peoples such Italians and Danes to kill Jews by arguing that, unlike Germans, they did not have eliminationist racist attitudes towards Jews and, in addition, were not affected by the siege mentality of war – at least, not to the same degree. It is obvious that Browning's theorising about these secondary factors is underdeveloped. It is true that he fails to justify the ranking he gives them. Moreover, a good case could be made that he understates or misinterprets, perhaps badly, the role of 'racism' in motivating ordinary Germans to be willing executioners. But the fact remains that he does not, contrary to what Goldhagen implies, ignore the role of racism as a precondition for perpetrator action during the Holocaust.[69] In short, Goldhagen fails to enhance the plausibility of his theory by severely criticising its rivals since he misrepresents the strongest of these rivals – Browning's theory. The latter certainly is empirically inadequate, but it is eminently plausible whereas Goldhagen's does not pass this minimum test of reliability.

But what about the criteria we have said very little about – those of originality? Does Goldhagen rank higher by this standard than Browning? In terms of novel use of evidence, they are fairly equal. Although Browning was the first to use war-crime trial testimonies as primary source material, Goldhagen's use of photographic evidence is far more imaginative. In relation to originality of approach, again not much distinguishes them. Browning must be given credit for devising the highly focused institutional case study to investigate everyday perpetrator actions; but Goldhagen must be given credit for extending the approach to work camps, a hitherto unexamined field of perpetrator action. As far as methodology is concerned, Goldhagen is clearly the more innovative. While Browning's study employs the standard tools of textual scholarship, Goldhagen's use of deductive argument to circumvent the evidential problems associated with perpetrator intentions, and his use of crucial cases to avoid the problems of unrepresentative cases, are ingenious, indeed brilliantly imaginative – even if their implementation goes astray. On the other hand, however, we could say that Browning's explanation was, for its time, original, whereas Goldhagen's was not: by the time Goldhagen began his research, antisemitism had long been a standard part of the explanation of the Holocaust, even though Goldhagen took it much further. In addition, Browning virtually discovered the phenomenon of compliance by ordinary men – and that discovery made Goldhagen's study possible.

In sum, the two theories are of roughly equal value in relation to our explanatory power principle; but Browning's is substantially superior in relation to the reliability principle and marginally superior perhaps in relation to the originality principle. All things considered, our verdict must be that Browning's theory is the best.

■ Conclusion

This chapter started by saying that social historians select from a wide range of criteria when they evaluate rival explanatory theories, and that the conventions governing the choice of these criteria were too loose. The chapter then proposed how the criteria could be prioritised and ordered into a more rational evaluative strategy built around the three fundamental principles of originality, explanatory power and reliability.

What can be learnt from the experience of testing the strategy against Browning's and Goldhagen's rival explanations? The first point to make is that the exercise of matching each rival against all those criteria was somewhat cumbersome and mechanical. So when we engage in evaluations of other sets of rival theories, we may consider combining some of the criteria and not using others. The second point to make is that although the strategy worked in this particular instance, one swallow does not make a summer – this particular set of rival explanations might not be typical of all the other sets. Although the strategy found a winner this time, it might have greater difficulty the next. Hence, we may have to consider giving different weights to the three guiding principles – but how we do this will obviously have to be justified with good arguments, not an easy thing for social historians given that they are not in the habit of defending the criteria they select for evaluating competing explanations.

Then there is the question about the sequence of the sieves we employed under the reliability principle. Why should we use the plausibility sieve first, then the credibility one, and end up sieving away with the probability criteria? Why should we proceed in this particular sequence and not in another? My answer to this is that the probability criteria must come last because their application requires the most resources which would be wasted if the other – and less resource-demanding criteria – showed that the explanation suffered from more serious problems. Moreover, the plausibility screening must come first because it is the most basic: it tells us quite decisively whether an explanation is impossible. If an explanation cannot pass the plausibility tests of logicality and falsifiability, then there is no point going to all the trouble of seeing how well it is supported by the empirical evidence, unless the rival also fails these tests. A theory that is neither logical nor testable will not fly no matter how much evidence supports it.

The last point is the harshness of our verdicts. We might consider being more generous to an explanatory theory which uses an unusual or innovative methodology to solve difficult evidential problems even though, like Goldhagen's, it may in its particular application create more problems than it solves. If the methodology has the potential to help us solve other kinds of difficult evidential problems, should we not give more credit to the person who showed us the way?

Notes, References and Further Reading

☐ Introduction (pp. 1–12)

1. A 1982 survey of methods courses in 103 history programmes in the USA found that only 43 per cent of history departments offered courses in quantitative analysis and/or data processing. A.G. Bogue 'The Quest for Numeracy: Data and Methods in American Political History', *Journal of Interdisciplinary History*, vol. 21, 1, 1990, pp. 89–116.
2. See, e.g., the otherwise excellent book by B.D. Palmer, *Descent into Discourse: The Reification of Language and the Writing of Social History*, Philadelphia, 1990, p. 52 where 'method' is unfavourably equated with cliometrics. The idea that history should be concerned with method is condemned by J. Barzun, *Clio and the Doctors: Psycho-History, Quanto-History & History*, Chicago, 1974.
3. Felix Gilbert in his 'Introduction' to *Historical Studies Today*, in F. Gilbert and S.R. Graubard, eds, New York, 1972, p. xxi, pointed out that the growing interest in new forms of history had not led to a corresponding expansion in the content of the handbooks summarising the principles of historical method: this seems to me to be as true now as it was then.

☐ Further Reading

The most comprehensive work on the dimensions of social history is Peter Stearns, ed., *Encyclopedia of Social History*, New York, 1994. Not only is the whole text worth browsing but all of its entries are accompanied with useful references. More specialised but also worth browsing and consulting is the monumental work, M. Cayton, E. Gorn, and P. Williams, eds, *Encyclopedia of American Social History*, 3 vols, New York, 1993.

Students can find informative overviews on the historiography of social history in P. Burke, ed., *New Perspectives on Historical Writing*, University Park, PA, 1992 (especially Burke's brief introduction and conclusion, and Sharpe's chapter); the essays in J. Le Goff and P. Nora, eds, *Constructing the Past: Essays in Historical Methodology*, Cambridge, 1985; the essays in T. Rabb and R.I. Rotberg, eds, *The New History: the 1980s and Beyond. Studies in Interdisciplinary History*, Princeton, 1982. The most recent surveys are Ignacio Olábarri, '"New" New History: A *Longue Durée*

Structure', *History and Theory*, vol. 34, 1995, pp. 1–29; John Tosh, *The Pursuit of History*, 2nd edn, London, 1992; and Miles Taylor, 'The Beginnings of British Social History?', *History Workshop Journal*, vol. 43, 1997, pp. 155–76. Also informative but now somewhat dated are Geoff Eley, 'Some Recent Tendencies in Social History', in G.G. Iggers and H.T. Parker, eds, *International Handbook of Historical Studies*, Westport, Conn., 1979; E.Breisach, *Historiography: Ancient Medieval, & Modern*, Chicago, 1983; E. Hobsbawm, 'From Social History to the History of Society', in F. Gilbert and S.R. Graubard, eds, *Historical Studies Today*, New York, 1972; 'Introduction', in P. Thane and A. Sutcliffe, eds, *Essays in Social History*, vol. 2, Oxford, 1986.

Clear and informative introductions for historians to the concepts and theories of certain of the social sciences are Peter Burke, *Sociology and History*, London, 1980 and *History and Social Theory*, Cambridge, 1992. Views on the relationship of social history to the social sciences abound: amongst them are Charles Tilly, *As Sociology Meets History*, New York, 1981; Philip Abrams, *Historical Sociology*, Ithaca, 1982; Denis Smith, *The Rise of Historical Sociology*, Philadelphia, 1991; Fernand Braudel, *On History*, London, 1980, part 2; and (for a traditionalist's viewpoint) Gertrude Himmelfarb, *The New History and the Old*, Cambridge, Mass., 1987. Criticisms by people inside the discipline include Lawrence Stone, *The Past and the Present Revisited*, London, 1987; and P.N. Stearns, 'Coming of Age', *Journal of Social History*, vol. 10, 2, 1976, pp. 246–55.

Criticisms of social history as a discipline can be found in Himmelfarb, *The New History*. No one work has tried overtly to survey all the 'bedrock' issues; but Christopher Lloyd touches on many of these as well as the debates that have gone on over some of the sub-disciplines in his 'The Methodologies of Social History: A Critical Survey and Defense of Structurism', in *History and Theory*, vol. 30, 1991, pp. 180–219.

The exclusive studies on the methodology of social history include Christopher Lloyd, *Explanation in Social History*, New York, 1985, and his article cited above. The works by Theda Skocpol and her associates on comparative methods are T. Skocpol, ed., *Vision and Method in Historical Sociology*, Cambridge, 1984 (which has an excellent annotated bibliography); and T. Skocpol and M. Somers, 'The Uses of Comparative History in Macrosocial Enquiry', *Comparative Studies in Society and History*, vol. 22, 2, 1980, pp. 174–97. Robert F. Berkhofer, *A Behavioral Approach to Historical Analysis*, New York, 1969, has interesting summary discussion on the viewpoint of the actor, the problems of explanation, and types of groups.

Short and lucid introductions to post-modernism for historians include F.R. Ankersmit, 'Historiography and Postmodernism,' *History and Theory*, vol. 28, 1989, pp. 137–53; K. Windschuttle, *The Killing of History*, Sydney, 1996; G.G. Iggers, 'Rationality and History', in Henry Kozicki, ed., *Developments in Modern Historiography*, New York, 1993; K. Jenkins, *Re-Thinking History*, London, 1991; A. Munslow, *Deconstructing History*, London, 1997.

☐ **1 The Problem of Absent Social Categories (pp. 13–38)**

1. L. Davidoff, *Worlds Between: Historical Perspectives on Gender and Class*, Cambridge, 1995, p. 14.
2. L.J. Moore, 'Good Old-Fashioned New Social History...', *Reviews in American History*, vol. 24, 4, Dec. 1996, p. 559.
3. Special issue of the *Journal of Social History*, Supplement, vol. 29, 1995: B.W. Bienstock, 'Everything Old is New Again...', pp. 62, 61; G.R. Andrews, 'Social History and the Populist Moment', p. 109; P.N. Stearns, 'Uncivil War...', p. 10; J. Kocka, 'What is Leftist about Social History Today?', p. 70.
4. See D. Little, *Varieties of Social Explanation: An Introduction to the Philosophy of Social Science*, Boulder, 1991.
5. E.P. Thompson, *The Making of the English Working Class*, London, 1965.
6. Thompson, *The Making*, p. 11.
7. Thus workplace customary rights are economically determined but Paine's *The Rights of Man* is not.
8. Thompson, *The Making*, p. 10.
9. Thompson, *The Making*, p. 194.
10. C. Hall, 'The Tale of Samuel and Jemima: Gender and Working-Class Culture in Early Nineteenth-Century England', in T. Bennett, C. Mercer and J. Woollacott, eds, *Popular Culture and Social Relations*, Milton Keynes, 1986.
11. Hall, 'Samuel and Jemima', p. 75, my emphasis.
12. Hall, 'Samuel and Jemima', p. 75.
13. See Thompson's much quoted and much criticised comment in *The Making* (p. 417) that the role of Female Reform Societies 'was confined to giving moral support to the men....'
14. Although the article's attack on *The Making* is oblique, in a later book co-authored with L. Davidoff she expressly states that it was this text she was criticising. See L. Davidoff and C. Hall, *Family Fortunes: Men and Women of the English Middle Class, 1780–1850*, London, 1987, p. 30 and p. 474 fn. 61.
15. Hall, 'Samuel and Jemima', p. 89.
16. Hall, 'Samuel and Jemima', pp. 75, 73.
17. Hall, 'Samuel and Jemima', pp. 74–5.
18. Hall, 'Samuel and Jemima', pp. 74 and 80.
19. F. Braudel, *The Mediterranean and the Mediterranean World in the Age of Philip London, II*, trs. S. Reynolds, 2 vols, 1972. An abbreviated version, edited by Richard Ollard, was published in 1992. The term *Annales* comes from the title of the journal which the leaders of the movement founded in 1929, *Annales d'histoire sociale et économique*. It is now called *Annales: économies, sociétés, civilisations*.

20. Bernard Bailyn quoted in J.H. Hexter, 'Fernand Braudel and the *Monde Braudellien*,' in *On Historians: Reappraisals of Some of the Makers of Modern History*, Cambridge, Mass., 1979, p. 135.

☐ **Further Reading**

There has been little systematic discussion by social historians on the problem of full accounts and absences. Some useful comments are in J. Hughes, *The Philosophy of Social Research*, 2nd edn, London, 1990, pp. 53, 106–7; and C. Behan McCullagh, 'The Truth of Historical Narratives', *History and Theory*, Beiheft 26, 1987, pp. 30–46.

The notion that the subject-matter of social history consists of large aggregates has not been accepted by some practitioners. See e.g. R. Cobb, 'Modern French History in Britain', *Proceedings of the British Academy*, 60, 1974, pp. 271–93; and T. Zeldon, 'Social History and Total History', *Journal of Social History*, vol. 10, 2, Winter 1976, pp. 237–45.

Thompson's works have attracted a great deal of discussion. The clearest and simplest introduction to his ideas, which also provides a comprehensive bibliography, is E.K. Trimberger, 'E.P. Thompson: Understanding the Process of History', in T. Skocpol, ed., *Vision and Method in Historical Sociology*, Cambridge, 1984. Also worth consulting is B.H. Moss, 'Republican Socialism and the Making of the Working Class in Britain, France, and the United States: A Critique of Thompsonian Culturalism', *Comparative Studies in Society and History*, vol. 35, 2, April 1993, pp. 390–413.

Other critiques by feminist historians of *The Making* include J.W. Scott, *Gender and the Politics of History*, New York, 1988, Ch. 4; S. Alexander, 'Women, Class and Sexual Differences', *History Workshop*, 17, Spring 1984, pp. 125–49. A tough rejoinder to Scott's critique of *The Making* is Palmer, *Descent into Discourse*, Ch. 2. A more sympathetic treatment of Thompson by a feminist historian is Anna Clark, *The Struggle for the Breeches: Gender and the Making of the British Working Class*, Berkeley, 1995.

Commentaries on Braudel's *The Mediterranean* abound. They should be read before *The Mediterranean* itself is tackled. The best is J.H. Hexter's article cited above.

Commentaries on the *Annales* school include T. Stoianovich, *French Historical Method: The Annales Paradigm*, Ithaca, 1976; P. Burke, *The French Historical Revolution: The Annales School, 1929–89*, Cambridge, 1990; G. Iggers, *New Directions in European Historiography*, rev. edn, London, 1984, Ch. 2; and the short article by Colin Lucas, 'Introduction', in J. Le Goff and P. Nora, eds, *Constructing the Past: Essays in Historical Methodology*, Cambridge, 1985.

2 The Problem of Generalising from Fragmentary Evidence (pp. 39–57)

1. T. Burnard, 'Ethnicity in Colonial American Historiography: A New Organising Principle?', *Australasian Journal of American Studies*, vol. 11, July 1992, p. 4. Note, however, that in France where the *Annales* school has been immensely influential, there has been a strong tendency for historians outside the school to follow the *Annales* paradigm in their local case studies. A prime example of collaborative research based on local case studies is that conducted by the Cambridge Population Group; this has produced standardised investigations on a range of demographic questions.

2. Davidoff and Hall, *Family Fortunes*.

3. Davidoff and Hall, *Family Fortunes*, pp. 279, 13. My emphasis.

4. It is not clear from the text whether the seven types of 'investment' have equal explanatory capacity or vary in explanatory capacity, whether the whole lot as a group were required to ensure the upward mobility of the male, or whether any one type would be sufficient, and whether some were crucial and others were dispensable.

5. Note that the authors do not cite or discuss counter-examples. The greater problem with the authors' method is that it does not tell us how important the contribution of women was in relation to a host of other possible factors driving male upward mobility. The authors make no attempt, for example, to show that the skills and social contacts, the access to capital and the good standing of the female kin exercised more influence on male upward mobility than other attributes possessed by the men.

6. Himmelfarb, *The New History*, p. 55.

7. J.J. Tobias, *Crime and Industrial Society in the 19th Century*, London, 1967.

8. Tobias, *Crime and Industrial Society*, p. 128. He also refers to them as 'well-informed', pp. 151, 214.

9. Tobias, *Crime and Industrial Society*, pp. 125ff.

10. M. Devitt and K. Sterelny, *Language and Reality; An Introduction to the Philosophy of Language*, Oxford, 1987, p. 8; also pp. 238ff. See too H.E. Longino, *Science as Social Knowledge*, Princeton, 1990, p. 45.

11. Keith Thomas, *Man and the Natural World: Changing Attitudes in England 1500–1800*, London, 1983.

12. Thomas, *Man and the Natural World*, pp. 242–54.

13. The ancient pastoral ideal, he writes, 'has survived into the modern industrial world. It can be seen in the rural imagery so often employed to advertise consumer goods; and in the vague desire of so many people to end their days in a country cottage. Sentimental

though they are, such feelings reflect the unease generated by the progress of human civilisation and a reluctance to accept the urban and industrial facts of modern life.' Thomas, *Man and the Natural World*, pp. 253–4.

14. A. Rosenberg, *Philosophy of Social Science*, 2nd edn, Boulder, 1995.
15. Thomas, *Man and the Natural World*, pp. 70ff.
16. Clifford Geertz, 'Common Sense as a Cultural System', in *Local Knowledge: Further Essays in Interpretive Anthropology*, New York, 1983, seems to argue that all common sense beliefs in a society are specific to it.

☐   **Further Reading**

Additional discussion of the problem of fragmentary evidence can be found in L. Stone, 'Prosopography', and J. Habakkuk, 'Economic History and Economic Theory', in Gilbert and Graubard, eds, *Historical Studies Today*.

A stinging attack on the method whereby historians look for positive examples and ignore counter-examples is Hexter, 'The Historical Method of Christopher Hill', in *On Historians*. Hexter's attack is rather unfair in that he fails to acknowledge that a great many historians, including leading historians, employ this method to support crucial claims far more often than he indicates.

In philosophy a version of the problem of fragmentary evidence is the problem of induction; the philosopher most associated with the attack on induction as a method is Karl Popper. A good introduction to Popper's thought is Lloyd, *Explanation in Social History*, pp. 55ff.

Some critiques of Davidoff and Hall are A. Vickery, 'Shaking the Separate Spheres; Did Women Really Descend into Graceful Indolence?', in *Times Literary Supplement*, 12 March 1993, pp. 6–7; J. Tosh, 'What should Historians do with Masculinity?', *History Workshop*, no. 38, 1994, pp. 179–202; and the review of the book by J. Saville in *History Workshop*, no. 26, 1988, pp. 188–90.

A penetrating and succinct discussion of the problems in Tobias is D. Philips, *Crime and Authority in Victorian England: the Black Country 1835–1860*, London, 1977. See also V.A.C. Gatrell and T.B. Hadden, 'Criminal Statistics and their Interpretation', in E.A. Wrigley, ed., *Nineteenth-century Society: Essays in the Use of Quantitative Methods for the Study of Social Data*, Cambridge, 1972.

A most accessible discussion by a philosopher of history on the use of common sense and its limitations in historical accounts is Patrick Gardiner, *The Nature of Historical Explanation*, London, 1952, Ch. 2. Also helpful is W.H. Walsh, *An Introduction to Philosophy of History*, London, 1967, Ch. 3, sections 4, 5.

A comprehensive discussion of the techniques of 'internal source criticism' is in R.J. Shafer, *A Guide to Historical Method*, rev. edn, Homewood, Ill., 1974.

3 Some Solutions for the Problem of Fragmentary Evidence (pp. 58–84)

1. A. Macfarlane, *Witchcraft in Tudor and Stuart England*, London, 1970, p. 168.
2. G. King, R.O. Keohane, and S. Verba, *Designing Social Inquiry; Scientific Inference in Qualitative Research*, Princeton, 1994, suggest and discuss a multitude of good techniques for the method.
3. See Carl Hempel, 'The Function of General Laws in History', in P. Gardiner, ed., *Theories of History*, Glencoe, 1959. The issue of whether there were covering laws in history was much debated in the 1950s and 1960s, as shown by the issues in the journal, *History and Theory*. For a summary of the debate see Louis O. Mink, 'Philosophy and Theory of History', in Iggers and Parker, eds, *International Handbook*. A good summary of Hempel is in Lloyd, *Explanation*, pp. 46ff, 61ff.
4. I. Lakatos, *The Methodology of Scientific Research Programmes, Philosophical Papers*, ed., J. Worrall and G. Currie, vol. l, Cambridge, 1978. For a useful summary of Lakatos see Lloyd, *Explanation*, pp. 78ff.
5. L. Stone, *The Crisis of the Aristocracy: 1558–1641*, Oxford, 1965. To my knowledge, Stone has not discussed his views on methodology, at least not systematically, in any publication. In a collection of essays, however, he hints that it consists of a 'feedback process' by which hunches are tested by data and the data in turn generate new hunches; see his *The Past and the Present Revisited*, p. 29.
6. Stone, *Crisis*, pp. 3, 7–8.
7. Stone, *Crisis*, pp. 12–13.
8. Stone, *Crisis*, pp. 746–7. For other discussions in the text on the importance of status see e.g. 223.
9. Note that Stone, *Crisis*, p. 746, confuses the issue about whether the preoccupation with status was peculiar to pre-modern societies. He quotes a sociologist, T.H. Marshall, to the effect that the high value placed on status is universal. His view that pre-modern societies place a much greater value on status than modern societies is much clearer in a later article on the long-term trends in violence in England, 'Homicide and Violence', in his *The Past and the Present Revisited*, pp. 295–310.
10. Stone, *Crisis*, pp. 747ff.
11. He summarises the causes himself in his conclusion, pp. 748–9.
12. Stone, *Crisis*, pp. 199–270. For praise of Stone on this issue, see Hexter, *On Historians*, p. 170.
13. When the book first emerged most of the critics tended to focus on his hypothesis that the aristocracy had declined in wealth. The preoccupation was perhaps inevitable given that the book came out near

the end of protracted and heated debate which R.H. Tawney had sparked in 1941 about whether the aristocracy or the gentry had experienced a decline in wealth prior to the Civil War.

14. Many philosophers of science claim that the problem of 'underdetermination' also prevails in the physical sciences. See L. Laudan, *Science and Relativism: Some Key Controversies in the Philosophy of Science*, Chicago, 1990, Ch. 2.

15. Translated by J. and A. Tedeschi, Baltimore, 1980.

16. Ginzburg, *Cheese and Worms*, pp. 8, 103. There were other members of the tribunal but Ginzburg is not entirely clear about who they were.

17. Ginzburg, *Cheese and Worms*, p. 75.

18. Ginzburg, *Cheese and Worms*, p. 66.

19. Ginzburg, *Cheese and Worms*, p. 53.

20. Ginzburg, *Cheese and Worms*, pp. 41, xxiii, xii; also xix, 20–1, 33, 58–9, 60–1, 68, 112, 117.

21. Ginzburg, *Cheese and Worms*, pp. 62–5, 68.

22. Ginzburg, *Cheese and Worms*, pp. 112ff. On the face of it, another kind of evidence that is inconsistent with the claim is that Menocchio's opinions were described as fantastic by his fellow villages. However, these descriptions are suspect given that they were responses to the inquisitor. Moreover, Ginzburg presents clear evidence that Menocchio was accepted, even respected, by his fellow villagers, see pp. 2, 95.

23. Ginzburg, *Cheese and Worms*, pp. 6–7.

24. Ginzburg, *Cheese and Worms*, pp. 18–19.

25. Ginzburg, *Cheese and Worms*, pp. 19–21.

26. Ginzburg, *Cheese and Worms*, pp. 50, 81. Although note that Ginzburg concedes that Menocchio knew such a man, a painter, who probably lent him books, see pp. 21–7.

27. K. Popper, 'The Rationality Principle' in *Popper Selections*, D. Miller, ed., Princeton, 1985. (An earlier edition of this is *The Pocket Popper*, D. Miller, ed., Oxford, 1983.)

☐   **Further Reading**

The work cited above – King, Keohane and Verba, *Designing Social Inquiry* – also discusses and criticises the crucial case method. The method of crucial cases is outlined by H. Eckstein, 'Case Study and Theory in Political Science', in F.I. Greenstein and N.W. Polsby, eds, *Strategies of Inquiry*, vol. 7 of *Handbook of Political Science*, Reading, Mass., 1975, pp. 79–138.

For another example of the method of extrapolating from comparable cases, see L. Stone's use of modern anthropological case studies to back up his arguments about family mores and household structure in early modern England in his *Family, Sex and Marriage in England 1500–1800*, New York, 1977. Withering criticism of Stone's use of these cases, however, is in a review of the book by A. Macfarlane in *History and Theory*, 18, 1979, pp. 103–26.

A good example of the application of the hypothetical-deductive method (eliminationism) is Dagfinn Føllesdal, 'Hermeneutics and the Hypothetico-Deductive Method', in M. Martin and L. McIntyre, eds, *Readings in the Philosophy of Social Science*, Cambridge, Mass., 1994. A more elaborate variant of the method is C. Behan McCullagh, *Justifying Historical Descriptions*, Cambridge, 1984, Ch. 2.

There are a multitude of critiques of Lawrence Stone's *Crisis*. Among the best is that by Hexter in Chapter 4 of *On Historians*. Stone's account of the influences upon his views about history can be seen in his 'Epilogue: Lawrence Stone – as Seen by Himself', in *The First Modern Society*, eds, A.L. Beier, D. Cannadine and J.M. Rosenheim, Cambridge, 1989.

A discussion of Ginzburg's work which focuses on his use of eliminationist method, is E. Muir, 'Introduction: Observing Trifles', in E. Muir and G. Ruggiero, eds, *Microhistory and the Lost Peoples of Europe*, trs. E. Branch, Baltimore, 1991, pp. xvi ff and fn. 41, p. xxvi.

Close criticism of Popper's logic of the situation model can be found in R. Nadeau, 'Confuting Popper on the Rationality Principle', *Philosophy of the Social Sciences*, vol. 23, 4, 1993, pp. 446–67. Very close to Popper's model is W.H. Dray's notion of the rationale of actions, developed specifically for historians; see, e.g., his *Laws and Explanation in History*, Oxford, 1957. I. Jarvie, an anthropologist, has applied Popper's model in a useful way to cargo cults; see his *The Revolution in Anthropology*, London, 1967.

4 The Problem of Establishing Important Causes (pp. 85–111)

1. E.H. Carr, *What is History?*, Harmondsworth, 1964, pp. 104–5.
2. For excellent summaries and discussions of the major comparative studies by these figures see Skocpol, ed., *Vision and Method in Historical Sociology*.
3. T. Skocpol, *States and Social Revolutions: A Comparative Analysis of France, Russia, and China*, Cambridge, 1979.
4. See her Introduction and concluding chapter, 'Emerging Agendas and Recurrent Strategies in Historical Sociology', in Skocpol, ed., *Vision and Method* ; and Skocpol and Somers, 'Uses of Comparative History in Macrosocial Enquiry', pp. 174–97.
5. *States and Social Revolutions*, pp. 37, 18. In her article, 'Emerging Agendas', she also implies the book was dealing with causal regularities

by citing it as an example in a section headed, 'Analyzing causal regularities in history', pp. 374ff.

6. *States and Social Revolutions*, p. 173.
7. *States and Social Revolutions*, p. 40.
8. *States and Social Revolutions*, p. 37.
9. She is less clear about what the decisive external crisis was for China, but in *States and Social Revolutions*, p. 77, she strongly implies it was the war of 1895–6.
10. *States and Social Revolutions*, pp. 149–50.
11. On Paris see e.g. G. Rudé, *The Crowd in the French Revolution*, Oxford, 1959.
12. *States and Social Revolutions*, p. 113.
13. *States and Social Revolutions*, pp. 149, also p. 154.
14. *States and Social Revolutions*, pp. 151, 153.
15. *States and Social Revolutions*, pp. 153,154.
16. *States and Social Revolutions*, p. 290, my emphasis.
17. *States and Social Revolutions*, p. 288.

☐   **Further Reading**

For an example of a historiographical work that explicitly equates causal regularity with causal importance see Raymond White, 'Causes, Conditions, and Causal Importance', *History and Theory*, vol. 21, 1982, pp. 53–74.

An accessible and helpful philosophical discussion of the problem of ascertaining important causes that is more advanced, is E.O. Wright, A. Levine and E. Sober, *Reconstructing Marxism: Essays on Explanation and the Theory of History*, London, 1992, Ch. 7, 'Causal Asymmetries'. They claim that the concept of causal frequency should be distinguished from that of causal potency. As they see it, important causes are usually identified with causal frequency and that the identification overlooks the question of causal potency.

The best account of historical sociology and works in this genre is P. Abrams, *Historical Sociology*, Ithaca, 1982. He also provides a perceptive and well argued idea about how the antitheses of agency and structure can be reconciled.

For discussion on the systematic comparative method, students are strongly recommended to consult the items mentioned above: the essay by Skocpol and Somers and the collection of essays edited by Skocpol, *Vision and Method*, which has an excellent annotated bibliography. Samuel H. Beer, 'Causal Explanation and Imaginative Re-enactment', *History and Theory*, vol. 3, 1, 1963, pp. 6–29, advances some of the standard objections to systematic comparison.

Also recommended are: N. Smelser, *Comparative Methods in the Social Sciences*, Englewood Cliffs, 1976; V.E. Bonnell, 'Theory, Concepts and Comparison in Historical Sociology', *Comparative Studies in Society and History*, vol. 22, 1980, pp. 156–73; and M. Bloch, 'A Contribution Towards a Comparative History of European Societies', trs. J.E. Anderson, *Land and Work in Medieval Europe: Selected Papers*, London, 1967 (a classic).

For critiques of *States and Social Revolutions* see e.g. J.L. Himmelstein and M.S. Kimmel, 'States and Revolutions: The Implications and Limits of Skocpol's Structural Model,' *American Journal of Sociology*, vol. 86, 1981, pp. 1145–54; and the review by P.T. Manicas in *History and Theory*, vol. 20, 1981, pp. 204–18.

5 The Problem of Establishing Similarities and Differences – of Lumping and Splitting (pp. 112–44)

1. Hexter, *On Historians*, pp. 241ff. The context was a discussion of the works by Christopher Hill and the generalising/particularising traits of historians.

2. Werner Sombart, *Why is There no Socialism in the United States?* ed., C.T. Husbands, White Plains, N.Y., 1976.

3. For a critical view of this argument see e.g. J. Black, *Convergence or Divergence?: Britain and the Continent*, New York, 1994.

4. Historians, as we all know, have evolved a stock of conventions that indicate how the particular entities they deal with can be appropriately categorised. Such conventions are established through common usage, from the unconscious or unthinking accumulation of precedents – when successive works in a given field follow the example of their predecessors and employ the same class term to designate the same specific entities, without their authors being much aware of the fact. For example, from the mass of literature on the First World War we know there is a convention that the Battle of the Somme in 1916 belongs to a general class of battles collectively called the 'First World War'. There is also a convention that the state of Virginia in 1840 can be put into the general class of past places designated the 'Antebellum South', that eleventh century France belongs to a general class of periods we name 'the medieval era', and that the growth of woollen mills in Bradford in the nineteenth century is a member of a general class of processes we know as 'industrialisation'. What these conventions imply, of course, is that the specific objects grouped under each class are comparable. Hence, when we categorise the Battle of the Somme of 1916 as an event in the First World War, we imply it is comparable with other battles during the same war such as Ypres, and Messines.

In many instances, we should not automatically assume that everyone will agree with our understanding about what a particular convention is. With these, we would be well-advised to defend our lumping or splitting decisions explicitly. The usual technique for doing this is to discuss the historical literature in the field, or salient areas of it, and demonstrate, by citing all the relevant texts, that it provides ample precedents for our decisions.

However, as I have noted in other places, social history is a largely pre-paradigmatic discipline and, as a consequence, its practitioners tend to possess sharply conflicting views about the ontology – the composition – of the social past. Symptomatic of this is the contentiousness of so many of the specialised class terms that social historians and historians have invented (or borrowed from the social sciences) to designate the constituent elements in the social past and their relationship. Some of these terms – for instance, 'bastard feudalism', 'refeudalisation', 'slave societies', 'class conflict', 'the Protestant ethic', 'modernisation', 'separate spheres', 'the bourgeois', 'the aristocracy of labour', 'patriarchy' – are very charged indeed. What makes them so is that are associated with intense debates over certain theories that have seldom been conclusive.

5. Indefinite particularity is not unique to social phenomena; it applies to other phenomena as well. J. Hospers, *An Introduction to Philosophical Analysis*, London, 1965, p. 20, says: 'The common characteristics which we take as criteria for the use of a class word are a matter of convenience. Our classifications depend on our interests and our need for recognizing both the similarities and the differences among things.... There are as many possible classes in the world as there are common characteristics or combinations thereof which can be made the basis of classification'.

6. New York, 1989.

7. Fischer, *Albion's Seed*, e.g. pp. 468–9, 651.

8. Fischer, *Albion's Seed*, p. 816.

9. Fischer, *Albion's Seed*, p. 7.

10. Fischer, *Albion's Seed*, e.g. pp. 373, 380, 476, 531, 502, 524, 485, 481, 505, 652, 488, 507, 596, 518, 563, 586, 510, 610–11, 653, 727, 772, 777, 788.

11. Fischer, *Albion's Seed*, pp. 783, 889; note that in the first context he indicates that the situation he is referring to in America's case is apparent in every decennial census, while in the second he says he is also talking about the situation 'today'.

12. Fischer, *Albion's Seed*, pp. 812 and 816.

13. Fischer, *Albion's Seed*, p. 345.

14. Fischer, *Albion's Seed*, pp. 360–5.

15. Fischer, *Albion's Seed*, pp. 368ff.
16. Fischer, *Albion's Seed*, p. 374.
17. Fischer, *Albion's Seed*, p. 383.
18. Fischer, *Albion's Seed*, p. 485.
19. Fischer, *Albion's Seed*, p. 496.
20. Fischer, *Albion's Seed*, p. 591.
21. Fischer, *Albion's Seed*, pp. 615, 621.
22. Fischer, *Albion's Seed*, p. 634.
23. Fischer, *Albion's Seed*, pp. 634–5.
24. Edinburgh, 1979.
25. Although the book advances an interesting argument about the survival of a peasantry under capitalism, it seems nonetheless to be based on something of a chimera. What makes the book interesting is the arresting paradox it postulates right at the beginning: that although capitalism's domination of agriculture was complete by the 1840s, its domination was compatible with a large and thriving peasantry. As he proceeds, however, he lets slip every now and then that capitalism was immature in 1840 and was still maturing in the late century, e.g. pp. 31, 96. Had he started off by postulating that capitalism was immature by 1840, would its compatibility with a large and thriving peasantry still be an interesting problem and an arresting paradox? Surely, we would expect an immature capitalism to co-exist with a peasantry – with a pre-capitalist social formation. Indeed, he con flates the two issues capitalistic domination and capitalistic maturity – on p. 21 where he states that between 1780 and 1840 '*capitalism matured to be the dominant mode of agricultural production in the region*' [my emphasis].
26. Carter, *Poor Man's Country*, p. 7.
27. Carter, *Poor Man's Country*. His definition was also influenced by the seminal work on peasant societies by T. Shanin, see fn. 15, pp. 4, 186.
28. Carter, *Poor Man's Country*, p.26.
29. Carter, *Poor Man's Country*, p. 26. See also p. 23.
30. Carter, *Poor Man's Country*, p. 28.
31. Carter, *Poor Man's Country*, p. 28, and fn. 81 p. 190.
32. Carter, *Poor Man's Country*, p.104.
33. Carter, *Poor Man's Country*, p. 107.
34. Carter, *Poor Man's Country*, p. 107.
35. Carter, *Poor Man's Country*, p. 21.
36. Carter, *Poor Man's Country*, calculated from Table 4.4. p. 106.
37. Oxford, 1978.
38. Macfarlane, *Individualism*, p.163.
39. Later in the text, Macfarlane indicates that the concept of joint family property rights refers to immoveable property, not to chattels. What

might be ambiguous, is whether he is referring to the actual practice of disposing of property or just to the law/custom on the matter – the latter does not entail the former.

40. Macfarlane, *Individualism*, p.17.
41. Macfarlane, *Individualism*, p.33.
42. Macfarlane, *Individualism*, p.18.
43. Macfarlane, *Individualism*, p.18.
44. Macfarlane, *Individualism*, Ch. 2 'When England Ceased to be a Peasant Society: Marx, Weber and the historians', pp. 34ff.
45. He finds it no coincidence that some of the most influential medievalists who propagated the standard interpretation were of east European origin: E.A. Kosminsky, Sir Paul Vinogradoff and M.M. Postan. He asserts that they, coming from eastern Europe where the 'central feature' was the norm, automatically presupposed it would prevail in England in the medieval period; see his p.18.

☐ Further Reading

For an historian's view of lumping and splitting see the Hexter article cited above. An admirably lucid discussion by an analytical philosopher of the question is Hospers, *Introduction to Philosophical Analysis*, 'Class Words and Classifications', pp. 14ff. The foundation theory for the classification of objects was by the eighteenth-century philosopher, David Hume, in his *A Treatise of Human Nature*, 1739–40, new edn, Oxford, 1978. Gérard Lenclud, 'The Factual and the Normative on Ethnography; Do Cultural Differences Derive from Description?', *Anthropology Today*, vol. 12, no. 1, Feb. 1996, pp. 7–11, provides interesting philosophical arguments against the tendency by anthropologists to emphasise the differences between societies as opposed to their similarities. The claim, that the assigning of objects into the same or different categories, is a completely arbitrary and culturally bound business has been advanced by another anthropologist, Mary Douglas, 'Classified as Edible', in her *Thought Styles*, London, 1996. The opposing view, that the drawing of boundaries is to a substantial extent based on universal cognitive principles, has been advanced by the cognitive psychologist Eleanor Rosch, 'Principles of Classification', in E. Rosch and B.B. Lloyd, eds, *Cognition and Categorization*, Hillsdale, N.J., 1978; and see also Amos Tversky and Itamar Gati, 'Studies of Similarity' in op. cit.; and A. Tversky, 'Features of Similarity', *Psychological Review*, vol. 84, 1977, pp. 327–52.

The widespread debate over David Fischer's *Albion's Seed* seldom touched on the classification issues dealt with here. A comprehensive idea of the terms of the debate can be gleaned from a series of articles in the *William and Mary Quarterly*, third series, vol. xlviii, April 1991.

For commentaries on Alan Macfarlane's *Individualism* see, e.g., Lawrence Stone, *New York Review of Books*, vol. 26, April 19, 1979. Also see M. Reed, 'The Peasantry of Nineteenth-century England: A Neglected Class?', *History Workshop Journal*, no. 18, 1984, pp. 53–76.

□ **6 To Count or Not to Count? (pp. 145–76)**

1. P. Burke, *Culture and Society in Renaissance Italy 1420–1540*, London, 1972, p. 38 and pp. 293ff.
2. R.W. Fogel and S. Engerman, *Time on the Cross*, Boston, 1974. For cogent criticisms see O. Handlin, *Truth in History*, Cambridge, Mass.,1979, pp. 206ff; H. Gutman, *Slavery and the Numbers Game: A Critique of Time on the Cross*, Urbana, 1975.
3. Scott, *Gender and the Politics of History*, p. 115, takes this line, though note that here she applies it to the original generators of statistical data and not to the cliometricians who draw on the data.
4. A. Schlesinger, 'The Humanist Looks at Empirical Social Research', *American Sociological Review*, vol. 27, 1962, p. 770, his emphasis.
5. M. Vovelle, *Piété baroque et déchristianisation en Provence au XVIIIè siècle*, Paris, 1973.
6. D. Baines, *Migration in a Mature Economy: Emigration and Internal Migration in England and Wales, 1861–1900*, Cambridge, 1985.
7. The example of eye-lid movements comes from C. Geertz, 'Thick Description: Toward an Interpretive Theory of Culture', in his *The Interpretation of Cultures*, New York, 1973, pp. 6–7. He borrowed it from the philosopher Gilbert Ryle.
8. It is perfectly possible for cliometric models to postulate structures that are not completely deterministic. For example, the models might assume that the structures restrict agency or even enable actors to do something they otherwise could not do.
9. K.D.M. Snell, *Annals of the Labouring Poor: Social Change and Agrarian England, 1660–1900*, Cambridge, 1985.
10. Cambridge, Mass., 1975.
11. Rudé, *The Crowd in the French Revolution*, Oxford, 1959.
12. Tilly et al., *Rebellious Century*, p. 11. It should be emphasised that the authors are not clear about whether 'hardship' and 'breakdown' are distinct explanations or different facets of the same explanation. In some contexts they are treated as if they were part of the same 'breakdown' explanation (e.g. pp. 74–5, 270). In others, their relationship is vague (e.g. Table 3, p. 81 is headed 'Correlations of collective violence with "breakdown" and "hardship" variables'). In most contexts, however, they are treated as distinctly different explanations. For example, when explaining collective violence in the German study, Richard Tilly starts by asking, 'Can this historical picture of Germany's

collective violence be explained by reference to some simple, obvious, but powerful economic factors?' After looking at the evidence, he concludes by saying, 'The great transition in the overall quantity of collective violence around mid-century demands a more satisfying explanation than food prices and the trade cycle can produce. Perhaps the history of urbanisation can provide it'. He then refers to the 'very substantial literature' attributing anti-social behaviour to the social breakdown wrought by urbanisation. Following this, he tests the linkage between urbanisation and collective violence; see pp. 213ff. For other contexts where the influence of the standard of living on collective violence is treated on its own as if it were a separate explanation see pp. 11, 75, 162, 167–8, 271–2. As most contexts seem to refer to two distinct explanations, and as in theory they surely can be treated as distinct, my summary assumes that the Tillys are referring to two separate theories.

13. Although the authors claim that urbanisation and industrialisation do not push up the incidence of collective violence, they also claim that these phenomena affect the ways in which collective violence is organised. This is an important ancillary argument in the book.

14. Some of my summary of the indicators used in the three studies may not be an accurate description. There is no explicit description or list of the indicators anywhere in the text, and the summary discussion of the data is often so abbreviated that it is unclear from the context what the indicators are.

15. Tilly et al., *Rebellious Century*, p. 314.

16. Tilly et al., *Rebellious Century*, pp. 75, 213–14.

17. Appendix D, p. 315, states that the French collective violence data are biased towards 'events of manifest significance to national politics'. Surely this necessarily implies that the bias is greatest in times of acute political crisis since such times produce events of greatest significance to national politics. By extension, the German data must be biased in the same way since these data are very similar in composition to the French. To explain the bias we could argue the following. Given that the state would be far more fearful of protest in periods of national political crisis than in non-crisis periods, it follows that the state would be far more prepared to use violence to break up protest gatherings in the crisis periods than in the normal periods. As a consequence, the definition is loaded towards the protest in the crisis periods and against the protest in the non-crisis ones.

18. Moreover, other kinds of evidence cited in the book corroborate the evidence of the indicators. For example, the evidence for Italy pp. 143, 161–2; and a prosopographical study cited for Germany, pp. 215–16.

19. Though note that none of the indicators expressed the concept of 'relative deprivation', a key variant of the concept of anomie.
20. Tilly et al., *Rebellious Century*, p. 281.
21. Tilly et al., *Rebellious Century*, pp. 278–80.
22. This judgment may be unduly harsh. Thompson's arguments (often called the 'moral economy' model) have been borrowed by a multitude of scholars attempting to explain social protest in a considerable range of societies.
23. Cambridge, Mass., 1973.
24. The other pioneer was Michael Katz, *The People of Hamilton, Canada West: Family and Class in a Mid-Nineteenth Century City*, Cambridge, Mass., 1975.
25. Thernstrom, *Other Bostonians*, p. 335 fn. 15.
26. Thernstrom, *Other Bostonians*, pp. 276–88.
27. See his discussion of the inverse relationship between transience and economic success, pp. 39–42.
28. That his samples undercount the 'residuum' is implied by the sources from which they were drawn. The samples, it will be remembered, were census manuscripts (1880), marriage records (1910), birth certificates (1930), and city directories (1958).
29. Thernstrom, *Other Bostonians*, pp. 70–1, 110.
30. Thernstrom, *Other Bostonians*, pp. 283, 72, 74.
31. Thernstrom, *Other Bostonians*, pp. 70–1
32. I have to emphasise here that he does not stick consistently to this relativistic position. In his last and summary chapter, he adopts a hermeneutic perspective: 'The meaning of mobility – whether a given level of it is perceived as high or low, whether it satisfies the people who experience it or only whets greater appetite – is influenced by societal values'; Thernstrom, *Other Bostonians*, p. 259.

☐ **Further Reading**

A good example of conditional criticisms of mass quantification are those by the well-known econometric historian, Robert Fogel in 'The Limits of Quantitative Methods in History', *American Historical Review*, vol. 80, 2, April 1975, pp. 329–50.

Prominent examples of fundamentalist criticisms include Himmelfarb, *The New History and the Old;* Barzun, *Clio and the Doctors;* Stone, *The Past and the Present Revisited*; Handlin, *Truth in History*, Ch. 8; Scott, 'A Statistical Representation of Work', in her *Gender and the Politics of History*.

Defences have been mounted by R. Floud in his 'Introduction' to *An Introduction to Quantitative Methods for Historians*, London, 1974; and in his

'Quantitative History and People's History: Two Methods in Conflict?', *History Workshop*, 17, Spring 1984, pp. 113–24.

For other contributions to the debate see Eric. E. Lampard, 'Two Cheers for Quantification History: An Agnostic Foreword', in L. Schnore, ed., *The New Urban History*, Princeton, 1975; J.M. Kousser, 'The Revivalism of Narrative: A Response to Recent Criticisms of Quantitative History', *Social Science History*, vol. 8, 1984, pp. 133–49; T.K. Rabb, 'The Development of Quantification in Historical Research', *Journal of Interdisciplinary History*, vol. 13, 4, 1983, pp. 591–601; W.H. Aydelotte, *Quantification in History*, Reading, Mass., 1971; Fogel and Elton, *Which Road to the Past?;* Tosh, *The Pursuit of History*, Ch. 9, gives a sensible summary of the trends in cliometrics.

The best short account of prosopography is Stone, *The Past and the Present Revisited*, Ch. 2.

Useful textbooks on statistics for historians include Aydelotte, *Quantification in History* and Floud in his *Introduction to Quantitative Methods for Historians*, both cited above; and K.H. Jarausch and K.A. Hardy, *Quantitative Methods for Historians: A Guide to Research, Data, and Statistics*, Chapel Hill, 1991. The essays in E.A. Wrigley, ed., *Nineteenth-century Society: Essays in the Use of Quantitative Methods for the Study of Social Data*, Cambridge, 1972, discuss a wide range of British raw statistics (including those on occupations and crime) and how to handle them. The journal *History & Computing* (published by Oxford University Press) has excellent articles on the creation of data bases.

For some of the more cogent criticisms of the methodology in *The Rebellious Century* see Stone, *The Past and the Present Revisited*, p. 34.

7 The Problem of Socially Constructed Evidence (pp. 177–202)

1. The commentary on Foucault's influential idea of the relationship between power and knowledge is considerable. Perhaps the best place to start is Alan Sheridan, *Michel Foucault; The Will to Truth*, London, 1980. A devastating critique of Foucault's concept of power/ knowledge is R. Nola, 'Post-Modernism, A French Cultural Chernobyl: Foucault on Power/Knowledge', *Inquiry*, 37, 1994, pp. 3–43. Also critical of Foucault, but from other angles, is Keith Windschuttle, 'The Discourses of Michel Foucault', in his *The Killing of History*.
2. P. Burke, *Popular Culture in Early Modern Europe*, London, 1978, pp. 68ff.
3. Note that the term 'deconstruction', invented by Derrida, is sometimes used interchangeably with 'discourse analysis'.
4. Scott, 'A Statistical Representation of Work', in her *Gender and the Politics of History*, p. 115.

5. In V.A.C. Gatrell, B. Lenman and G. Parker, eds, *Crime and the Law; The Social History of Crime in Western Europe since 1500*, London, 1980.
6. Examples of radical social control theory are J. Ditton, *Controlology; Beyond the New Criminology*, London, 1979; E. Lemert, *Human Deviance, Social Problems and Social Control*, New Jersey, 1967. The nearest thing to its application to a historical situation is G. Pearson, *Hooligan: A History of Respectable Fears*, London, 1983.
7. Gatrell, 'The Decline of Theft and Violence', pp. 276, 292.
8. Gatrell, 'The Decline of Theft and Violence', p. 291.
9. New York, 1985.
10. Michael W. Dois, *Majnun, The Madman in Medieval Islamic Society*, ed., D.E. Immisch, Oxford, 1992.
11. Showalter, *The Female Malady*, pp. 17, 73.
12. Showalter, *The Female Malady*, e.g. p. 204, Ch. 9.
13. Showalter, *The Female Malady*, pp. 63, 72–3, 213.
14. Showalter, *The Female Malady*, pp. 57,161.
15. A weaknesses in her argument is that she does not explain how real mental disease entities are discovered. Nor does she explain how and why male mental disease entities are 'constructed'.
16. Showalter, *The Female Malady*, pp. 72, 142, 144, 192–3.
17. Showalter, *The Female Malady*, p. 210.
18. Showalter, *The Female Malady*, p. 136.
19. Showalter, *The Female Malady*, p. 137.
20. Showalter, *The Female Malady*, p. 143.
21. New York, 1974.
22. Genovese, *Roll, Jordan* p. xvi.
23. Genovese, *Roll, Jordan*, pp. 3–149. I think this is the weakest of the three arguments. Genovese provides little evidence that slaves had a sense of rights and does not suggest any criteria for the existence of 'self-respect'.
24. Genovese, *Roll, Jordan*, pp. 646, 645, 84, 675; also 86, 133.
25. Genovese, *Roll, Jordan*, p. 675.
26. Genovese, *Roll, Jordan*, p. 675.
27. There is overwhelming evidence that peoples' memories of distant events in their own lives are unreliable. For example, P.M. Blau and O.D. Duncan, *The American Occupational Structure*, New York, 1967, compared the occupations that men gave in census manuscripts with those attributed to them by their sons and found a 30 per cent discrepancy. D. Stannard, *Shrinking History: On Freud and the Failure of Psychohistory*, New York, 1980, pp. 101ff cites many studies demonstrating the fallibility of parental memory in respect of the milestones in the lives of their children when they went through infancy. Also see T.S. Sarbin review in *History and Theory*, vol. 26, 1987, pp. 352–64.

28. Genovese, *Roll, Jordan*, p. 675.
29. The Rosenthal effect is the term given to the famous experiments by the American psychologist, Robert Rosenthal, who found that the expectations of the researcher influence the responses of subjects, even under the strictest laboratory conditions. It has echoes, of course, of social-constructionist theories. A superb discussion of the effect and of how to deal with it is by M. Martin, 'The Philosophical Importance of the Rosenthal Effect', in Martin and McIntyre, eds, *Readings in the Philosophy of Social Science*, Ch. 37.

A third problem with oral history which I have not dealt with here is the typicality of the respondents. There is good evidence that slave narratives were quite atypical; see C. Vann Woodward, 'History from Slave Sources', *American Historical Review*, 79, pp. 470–81; and D.J. Spindel, 'Assessing Memory: Twentieth-Century Slave Narratives Reconsidered', *Journal of Interdisciplinary History*, xxvii, no.2, Autumn 1996, pp. 247–61.

My strictures about oral history are not meant to suggest that oral history is a fundamentally and fatally flawed empirical technique which should never be applied. Instead I am suggesting that its practitioners are often far too casual in their use of their data and badly need to verify the observations in the data with devises similar to the techniques of textual criticism which conventional scholars apply to documentary sources.
30. Genovese, *Roll, Jordan*, pp. 285–324.

☐   **Further Reading**

A vast amount has been written on the theory of social constructionism. A sharp and readable critique of the theory is Laudan, *Science and Relativism*, especially Ch. 2.

Of recent exponents of social constructionism in the philosophy of science, the most influential are B. Latour and S. Woolgar, *Laboratory Life: The Social Construction of Scientific Facts*, 2nd edn, Princeton, 1985. Also Longino, *Science as Social Knowledge*; Joseph Rouse, *Knowledge and Power: Toward a Political Philosophy of Science*, Ithaca, 1987; D. Bloor, *Knowledge and Social Imagery*, London, 1976. The notion of 'theory-laden observation' is otherwise known as the **hermeneutic circle** (the idea that observation and the interpretation of meanings are inseparable). Michael Martin provides a comprehensive discussion of how the problem can be overcome in his 'Taylor on Interpretation and the Sciences of Man', in Martin and McIntyre, eds, *Readings in the Philosophy of Social Science*, Ch. 14. Also of value is S.D. Hunt, 'A Realist Theory of Empirical Testing; Resolving the Theory-Ladenness/Objectivity Debate', *Philosophy of the Social Sciences*, vol. 24, 2, June 1994, pp. 133–58.

Good critiques for historians of social constructionism are M.E. Hobart, 'The Paradox of Historical Constructionism', *History and Theory*, vol. 28, 1989, pp. 43–58.

Accounts of the history of madness include Andrew Scull, *The Most Solitary of Afflictions; Madness and Society in Britain, 1700–1900*, New Haven, 1993.

Strong social constructionist approaches to medicine include O. Temkin, 'The Meaning of Medicine in Historical Perspective', in his *The Double Face of Janus and Other Essays*, Baltimore, 1977; B.S. Turner, *The Body and Society: Explorations in Social Theory*, London, 1984; and the classic work, L. Fleck, *The Genesis and Development of a Scientific Fact*, Chicago, 1935 (1979). A good place to start with Foucault's difficult ideas of social constructionism is Munslow, *Deconstructing History*.

☐ **8 The Problem of Appropriate Concepts (pp. 203–34)**

1. For example, E.P. Thompson, 'The Peculiarities of the English', *Socialist Register*, 1965, p. 338, 'History is made up of episodes, and if we cannot get inside them we cannot get inside history at all'. G.R. Elton, *The Practice of History*, Sydney, 1967, pp. 47–8, 'The task is to understand the past, and if the past is to be understood it must be given full respect in its own right. And unless it is properly understood, any use of it in the present must be suspect and can be dangerous.' Muir, 'Introduction: Observing Trifles' in Muir and Ruggiero, eds, *Microhistory and the Lost Peoples of Europe*, p. xi, ' . to write history without the taint of anachronism [is] a task advocated by most historians but difficult to accomplish.'

   It should be noted that 'presentism' is often used by theorists in a sense which is quite different from anachronism. According to this alternative usage (which is closely associated with John Dewey, the American philosopher), 'presentism' consists of all the benefits (mainly personal) that people in the present can gain by studying history; in his phrase, history is a 'usable past'. A critical discussion of Dewey's notion is in W.H. Dray, *On History and Philosophers of History*, Leiden, 1989, Ch. 8, 'Some Varieties of Presentism'.

2. R.G. Collingwood, *The Idea of History*, Oxford, 1946.

3. *Reappraisals in History*, London, 1961, p. 9.

4. Robert Darnton, *The Great Cat Massacre and Other Episodes in French Cultural History*, New York, 1984, pp. 4–6.

5. R. Isaac, *The Transformation of Virginia, 1740–1790*, Chapel Hill, 1982, p. 324.

6. David Sabean, *Power in the Blood: Popular Culture and Village Discourse in Early Modern Germany*, Cambridge, 1984, p. 3.

7. Geertz, 'Thick Description: Toward an Interpretive Theory of Culture', in his *The Interpretation of Cultures*.
8. Recently joining the anti-naturalist tradition, are the various forms of post-modernism. For discussion of the difference between the naturalistic and the anti-naturalistic traditions in the social sciences, see Little, *Varieties of Social Explanation*, pp. 222–36; and Rosenberg, *Philosophy of Social Science*.

    Although hermeneutics is sometimes called interpretive theory, I will avoid the latter term since it might confuse historians who generally talk about 'interpretation' in another sense, as a generic term for an historical argument/theory/view.
9. An early example of ethnomethodology in sociology was P. Berger and T. Luckmann, *The Social Construction of Reality: A Treatise in the Sociology of Knowledge*, New York, 1980. In anthropology the pioneer of interpretive techniques was the Africanist, E.E. Evans-Pritchard, *Witchcraft, Oracles and Magic Among the Azande*, Oxford, 1937.
10. P. Winch, *The Idea of a Social Science and its Relation to Philosophy* , London, 1958, and 'Understanding a Primitive Society', in B.R. Wilson, ed., *Rationality*, Oxford, 1970. The sway now exercised by the rule-following version is apparent in its virtual identification with hermeneutics in leading texts on the philosophy of the social sciences, for example, David Braybrooke, *Philosophy of Social Science*, Englewood Cliffs, N.J., 1987; Martin Hollis, *The Philosophy of Social Science: An Introduction*, Cambridge, 1994; J.R. Searle, 'Intentionalistic Explanations in the Social Sciences', *Philosophy of the Social Sciences*, vol. 21, September 1991, pp. 332–44; Rosenberg, *Philosophy of Social Science*. It should be emphasised, however, that there are many sub-variants of the rule-following version which diverge from or criticise aspects of Winch's views. It should also be stressed that the rule-following version(s) does not currently prevail in interpretive social science. Since the late 1960s it has been at least as influential as the 'continental' versions associated with the German hermeneutic philosopher, H.-G. Gadamer; see W. Outhwaite, *New Philosophies of Social Science: Realism, Hermeneutics and Critical Theory*, Houndmills, 1987, pp. 11ff.
11. Note there is a widespread confusion amongst hermeneuticians about whether the mind has concepts which are independent of words; frequently the distinction is not made nor clear.
12. Rosenberg, *Philosophy of Social Science*, p. 28.
13. Isaac, *Transformation of Virginia*, pp. 324–5.
14. C. Lévi-Strauss, *Structural Anthropology*, London, 1968; Ernest Gellner, 'Concepts and Society', in B.R. Wilson, ed., *Rationality*, Oxford, 1970.
15. See Burke, *Popular Culture in Early Modern Europe*, p. 149.

16. This objection has been expressed most forcibly by Ernest Gellner, the social anthropologist and philosopher, in his *Postmodernism, Reason and Religion*, London, 1992, p. 63.

17. *Clues, Myths, and the Historical Method*, trs. J. and A.C. Tedeschi, Baltimore, 1989. Ginzburg's name for drawing significant patterns from tiny clues is the 'evidential paradigm'.

□ Further Reading

Theoretical discussions of microhistory can be found in Giovanni Levi, 'On Microhistory', in P. Burke, ed., *New Perspectives on Historical Writing*, Cambridge, 1991; Darnton, *Great Cat Massacre*, 'Introduction' and 'Conclusion'; Muir, 'Introduction: Observing Trifles' in Muir and Ruggiero, eds, *Microhistory and the Lost Peoples of Europe*; June Philip, 'Traditional Historical Narrative and Action-Oriented (or Ethnographic History)', *Historical Studies*, vol. 20, p. 339–52; Isaac, *Transformation of Virginia*, 'A Discourse on the Method: Action, Structure, and Meaning'; Hans Medick, '"Missionaries in the Row Boat"? Ethnological Ways of Knowing as a Challenge to Social History', *Comparative Studies in Society and History*, vol. 29, 1, 1987, pp. 76–98; and the Italian Preface to Ginzburg, *The Cheese and the Worms*. An introductory discussion on 'internalist' and 'externalist' models is Peter Caws, 'Operational, Representational, and Explanatory Models', *American Anthropologist*, vol. 76, 1974, pp. 1–10.

Simple and short introductions to the philosophy of hermeneutics include Lloyd, *Explanation in Social History*, Ch. 6; and Little, *Varieties of Social Explanation*, Ch. 4, and pp. 232–6. For more extended discussions on the philosophy of hermeneutic social science, the following are highly recommended: Rosenberg, *Philosophy of Social Science*; A. Ryan, *The Philosophy of the Social Sciences*, London, 1970, Ch. 6; Hughes, *The Philosophy of Social Research*; and the debate between various anthropologists and philosophers over P. Winch's theories in Wilson, ed., *Rationality*. A searing attack on hermeneutics, although it does tend to conflate hermeneutics with post-modernism, is Gellner, *Postmodernism, Reason and Religion*.

The best known of the interpretive anthropologists is Clifford Geertz. His 'Thick Description: Toward an Interpretive Theory of Culture', in *Interpretation of Cultures*, can be read with profit; as can his '"From the Native's Point of View"': on the Nature of Anthropological Understanding' in *Local Knowledge: Further Essays in Interpretive Anthropology*, New York, 1983. A later representative in anthropology who veers towards post-modernism, is R. Rosaldo, *Culture & Truth; the Remaking of Social Analysis*, Boston, 1989. A classic discussion by a sociologist is R.K. Merton, 'The Perspectives of Insiders and Insiders', in N.W. Storer, ed., *The Sociology of Science: Theoretical and Empirical Investigations*, Chicago, 1973.

The more accessible hermeneutic circle arguments are in H.-G. Gadamer, 'The Problem of Historical Consciousness', in P. Rabinow and W.M. Sullivan, eds, *Interpretive Social Science: A Reader*, Berkeley, 1979; and Charles Taylor, 'Interpretation and the Sciences of Man', in P. Rabinow and W.M. Sullivan, eds, *Interpretive Social Science: A Second Look*, Berkeley, 1987.

In the philosophy of history, the foremost and clearest exponent of hermeneutics, but in the older tradition of intuitionism, is Collingwood, *The Idea of History*. Some of the later modifications of Collingwood's approach, which went in the direction of recreating the rationality behind the actions of historical actors, were led by Dray, *Laws and Explanation in History*; and K. Popper, 'The Rationality Principle', in D. Miller, ed., *The Popper Selections*, Princeton, 1985. Note that Popper did not think of his principle as being in the hermeneutic tradition. For criticisms of Popper's logic of the situation, see Nadeau, 'Confuting Popper on the Rationality Principle'.

Critiques by philosophers of hermeneutic circle arguments include Martin, 'Taylor on Interpretation and the Sciences of Man', in Martin and McIntyre, eds, *Readings in the Philosophy of Social Science*, Ch. 17.

The standard discussions by historians of presentism are H. Butterfield, *The Whig Interpretation of History*, London, 1931; P.B.M. Blaas, *Continuity and Anachronism: Parliamentary and Constitutional Development in Whig Historiography and in the Anti-Whig Reaction between 1890 and 1930*, The Hague, 1978; D.L. Hull 'In Defense of Presentism', *History and Theory*, vol. 18, 1979, pp. 1–15; A. Wilson and T.G. Ashplant, 'Whig History and Present-Centred History', *Historical Journal*, vol. 31, 1, 1988, pp. 1–16; and 'Present-centred History and the Problem of Historical Knowledge', *Historical Journal*, vol. 31, 2, 1988, pp. 253–74.

9 The Problem of Determining the Best Explanation (pp. 235–80)

1. Karl Popper, *Conjectures and Refutations: The Growth of Scientific Knowledge*, 3rd rev. edn., London, 1969, Ch. 10: 'Truth, Rationality, and the Growth of Knowledge'. Popper's verisimilitude principle offers three basic tests for distinguishing the best theory: (1) it will not only explain the same facts as its rivals but avoid their errors and explain facts which the rivals cannot account for; (2) it will unify hitherto unconnected problems; (3) it will make surprising predictions which are successful.

2. This is Popper's famous principle of falsification expounded in his *The Logic of Scientific Discovery*, first published in German in 1934, now available in English. The verisimilitude principle departed quite substantially from the falsification notion.

3. A special case is one where extraordinary circumstances break a pattern – such as the intervention of freak events or the dominating presence of a leader.

4. I give much less weight to the common-sense part of this criterion than to the two other plausibility criteria. The more an explanation coheres with our common-sense beliefs, the less original it is likely to be. The other two plausibility criteria do not conflict with either the explanatory power principle or the originality principle.

5. An extra proviso here is that where accounts employ multivariate analyses, and if we have the appropriate technical knowledge of their techniques, then we should also assess the robustness of the analyses.

6. C.R. Browning, *Ordinary Men: Reserve Police Battalion 101 and the Final Solution in Poland*, New York, 1992. Hereafter the Battalion will be referred to as 'Police Battalion 101' or the 'Battalion'.

7. Browning, *Ordinary Men*, p. 142.

8. Browning, *Ordinary Men*, p. 48.

9. Browning, *Ordinary Men*, p. 65.

10. Browning, *Ordinary Men*, pp. 128–9.

11. Browning, *Ordinary Men*, p. 159.

12. Browning, *Ordinary Men*, pp. 184–5; also 71–2.

13. Browning, *Ordinary Men*, pp. 185, 72, 129; also 66,116.

14. Browning, *Ordinary Men*, p. 150.

15. Browning, *Ordinary Men*, pp. 73, 186, 153.

16. Browning, *Ordinary Men*, pp. 153, 73; also 186, 188–9.

17. Browning, *Ordinary Men*, pp. 2, 73.

18. Browning, *Ordinary Men*, pp. 75–6, 169–70.

19. Browning, *Ordinary Men*, p. 87.

20. Browning, *Ordinary Men*, pp. 87, 127–8.

21. Browning, *Ordinary Men*, pp. 76–7.

22. Browning, *Ordinary Men*, pp. 76–7.

23. Browning, *Ordinary Men*, pp. 188–9.

24. Browning, *Ordinary Men*, pp. 75–6, 169–70.

25. Browning, *Ordinary Men*, p. 185.

26. Browning, *Ordinary Men*, p. 76.

27. The primary factor – that peer pressure induced the men to comply – would not be testable if he had argued that most of the men complied because peer pressure was so powerful, and had then cited the lack of non-complying as evidence for the power of peer pressure. This would have been a circular argument.

28. Browning, *Ordinary Men*, p. 103.

29. Browning, *Ordinary Men*, e.g. pp. 103, 116.

30. He provides one example of this. The example refers to one particular officer, Captain Wohlauf, who was regarded as a misfit – the men disapproved of his pretentious ways and roundly condemned him

when he brought his young bride to watch a brutal ghetto clearance. The example is a most telling one. But it is an aside and its implication for the tightness of conformity within the Battalion is not made explicit; see Browning, *Ordinary Men*, pp. 91–3. To be fair, the testimonies may not have provided much information about the range of norms within the Battalion.

31. Browning, *Ordinary Men*, pp. 174–5. The finding which Browning cites was the outcome of one of Milgram's less well known experiments. The experiment in question showed that naive subjects, when asked by a scientist authority figure, were less likely to inflict pain in the absence of collaborators than naive subjects who had witnessed collaborators inflicting pain. Stanley Milgram, *Obedience to Authority: An Experimental View*, New York, 1974.

32. It has to be stressed that Browning candidly admits that the testimonies have most of these defects. He defends their use on the ground that they are rich and that they provide virtually the only information we have about the Battalion's deeds and internal dynamics. See his Preface to *Ordinary Men*, where he also describes, in very generalised fashion, his method for dealing with their problems.

33. Browning, *Ordinary Men*, p. 72.

34. The argument takes up all of Chapter 18.

35. *Hitler's Willing Executioners: Ordinary Germans and the Holocaust*, London, 1996.

36. Goldhagen, *Willing Executioners*, p. 9. Other passages that explicitly state that he is dealing with *ordinary Germans* include pp. 14, 177–8, 454. It should be noted, however, and I will return to the point later, that Goldhagen does not formulate the core claim consistently.

37. Goldhagen, *Willing Executioners*, p. 418.

38. Goldhagen, *Willing Executioners*, pp. 49–53.

39. Goldhagen, *Willing Executioners*, pp. 53–70.

40. Goldhagen, *Willing Executioners*, p. 71.

41. Goldhagen, *Willing Executioners*, p. 72. He theorises about the importance of institutions in embedding ideology into the common sense of a society on p. 46.

42. Note that although he does not call to our attention the fact that the procedure consists of deductive reasoning, it is clearly a deductive argument nonetheless.

43. Goldhagen labels it as monocausal on p. 416.

44. Goldhagen, *Willing Executioners*, pp. 206ff.

45. Goldhagen, *Willing Executioners*, p. 465.

46. Goldhagen, *Willing Executioners*, pp. 293ff.

47. Goldhagen, *Willing Executioners*, p. 69.

48. Goldhagen, *Willing Executioners*, p. 69.

49. Goldhagen, *Willing Executioners*, p. 70.
50. Goldhagen, *Willing Executioners*, p. 71.
51. Goldhagen, *Willing Executioners*, pp. 74–5.
52. Goldhagen, *Willing Executioners*, pp. 23, 419, 443, 446, 447.
53. Goldhagen, *Willing Executioners*, pp. 32, 443, 444.
54. Goldhagen, *Willing Executioners*, p. 442.
55. Goldhagen, *Willing Executioners*, pp. 127. See also p. 414 on the ideology's 'multipotentiality'.
56. Goldhagen, *Willing Executioners*, p. 208.
57. Goldhagen, *Willing Executioners*, p. 207–8.
58. Goldhagen, *Willing Executioners*, p. 208.
59. Goldhagen, *Willing Executioners*, p. 167.
60 What aggravates the confusion is that when discussing the ill-treatment of Jewish Polish POWs in the Lipowa work camp on p. 298, he says that the German army had previously treated the same POWs 'relatively decently' – were these particular elements in the German army 'ordinary Germans'?
61. Goldhagen, *Willing Executioners*, p. 338–9.
62. Goldhagen, *Willing Executioners*, p. 337.
63. Goldhagen, *Willing Executioners*, pp. 338–52.
64. Goldhagen, *Willing Executioners*, pp. 338–9.
65. Goldhagen, *Willing Executioners*, p. 76.
66. The only place where Goldhagen mentions the antisemitism of other societies is p. 419.
67. The most notable examples being France during the Dreyfus affair and certain Eastern European societies, particularly the Ukraine and the Baltic states, from whom the Nazis recruited many 'Hiwis'.
68. See Goldhagen, *Willing Executioners*, e.g. pp. 151, 299, 335. Note, too, on p. 209 he says that Police Battalion 101 contained about a dozen men from Luxemburg.
69. Note here the middle paragraph of p. 186 in Browning's concluding chapter:

> Pervasive racism and the resulting exclusion of the Jewish victims from any common ground with the perpetrators made it all the easier for the majority of the policemen to conform to the norms of their immediate community (the battalion) and their society at large (Nazi Germany). Here the years of anti-semitic propaganda (and prior to the Nazi dictatorship, decades of shrill German nationalism) dovetailed with the polarizing effects of war. The dichotomy of racially superior Germans and racially inferior Jews, central to Nazi ideology, could easily merge with the image of a beleaguered Germany surrounded by warring enemies.... In wartime, when it was all too usual to exclude the enemy from the community of human obligation, it was also too easy to subsume the Jews into the 'image of the enemy,' or *Feindbild*.

☐ **Further Reading**

A searching critique of the sociology of knowledge is M. Bunge, 'A Critical Examination of the New Sociology of Science', Part I, *Philosophy of the Social Sciences*, vol. 21, 4, Dec. 1991, pp. 524–60; and Part II, vol. 22, 1, March 1992, pp. 46–76.

Critical discussion of Popper's falsification and verisimilitude principles are in Lloyd, *Explanation in Social History*, pp. 55ff; Lakatos, *Methodology of Scientific Research Programmes*, vol. I, pp.9ff; P.A. Schilpp, ed., *The Philosophy of Karl Popper*, La Salle, Ill., 1974.

The method of crucial cases is outlined by Eckstein, 'Case Study and Theory in Political Science', in Greenstein and Polsby, eds, *Strategies of Inquiry*, pp. 79–138. Critical discussion of the method is in King, Keohane and Verba, *Designing Social Inquiry*.

A good introduction to the Holocaust and its historiography is Michael Marrus, *The Holocaust in History*, London, 1989; the classic text is Raul Hilberg, *The Destruction of the European Jews*, 3 vols, rev. edn, New York, 1985. Some idea of the extraordinarily heated debate engendered by Goldhagen's book – most of it highly critical, some of it unnecessarily *ad hominem* – can be gleaned from Hans-Ulrich Wehler, 'The Goldhagen Controversy: Agonizing Problems, Scholarly Failure and the Political Dimension', *German History*, vol. 15, 1, 1997; B. Rieger, '"Daniel in the Lion's Den?" The German Debate about Goldhagen's *Hitler's Willing Executioners*', *History Workshop Journal*, 43, 1997, pp. 226–33; C. Glass, 'Hitler's (Un)willing Executioners', *New Statesman*, 23 January 1998; Josef Joffe, 'Goldhagen in Germany', *New York Review of Books*, November 1996; N.G. Finkelstein and R.B. Birn, *A Nation on Trial: the Goldhagen Thesis and Historical Truth*, New York, 1998; and the contributions to the H-NET List on German History, H-GERMAN www site, 'Goldhagen Finale'. Discussion of Browning's and Goldhagen's scholarly backgrounds can be found in Adam Shatz, 'Browning's Version: a Mild-Mannered Historian's Quest to Understand the Perpetrators of the Holocaust', *Lingua Franca*, February 1997. A sample of Goldhagen's replies includes *New Republic*, 23 Dec. 1996; and *New York Review of Books*, 6 Feb. 1997.

Glossary of Terms

action   Conduct which arises from choice and conscious reasoning. Often contrasted with 'behaviour', that is, involuntary conduct motivated by forces that the actor may be unconscious of and cannot control.

agency   Generally, the capacity of individuals or groups to adapt to events and circumstances. More specifically, (a) the capacity of individuals to make choices; (b) the capacity of individuals to relate means to ends adequately; (c) the capacity of individuals to make the best possible linkage between ends and means; and (d) the capacity of individuals to control or influence outcomes.

bench-mark years   A sequence of years, usually spaced out at regular intervals, at which the same phenomenon is studied.

closure   The degree to which vertical mobility occurs within a social hierarchy.

comparative method   In a broad sense, any type of history which compares cases. More specifically, (a) the act of alluding to another case or other cases in order to illustrate or highlight aspects of a particular case; (b) the systematic comparison of cases to test or demonstrate a hypothesis about a general cause and effect relationship.

counter-examples   Examples which contradict a claim; also called **anomalies** or **refuting instances**. Often very difficult to differentiate from exceptions.

counter-factual   A term given to a situation which does not exist. Usually a counter-factual is a model of a real-life situation where one or more features have been removed in order to see what effect the absence of these features has on the real-life situation.

covering law   A term devised by the philosopher Carl Hempel to refer to any well founded, precisely formulated, and universal theory about the world; a law of physics would be an example. Whether human societies are subject to covering laws is highly debatable. See also **explanation sketch**.

cross-sectional analysis   The examination of quantitative data taken from different places but existing at the same time. See also **longitudinal analysis**.

crucial case   A case that is inherently biased against a claim yet confirms the claim nonetheless.

ecological fallacy   The erroneous belief that because several things occupy the same space they must be causally connected.

epidemiological study   The study of the relationship – usually statistical – between several aggregate measures within the same case or series of cases. The term is derived from medical science where it refers to the study of the factors in an environment which are conducive to certain diseases. See also **prosopography**.

epistemology   The study of theories about how we should know the world and the justification of these theories.

event-oriented history   A term used by *Annales* historians as a synonym for history that is largely or wholly narrative in its form.

explanation sketch   A term devised by the philosopher Carl Hempel to refer to a generalisation that is of lower standing than a **covering law**. Hence it consists of any generalising explanation which is imprecisely formulated, unproven, and subject to exceptions.

expressive rationality   The faculty for taking a deliberate course of action which is not a means to an end but an appropriate end in itself. It is contrasted with **instrumental rationality** where the course of action is the appropriate means to an end.

externalist accounts   Accounts of a situation which are written from the viewpoint of an outside observer and may draw attention to things which were not apparent to the insiders.

fallacy of affirming the consequent   An illogical form of reasoning whereby conclusions are deduced from a premise that do not necessarily follow from the premise.

hermeneutics   In the social sciences, a form of investigation of actions and practices that endeavours to interpret what these mean to the actors.

hermeneutic circle   A term with many senses. In H.-G. Gadamer's, it is the idea that observation is inseparable from interpretation. In this sense it can be equated with the concept of 'theory-ladenness'.

hypothetico-deductive   A method of investigation which advances a series of competing hypotheses, deduces the consequences of each, searches for empirical evidence for and against each hypothesis, and vigorously appraises the hypotheses to establish the best one.

idiographic   An historical account that focuses exclusively on particular entities; its antithesis is **nomothetic**.

intergenerational mobility   The movement of people belonging to one generation away from the position in the social hierarchy held by their parents. See also **intragenerational mobility**.

internalist accounts   Accounts of a situation from the viewpoint of those who were part of it. See also **externalist accounts**.

intragenerational mobility   The movement of people belonging to one generation in the social hierarchy over the course of their adult lives.

longitudinal analysis   The analysis of statistical data taken from different points in time. Otherwise known as **time-series analysis** and by *Annales* historians as **serial analysis**. Its counterpart for the study of data taken from different places but contemporaneous in time is **cross-sectional analysis**.

mass quantification The use of statistics to elucidate or explain behaviour of large populations – aggregates.

microhistory A close-grained historical investigation on a tiny scale that is primarily intended to reveal how the actors understood themselves and their world.

model A simplified representation of reality. Often a distinction is drawn between **isomorphic models** (which attempt to produce an absolute replica of reality) and **homomorphic models** (which are simplified representations).

nomothetic A history which focuses on general classes of entities and their relationships; its antithesis is **idiographic**.

ontology In general terms, the study of how the world is composed. More specifically, any theory about what entities exist in the world and their relationship.

potential falsifier A term devised by the philosopher Karl Popper for the situation whereby someone who has proposed a theory specifies the tests that the theory must fail in order to satisfy the theorist that the theory is false.

probablistic explanation A variant of causal explanation where the explanation does not purport to apply to all the outcomes of a given class but to most of them and thus admits to exceptions.

prosopography Group biography. The study of the interrelationship between the attributes of every member of a large collection of people. See also **epidemiology**.

proxy variable A variable that stands in the place of another. Thus the ownership of large houses might be taken as a proxy variable of high income levels.

qualitative evidence Evidence that is not measurable.

quantitative evidence Evidence that is expressed in measurable form.

quantification The use of statistics as evidence or to represent the world.

record-linkage Research that systematically traces the same people listed in different kinds of primary sources or listed in the same kinds of sources at different points of time. The objective may be to see how far the attributes of these people changed over time, or to see how certain attributes described in one source are connected with different attributes described in another source.

Rosenthal effect A term named after an American social psychologist, Robert Rosenthal, who found that the expectations of experimenters about the outcomes of their research on humans or animals substantially affected these outcomes, even under the strictest laboratory conditions.

sensitive dependent   Situations where relatively small differences in antecedent conditions produce disproportionately large differences in outcomes. An example is in the nursery rhyme where the loss of a horse-shoe nail leads to the loss of a kingdom.

situational logic   A concept devised by the philosopher Karl Popper for a method which seeks to explain an action by reconstructing the reasoning that led the actor to act as he or she did, given that the action was appropriate in the circumstances. Very similar to the concept which a philosopher of history, W.H. Dray, has called the 'rationale of action'.

social mobility   (a) The migration of people; (b) the movement of people up or down or laterally in respect of some sort of social hierarchy.

special case   A case that is incompatible with a theory without invalidating it since the case is the product of freak circumstances.

statistical explanation   An explanation where statistical techniques are used to show that one or more things have a close association with one or more other things without assuming a cause and effect relationship between them.

structure-oriented history   A term used by *Annales* historians to refer to history that has a large analytical component and that deals with the underlying forces which limit human choices.

sufficient and necessary conditions   A **necessary condition** is a factor or group of factors that is always present where the phenomenon occurs but by itself is not enough to constitute the phenomenon. A **sufficient condition** is a factor or group of factors that is always enough to constitute the phenomenon but other factors can take its place. A **sufficient and necessary condition** is a factor or group of factors that is always present where the phenomenon occurs and no other factors can take its place. Usually these concepts are employed to establish the relative significance of postulated causal factors to an outcome.

underdetermined   A term usually applied to a theory which lacks adequate supporting empirical evidence.

unintended consequences   Outcomes of an action which were unintended by the actors concerned.

Bibliography

P. Abrams, *Historical Sociology*, Ithaca, 1982.

S. Alexander, 'Women, Class and Sexual Differences', *History Workshop*, vol. 17, Spring 1984, pp. 125–49.

G.R. Andrews, 'Social History and the Populist Moment', *Journal of Social History*, Supplement, vol. 29, 1995, pp. 109–13.

F.R. Ankersmit, 'Historiography and Postmodernism', *History and Theory*, vol. 28, 1989, pp. 137–53.

W.H. Aydelotte, *Quantification in History*, Reading, Mass., 1971.

D. Baines, *Migration in a Mature Economy: Emigration and Internal Migration in England and Wales, 1861–1900*, Cambridge, 1985.

J. Barzun, *Clio and the Doctors: Psycho-History, Quanto-History & History*, Chicago, 1974.

S.H. Beer, 'Causal Explanation and Imaginative Re-enactment', *History and Theory*, vol. 3, 1, 1963, pp. 6–29.

P. Berger and T. Luckmann, *The Social Construction of Reality: A Treatise in the Sociology of Knowledge*, New York, 1980.

R.F. Berkhofer, *A Behavioral Approach to Historical Analysis*, New York, 1969.

B.W. Bienstock, 'Everything Old is New Again...', *Journal of Social History*, Supplement, vol. 29, 1995, pp. 59–63.

J. Black, *Convergence or Divergence?: Britain and the Continent*, New York, 1994.

P.B.M. Blaas, *Continuity and Anachronism: Parliamentary and Constitutional Development in Whig Historiography and in the Anti-Whig Reaction between 1890 and 1930*, The Hague, 1978.

P.M. Blau and O.D. Duncan, *The American Occupational Structure*, New York, 1967.

M. Bloch, 'A Contribution towards a Comparative History of European Societies', *Land and Work in Medieval Europe: Selected Papers*, trs. J.E. Anderson, London, 1967.

A.G. Bogue 'The Quest for Numeracy: Data and Methods in American Political History', *Journal of Interdisciplinary History*, vol. 21, 1, 1990, pp. 89–116.

V.E. Bonnell, 'Theory, Concepts and Comparison in Historical Sociology', *Comparative Studies in Society and History*, vol. 22, 1980, pp. 156–73.

F. Braudel, *The Mediterranean and the Mediterranean World in the Age of Philip II*, trs. S. Reynolds, 2 vols, London, 1972.

F. Braudel, *On History*, London, 1980.

D. Braybrooke, *Philosophy of Social Science*, Englewood Cliffs, N.J. 1987.

E. Breisach, *Historiography; Ancient, Medieval, & Modern*, Chicago, 1983.

C.R. Browning, *Ordinary Men:Reserve Police Battalion 101 and the Final Solution in Poland*, New York, 1992.

M. Bunge, 'A Critical Examination of the New Sociology of Science', Part I, *Philosophy of the Social Sciences*, vol. 21, 4, Dec. 1991, pp. 524–60; and Part II, vol. 22, 1, March 1992, pp. 46–76.

P. Burke, *Culture and Society in Renaissance Italy 1420–1540*, London, 1972.

P. Burke, *Popular Culture in Early Modern Europe*, London, 1978.

P. Burke, *Sociology and History*, London, 1980.

P. Burke, *The French Historical Revolution: The Annales School, 1929–89*, Cambridge, 1990.

P. Burke, *History and Social Theory*, Cambridge, 1992.

P. Burke, ed., *New Perspectives on Historical Writing* , Cambridge, 1992.

T. Burnard, 'Ethnicity in Colonial American Historiography: a New Organising Principle?', *Australasian Journal of American Studies*, vol. 11, July 1992.

H. Butterfield, *The Whig Interpretation of History*, London, 1931.

E.H. Carr, *What is History?*, Harmondsworth, 1964.

I. Carter, *Farm Life in Northeast Scotland, 1840–1914: The Poor Man's Country*, Edinburgh, 1979.

P. Caws, 'Operational, Representational, and Explanatory Models', *American Anthropologist*, vol. 76, 1974, pp. 1–10.

M. Cayton, E. Gorn and P. Williams, eds, *Encyclopedia of American Social History*, 3 vols, New York, 1993.

A. Clark, *The Struggle for the Breeches: Gender and the Making of the British Working Class*, Berkeley, 1995.

R. Cobb, 'Modern French History in Britain', *Proceedings of the British Academy*, 60, 1974, pp. 271–93.

R.G. Collingwood, *The Idea of History*, Oxford, 1946.

R. Darnton, *The Great Cat Massacre and Other Episodes in French Cultural History*, New York, 1984.

L. Davidoff, *Worlds Between: Historical Perspectives on Gender and Class*, Cambridge, 1995.

L. Davidoff and C. Hall, *Family Fortunes; Men and Women of the English Middle Class, 1780–1850*, London, 1987.

G.E.M. de Ste. Croix, *The Class Struggle in the Ancient Greek World*, London, 1981.

M. Devitt and K. Sterelny, *Language and Reality; An Introduction to the Philosophy of Language*, Oxford, 1987.

J. Ditton, *Controlology; Beyond the New Criminology*, London, 1979.

M.W. Dois, *Majnun, The Madman in Medieval Islamic Society*, D.E. Immisch, ed., Oxford, 1992.

M. Douglas, *Thought Styles*, London, 1996.

W.H. Dray, *Laws and Explanation in History*, Oxford, 1957.

W.H. Dray, *On History and Philosophers of History*, Leiden, 1989.

H. Eckstein, 'Case Study and Theory in Political Science', in F.I. Green-stein and N.W. Polsby, eds, *Strategies of Inquiry*, Reading, Mass., 1975.

G. Eley, 'Some Recent Tendencies in Social History', in G.G. Iggers and H.T. Parker, eds, *International Handbook of Historical Studies*, Westport, Conn., 1979.

G.R. Elton, *The Practice of History*, Sydney, 1967.

E.E. Evans-Pritchard, *Witchcraft, Oracles and Magic Among the Azande*, Oxford, 1937.

P. Feyerabend, *Against Method*, London, 1975.

D.H. Fischer, *Albion's Seed: Four British Folkways in America*, New York, 1989.

L. Fleck, *Genesis and Development of a Scientific Fact*, Chicago, 1935 (1979).

R. Floud, *An Introduction to Quantitative Methods for Historians*, London, 1974.

R. Floud, 'Quantitative History and People's History: Two Methods in Conflict?', *History Workshop*, vol.17, Spring 1984, pp. 113–24.

R.W. Fogel in 'The Limits of Quantitative Methods in History', *American Historical Review*, vol. 80, 2, April 1975, pp. 329–50.

R.W. Fogel and S. Engerman, *Time on the Cross*, Boston, 1974.

R.W. Fogel and G.R. Elton, *Which Road to the Past?*, New Haven, 1983.

D. Føllesdal, 'Hermeneutics and the Hypothetico-Deductive Method', in M. Martin and L. McIntyre, eds, *Readings in the Philosophy of Social Science*, Cambridge, Mass., 1994.

H.-G. Gadamer, 'The Problem of Historical Consciousness', in P. Rabinow and W.M. Sullivan, eds, *Interpretive Social Science: A Reader*, Berkeley, 1979.

V.A.C. Gatrell and T.B. Hadden, 'Criminal Statistics and their Interpretation', in E.A. Wrigley, ed., *Nineteenth-century Society: Essays in the Use of Quantitative Methods for the Study of Social Data*, Cambridge, 1972.

V.A.C. Gatrell, 'Theft and Violence in Victorian and Edwardian England', in V.A.C. Gatrell, B. Lenman, and G. Parker, eds, *Crime and the Law: The Social History of Crime in Western Europe since 1500*, London, 1980.

P. Gardiner, *The Nature of Historical Explanation*, London, 1952.

C. Geertz, 'Thick Description: Toward an Interpretive Theory of Culture', in his *The Interpretation of Cultures*, New York, 1973.

C. Geertz, 'Common Sense as a Cultural System', in his *Local Knowledge: Further Essays in Interpretive Anthropology*, New York, 1983.

C. Geertz, '"From the Native's Point of View": on the Nature of Anthropological Understanding' in *Local Knowledge: Further Essays in Interpretive Anthropology*, New York, 1983.

E. Gellner, 'Concepts and Society', in B. R. Wilson, ed., *Rationality*, Oxford, 1970.

E. Gellner, *Postmodernism, Reason and Religion*, London, 1992.

E. Genovese, *Roll, Jordan, Roll: the World the Slaves Made*, New York, 1974.

F. Gilbert, 'Introduction', in F. Gilbert and S. R. Graubard, eds, *Historical Studies Today*, New York, 1972.

C. Ginzburg, *The Cheese and the Worms; The Cosmos of a Sixteenth-Century Miller*, trs J. and A. Tedeschi, Baltimore, 1980.

C. Ginzburg, *Clues, Myths, and the Historical Method*, trs. J. and A. Tedeschi, Baltimore, 1989.

D. Goldhagen, *Hitler's Willing Executioners: Ordinary Germans and the Holocaust*, London, 1996.

H. Gutman, *Slavery and the Numbers Game: A Critique of Time on the Cross*, Urbana, 1975.

J. Habakkuk, 'Economic History and Economic Theory', in F. Gilbert and S. R. Graubard, *Historical Studies Today*, New York, 1972.

C. Hall, 'The Tale of Samuel and Jemima: Gender and Working-Class Culture in Early Nineteenth-century England', in T. Bennett, C. Mercer and J. Woollacott, eds, *Popular Culture and Social Relations*, Milton Keynes, 1986.

O. Handlin, *Truth in History*, Cambridge, Mass., 1979.

C. Hempel, 'The Function of General Laws in History', in P. Gardiner, ed., *Theories of History*, Glencoe, 1959.

J.H. Hexter, *The History Primer*, London, 1972.

J.H. Hexter, *On Historians: Reappraisals of Some of the Makers of Modern History*, Cambridge, Mass., 1979.

R. Hilberg, *The Destruction of the European Jews*, 3 vols, rev. edn, New York, 1985.

G. Himmelfarb, *The New History and the Old* Cambridge, Mass., 1987.

J.M. Himmelstein and M.S. Kimmel, 'States and Revolutions: The Implications and Limits of Skocpol's Structural Model, ' *American Journal of Sociology*, vol. 86, 1981, pp. 1145–54.

M. E. Hobart, 'The Paradox of Historical Constructionism', *History and Theory*, vol. 28, 1989, pp. 43–58.

E. Hobsbawm, 'From Social History to the History of Society', in F. Gilbert and S.R. Graubard, eds, *Historical Studies Today*, New York, 1972.

M. Hollis, *The Philosophy of Social Science: An Introduction*, Cambridge, 1994.

J. Hospers, *An Introduction to Philosophical Analysis*, London, 1965.

J. Hughes, *The Philosophy of Social Research*, 2nd edn, London, 1990.

D.L. Hull 'In Defense of Presentism', *History and Theory*, vol, 18, 1979, pp.1–15.

D. Hume, *A Treatise of Human Nature*, 1739–40, new edn, Oxford, 1978.

S.D. Hunt, 'A Realist Theory of Empirical Testing; Resolving the Theory-Ladenness/Objectivity Debate', *Philosophy of the Social Sciences*, vol. 24, 2, June 1994, pp.133–58.

G.G. Iggers, *New Directions in European Historiography*, rev. edn, London, 1984.

G.G. Iggers, 'Rationality and History', in Henry Kozicki, ed., *Developments in Modern Historiography*, New York, 1993.

G.G. Iggers and H.T. Parker, eds, *International Handbook of Historical Studies*, Westport, Conn., 1979.

R. Isaac, *The Transformation of Virginia, 1740–1790*, Chapel Hill, 1982.

I. Jarvie, *The Revolution in Anthropology*, London, 1967.

K.H. Jarausch and K.A. Hardy, *Quantititative Methods for Historians: A Guide to Research, Data, and Statistics*, Chapel Hill, 1991.

M. Katz, *The People of Hamilton, Canada West: Family and Class in a Mid-Nineteenth Century City*, Cambridge, Mass., 1975.

G. King, R.O. Keohane, and S. Verba, *Designing Social Inquiry: Scientific Inference in Qualitative Research*, Princeton, 1994.

J. Kocka, 'What is Leftist about Social History Today?', *Journal of Social History*, Supplement, vol. 29, 1995.

J.M. Kousser, 'The Revivalism of Narrative: A Response to Recent Criticisms of Quantitative History', *Social Science History*, vol. 8, 1984, pp. 133–49.

I. Lakatos, *The Methodology of Scientific Research Programmes, Philosophical Papers*, ed., J. Worrall and G. Currie, vol. 1, Cambridge, 1978.

E.E. Lampard, 'Two Cheers for Quantification History: An Agnostic Foreword', in L. Schnore, ed., *The New Urban History*, Princeton, 1975.

B. Latour and S. Woolgar, *Laboratory Life: The Social Construction of Scientific Facts*, 2nd edn, Princeton, 1985.

L. Laudan, *Science and Relativism: Some Key Controversies in the Philosophy of Science*, Chicago, 1990.

J. Le Goff and P. Nora, eds, *Constructing the Past: Essays in Historical Methodology*, Cambridge, 1985.

E. Lemert, *Human Deviance, Social Problems and Social Control*, Englewood Cliffs, N.J., 1967.

G. Lenclud, 'The Factual and the Normative on Ethnography; Do Cultural Differences Derive from Description?', *Anthropology Today*, vol. 12, 1, Feb. 1996, pp. 7–11.

G. Levi, 'On Microhistory', in P. Burke, ed., *New Perspectives on Historical Writing*, Cambridge, 1991.

C. Lévi-Strauss, *Structural Anthropology*, London, 1968.

D. Little, *Varieties of Social Explanation: An Introduction to the Philosophy of Social Science*, Boulder, 1991.

C. Lloyd, *Explanation in Social History*, New York, 1985.

C. Lloyd, 'The Methodologies of Social History: a Critical Survey and Defense of Structurism', in *History and Theory*, vol. 30, 1991, pp. 180–219.

H. Longino, *Science as Social Knowledge: Values and Objectivity in Scientific Inquiry*, Princeton, 1990.

C. Lucas, 'Introduction', in J. Le Goff and P. Nora, eds, *Constructing the Past: Essays in Historical Methodology*, Cambridge, 1985.

A. Macfarlane, *Witchcraft in Tudor and Stuart England*, London, 1970.

A. Macfarlane, *The Origins of English Individualism: The Family, Property and Social Transition*, Oxford, 1978.

M. Martin, 'The Philosophical Importance of the Rosenthal Effect', in M. Martin and L. McIntyre, eds, *Readings in the Philosophy of Social Science*, Cambridge, Mass., 1994.

M. Martin, 'Taylor on Interpretation and the Sciences of Man', in M. Martin and L. McIntyre, eds, *Readings in the Philosophy of Social Science*, London, 1994.

M. Martin and L. McIntyre, eds, *Readings in the Philosophy of Social Science*, Cambridge, Mass., 1994.

M.R. Marrus, *The Holocaust in History*, London, 1989.

C.B. McCullagh, *Justifying Historical Descriptions*, Cambridge, 1984.

C.B. McCullagh, 'The Truth of Historical Narratives', *History and Theory*, Beiheft 26, 1987, pp. 30–46.

H. Medick, '"Missionaries in the Row Boat"? Ethnological Ways of Knowing as a Challenge to Social History', *Comparative Studies in Society and History*, vol. 29, 1987, pp. 76–98.

R.K. Merton, 'The Perspectives of Insiders and Insiders', in N.W. Storer, ed., *The Sociology of Science: Theoretical and Empirical Investigations*, Chicago, 1973.

S. Milgram, *Obedience to Authority: An Experimental View*, New York, 1969.

L.O. Mink, 'Philosophy and Theory of History', in G.G. Iggers and H.T. Parker, eds, *International Handbook of Historical Studies*, Westport, Conn., 1979.

L.J. Moore, 'Good Old-Fashioned New Social History...', *Reviews in American History*, vol.24, 4, Dec. 1996, pp. 555–73.

B.H. Moss, 'Republican Socialism and the Making of the Working Class in Britain, France, and the United States: A Critique of Thompsonian Culturalism', *Comparative Studies in Society and History*, vol. 35, 1993, pp. 390–413.

E. Muir and G. Ruggiero, eds, *Microhistory and the Lost Peoples of Europe*, trs. E. Branch, Baltimore, 1991.

E. Muir, 'Introduction: Observing Trifles', in E. Muir and G. Ruggiero, eds, *Microhistory and the Lost Peoples of Europe*, trs. E. Branch, Baltimore, 1991.

A. Munslow, *Deconstructing History*, London, 1997.

R. Nadeau, 'Confuting Popper on the Rationality Principle', *Philosophy of the Social Sciences*, vol. 23, 4, 1993, pp. 446–67.

R. Nola, 'Post-Modernism, A French Cultural Chernobyl: Foucault on Power/Knowledge', *Inquiry*, 37, 1994, pp. 3–43.

I. Olábarri, '"New" New History: A *Longue Durée* Structure', *History and Theory*, vol. 34, 1995, pp. 1–29.

W. Outhwaite, *New Philosophies of Social Science: Realism, Hermeneutics, and Critical Theory*, Houndmills, 1987.

B.D. Palmer, *Descent into Discourse: The Reification of Language and the Writing of Social History*, Philadelphia, 1990.

G. Pearson, *Hooligan: A History of Respectable Fears*, London, 1983.

J. Philip, 'Traditional Historical Narrative and Action-Oriented (or Ethnographic History)', *Historical Studies*, vol. 20, pp. 339–52.

D. Philips, *Crime and Authority in Victorian England: the Black Country 1835–1860*, London, 1977.

K. Popper, *Conjectures and Refutations: The Growth of Scientific Knowledge*, 3rd rev. edn, London, 1969.

K. Popper, 'The Rationality Principle', in *Popper Selections*, D. Miller, ed., Princeton, 1985.

T. Rabb, 'The Development of Quantification in Historical Research', *Journal of Interdisciplinary History*, vol. 13, 4, 1983, pp. 591–601

T. Rabb and R. I. Rotberg, eds, *The New History: The 1980s and Beyond. Studies in Interdisciplinary History*, Princeton, 1982.

M. Reed, 'The Peasantry of Nineteenth-century England: a Neglected Class?', *History Workshop Journal*, no. 18, 1984, pp. 53–76.

E. Rosch, 'Principles of Classification', in E. Rosch and B. B. Lloyd, eds, *Cognition and Categorization*, Hillsdale, N.J., 1978.

R. Rosaldo, *Culture & Truth; the Remaking of Social Analysis*, Boston, 1989.

A. Rosenberg, *Philosophy of Social Science*, 2nd edn, Boulder, 1995.

G. Rudé, *The Crowd in the French Revolution*, Oxford, 1959.

J. Rouse, *Knowledge and Power: Toward a Political Philosophy of Science*, Ithaca, 1987.

D. Sabean, *Power in the Blood: Popular Culture and Village Discourse in Early Modern Germany*, Cambridge, 1984.

A. Schlesinger, 'The Humanist Looks at Empirical Social Research', *American Sociological Review*, vol. 27, 1962, pp. 768–71.

J.W. Scott, *Gender and the Politics of History*, New York, 1988.

P.A. Schilpp, ed., *The Philosophy of Karl Popper*, La Salle, Ill., 1974.

J. Schumpeter, *Capitalism, Socialism and Democracy*, New York, 1942.

A. Scull, *The Most Solitary of Afflictions; Madness and Society in Britain, 1700–1900*, New Haven, 1993.

J.R. Searle, 'Intentionalistic Explanations in the Social Sciences', *Philosophy of the Social Sciences*, vol. 21, 1991, pp. 332–44.

R.J. Shafer, *A Guide to Historical Method*, rev. edn, Homewood, Ill., 1974.

A. Sheridan, *Michel Foucault; The Will to Truth*, London, 1980.

E. Showalter, *The Female Malady: Women, Madness and English Culture 1830–1980*, New York, 1985.

T. Skocpol, ed., *Vision and Method in Historical Sociology*, Cambridge, 1984.

T. Skocpol, 'Emerging Agendas and Recurrent Strategies in Historical Sociology', in T. Skocpol, ed., *Vision and Method in Historical Sociology*, Cambridge, 1984.

T. Skocpol and M. Somers, 'The Uses of Comparative History in Macrosocial Enquiry', *Comparative Studies in Society and History*, vol. 22, 1980, pp. 174–97.

T. Skocpol, *States and Social Revolutions: A Comparative Analysis of France, Russia, and China*, Cambridge, 1979.

N. Smelser, *Comparative Methods in the Social Sciences*, Englewood Cliffs, 1976.

D. Smith, *The Rise of Historical Sociology*, Philadelphia, 1991.

K.D.M. Snell, *Annals of the Labouring Poor: Social Change and Agrarian England, 1660–1900*, Cambridge, 1985.

W. Sombart, *Why is There no Socialism in the United States?*, ed., C.T. Husbands, White Plains, N.Y., 1976.

D.J. Spindel, 'Assessing Memory: Twentieth-Century Slave Narratives Reconsidered', *Journal of Interdisciplinary History*, vol.27, 2, Autumn 1996, pp.247–61.

D. Stannard, *Shrinking History: On Freud and the Failure of Psychohistory*, New York, 1980.

P. Stearns, 'Coming of Age', *Journal of Social History*, vol. 10, 2, 1976, pp. 246–55.

P. Stearns, ed., *Encyclopedia of Social History*, New York, 1994.

P. Stearns, 'Uncivil War...', *Journal of Social History*, Supplement, vol. 29, 1995, pp. 7–15.

T. Stoianovich, *French Historical Method: The Annales Paradigm*, Ithaca, 1976.

L. Stone, *The Crisis of the Aristocracy: 1558–1641*, Oxford, 1965.

L. Stone, 'Prosopography', in F. Gilbert and S.R. Graubard, eds, *Historical Studies Today*, New York, 1972.

L. Stone, *Family, Sex and Marriage in England 1500–1800*, New York, 1977.

L. Stone, 'Interpersonal Violence in English Society 1300–1980', *Past and Present*, Nov. 1983, pp. 22–33.

L. Stone, *The Past and the Present Revisited*, London, 1987.

C. Taylor, 'Interpretation and the Sciences of Man', in P. Rabinow and W.M. Sullivan, eds, *Interpretive Social Science: A Second Look*, Berkeley, 1987.

M. Taylor, 'The Beginnings of British Social History?', *History Workshop Journal*, vol. 43, 1997, pp. 155–76.

O. Temkin, 'The Meaning of Medicine in Historical Perspective', in his *The Double Face of Janus and Other Essays*, Baltimore, 1977.

S. Thernstrom, *The Other Bostonians: Poverty and Progress in the American Metropolis 1880–1970*, Cambridge, Mass., 1973.

K. Thomas, *Man and the Natural World: Changing Attitudes in England 1500–1800*, London, 1983.

C. Tilly, *As Sociology Meets History*, New York, 1981.

C. Tilly, L. Tilly and R.Tilly, *The Rebellious Century: 1830–1930*, Cambridge, Mass., 1975.

E.P. Thompson, *The Making of the English Working Class*, London, 1965.

E.P. Thompson, 'The Peculiarities of the English', *Socialist Register*, 1965.

J.J. Tobias, *Crime and Industrial Society in the 19th Century*, London, 1967.

J. Tosh, 'What Should Historians do with Masculinity?', *History Workshop*, no. 38, 1994, pp.179–202.

J. Tosh, *The Pursuit of History*, 2nd edn, New York, 1995.

E.K. Trimberger, 'E.P. Thompson: Understanding the Process of History', in T. Skocpol, ed., *Vision and Method in Historical Sociology*, Cambridge, 1984.

B.S. Turner, *The Body and Society: Explorations in Social Theory*, London, 1984.

A. Tversky, 'Features of Similarity', *Psychological Review*, vol. 84, 1977, pp. 327–52.

A. Vickery, 'Shaking the Separate Spheres. Did Women Really Descend into Graceful Indolence?', in *Times Literary Supplement*, 12 March 1993, pp. 6–7.

M. Vovelle, *Piété Baroque et Déchristianisation en Provence au XVIIIe siècle*, Paris, 1973.

W.H. Walsh, *An Introduction to Philosophy of History*, London, 1967.

R. White, 'Causes, Conditions, and Causal Importance', *History and Theory*, vol. 21, 1982, pp. 53–74.

A. Wilson and T.G. Ashplant, 'Whig History and Present-centred History', *Historical Journal*, vol. 31, 1, 1988, pp. 1–16.

A. Wilson and T.G. Ashplant, 'Present-centred History and the Problem of Historical Knowledge', *Historical Journal*, vol. 31, 2, 1988, pp. 253–74.

B.R. Wilson, ed., *Rationality*, Oxford, 1970.

P. Winch, *The Idea of a Social Science and its Relation to Philosophy*, London, 1958.

P. Winch, 'Understanding a Primitive Society', in B.R. Wilson, ed., *Rationality*, Oxford, 1970.

K. Windschuttle, *The Killing of History; The Killing of History*, Sydney, 1994.

C. Vann Woodward, 'History from Slave Sources', *American Historical Review*, vol. 79, pp. 470–81.

E.O. Wright, A. Levine and E. Sober, *Reconstructing Marxism: Essays on Explanation and the Theory of History*, London, 1992.

E.A. Wrigley, ed., *Nineteenth-century Society: Essays in the Use of Quantitative Methods for the Study of Social Data*, Cambridge, 1972.

T. Zeldon, 'Social History and Total History', *Journal of Social History*, vol. 10, 2, Winter 1976, pp. 237–45.

Index